YEAR
OF
FEAR

YEAR OF FEAR

A Jewish Prisoner
Waits for Auschwitz

Philip Mechanicus

translated from the Dutch by

Irene R. Gibbons

Hawthorn Books, Inc.   Publishers,   New York

INTRODUCTION TO THE ENGLISH LANGUAGE EDITION

DURING the Second World War—from May 1940 until May 1945—the Netherlands were occupied by the Germans. These five years gave the Germans the opportunity to carry out in Holland, as elsewhere, their programme of annihilating the Jews—*"Endlösung der Judenfrage"* (Final Solution of the Jewish Problem): the systematic, well planned and carefully executed process of torture, degradation, deprivation of rights, looting, isolation, herding together and exile, culminating in death by asphyxiation in the Polish gas chambers. A programme which differed only in minor details, according to local circumstances, from those carried out against the Jews in other occupied territories. Within the Dutch borders, on the basis of the racial characteristics laid down by the Germans, there were some 140,000 so-called "full Jews"—among them over 14,000 German Jews and 7,500 of other nationalities. The great majority of these Jews lived in the western part of the country, especially Amsterdam.

The diary of Philip Mechanicus gives a unique picture of one phase of the plan: the herding together of the Jews in Camp Westerbork, prior to deportation. The reader will find also the names of other camps containing Jews: Ellecom, Amersfoort, Vught. Westerbork served as a Dutch departure point; from here deportation was carried out. But what *was* Westerbork?

In the Netherlands, the most heavily populated country in Europe, uninhabitable or uninhabited areas are unknown today, although there are, here and there, unhealthy and unattractive ones. In one of these, in the province of Drente in the north-eastern part of the country, the Dutch Government had established in 1939 a camp for German-Jewish refugees who had left their country as victims of Nazi persecution, and with whom they did not know how to deal. The camp proper, a collection of wooden barracks, was relatively small, about five hundred square metres. It was not a pleasant place, for it was perpetually windy and the peat bogs were very damp. In May 1940 Westerbork contained about

750 people. Then the Netherlands became involved in the war and this radically changed the purpose of the camp: in July 1942 it was made a *"Polizeiliches Durchgangslager"* (Police Transit Camp), the depot in which the Germans concentrated the Jews before taking them to Poland. It remained so until the autumn of 1944. During this period about 100,000 Jews stayed at the camp, most of them a few days, some for a longer period, a few until the liberation (12th April 1945, when there were about 900 Jews left).

For a better understanding of Mechanicus' text one should bear in mind that Westerbork as a camp was organized in a virtually unique manner: it was a unit managed almost entirely by the German-Jewish camp inmates themselves, who had taken the initiative in this at an early stage so as to avoid the intervention of the dreaded SS. Because of this the Germans needed only the absolute minimum of guard personnel. Obviously they only allowed this situation to exist because the Jewish camp organization proved to be entirely satisfactory in the matter which was of prime importance to them: the deportation, without difficulties or fuss, of about 100,000 Jews. The Jews themselves did this so perfectly that the Germans were able to make staffing economies running perhaps into hundreds. In practice this meant collaboration, barely disguised and degrading, with an increasingly small number of Jews trying to save themselves by sending away larger and larger numbers of their own people. So, especially under its Commander *Obersturmführer* Albert Konrad Gemmeker (1942–1945), the *Musterlager* (Model Camp) of Westerbork functioned as a well-oiled part of the great German defence machine.

The camp organization also worked reasonably well in another respect: it tried to make Westerbork into a liveable place, relatively speaking, for those forced to stay there. Furthermore, by creating opportunities for work on behalf of the German war effort, the organizers tried to give the camp inmates a chance to make themselves useful in the eyes of their oppressors, hoping this might put a brake on the deportations. However, this hope proved to be illusory, and the siphoning off went on week after week since the extermination of the Jews had absolute priority in Berlin. The first aim did succeed up to a certain point. This is best illustrated by a brief outline of the so-called "Medical Service", selected here because a great part of this diary deals with the camp hospital.

The hospital had, at its peak, 1,725 beds, 120 doctors and a staff of over 1,000. And all the specialists you can think of. There were isolation rooms, a department for the mentally sick, a magnificent dispensary, a separate diet kitchen, all sorts of stores, draughtsmen, orthopaedists, hairdressers, photographers, laboratories, social welfare, the chaplain service, first aid posts, a hygiene service, dental clinics, despatch riders, porters, a postal service, an operating theatre, an out-patients' department with fixed consulting hours, an X-ray scheme to test all camp residents for tuberculosis, immuniza-tion against typhoid and paratyphoid, the testing of blood groups. The doctors held weekly meetings to deal with scientific and clinical subjects. And this whole organization was for the benefit of people who were to be destroyed a little later on! In the camp there were folk who looked on the black side and feared the worst as far as Poland was concerned, but is it any wonder that they were given little credence? The Germans surely could not be so stupid as to look after the people so well in the west if they had such evil intentions towards them in the east! That seemed crazy and impossible, but it turned out to be crazy—and possible.

In spite of all its excellence, there was one thing that the Medical Service was not able to do and that was to stop people being sent away—to stop deportation, the dynamic factor in the life at Westerbork, the factor governed by fate. In this reservoir, which seemed to be a combination of a Potemkin village and a doss-house and a *Huis-Clos*, people lived from one Tuesday to the next, for that was the day on which, again and again, the infernal train swallowed up its thousand victims, bound for a destination that people hardly dared to think about and yet thought about all the time, about which people could say nothing and yet spoke of incessantly. Every week the emotional curve showed the same pattern—moving rapidly upwards from dejection and utter weariness to a peak, followed by a gradual decline, passing through uneasiness, alarm, agitation, till it reached panic. For months on end.

Again and again this diary mentions the tensions prevailing in the camp. How could it be otherwise? The people dragged to Westerbork were "ordinary" human beings, behaving more or less just as any normal group of people placed in such ab-normal conditions would have behaved. Their previous history

7

should not be forgotten here. Any comparison with non-Jews or even with Jews living under other conditions (the ghetto in Warsaw or Israel) would be unjust. As we have said, these were "ordinary" human beings—Jews in this particular case. Perhaps I ought to write "Jews" in inverted commas—the human beings, men, women and children, whom the Germans chose to consider as such and on that basis chose to wipe out and exterminate, just as one exterminates vermin, in cold blood, in a premeditated, systematic and scientific way. At Westerbork there were all types of Jews—orthodox and non-orthodox, with all kinds of gradations in between. There were many kinds of baptized Jews, including monks or nuns wearing the Jewish star. There were Zionists, assimilated Jews, National Socialists of the NSB, anti-Semites, also a great number of different nationalities, including citizens of Liberia and Honduras and people with dual nationality. We find the right wing and the left wing represented, Catholics, anti-revolutionaries, the Christian Historical group, Liberals, Socialists, Communists. There were great men and artisans, tradesmen and farmers, working class folk with or without a white collar, also intellectuals, artists and representatives of the liberal professions. There were the very old (one woman over a hundred) and infants, and these too were intended for the "Labour Pool" (i.e., the abattoir), for which they "departed" (i.e., were dragged off). In short, there were all kinds, good and bad, just and unjust, fine men and scum—practically every type one would come across in a random sample of about a hundred thousand "ordinary" Dutchmen.

At Westerbork there was even an aristocracy. Not counts or barons or knights or squires, but the Long-Term Residents, the lucky ones who had been there before July 14th 1942 and now formed the oligarchy and enjoyed all sorts of small, but very important, benefits and the privilege that surpassed all others—a better guarantee of safety. In the pseudo-autonomous organization of Westerbork the upper stratum of these Long-Term Residents supplied the men at the top, the so-called "prominent" men, the VIP's, in this camp sometimes called MSW ("*macht sich wichtig*"—i.e., "throws his weight about"). Right at the top stood Schlesinger who is repeatedly mentioned in the diary—the powerless and yet so powerful grand vizier of the all-powerful Camp Commandant. He and his round table were largely responsible for

8

making up the transports for the weekly train from the "transport material" available (this term was actually used). In the eyes of the others, these paladins, nearly all of them German Jews, had control over life and death and were accordingly flattered, influenced, bribed, envied and hated, and indeed loathed. Compared with these, the others were pariahs, but even among these pariahs any sort of unity was hard to find. Those highest up were granted small houses by the "Accommodation Office" (yes, even Westerbork had one) and so they acquired the most precious thing of all—something that people in camps everywhere were deprived of in wartime—a little, just a very little privacy. And in their turn the occupants of the damp and grimy huts differentiated between one another. One hut called itself the "bend of the Heerengracht" because it was an elegant hut. It was not everyone who could get in there—only the angel of death could not be kept out. What took place inside each hut the reader will learn from the pages that follow.

The lowest of the bottom strata was formed by the so-called S-men and women, the "punishment cases", who were beyond saving, although occasionally one of them—including Mechanicus himself—would succeed in getting rid of his S. We now know, after the event, that every Jew, great or small, was considered as a "punishment case" in Poland because he was a Jew, and was indeed punished—by death.

We must also remember that by a satanic application of the dictum "divide and rule" the Germans introduced a wicked system of distinctions in 1942. The Jews were issued with stamps on their personal identity cards which granted a postponement of deportation "until further notice"—postponement, but not a cancellation. In the autumn of that year there was a mad rush for these stamps, as demoralizing as it was unavailing, because the persons favoured in this way were sent off to Westerbork sooner or later in spite of them, although rather later than those who had no stamps at all.

After this, from 1941 onwards, other equally deceptive paths for escape were opened up—the holes in the net that had been tightened so expertly. Now one had to get on one or other of the "lists", all indicated by names, the magical powers of which the reader will get plenty of proof of later on. One of the most sought after lists was that organized by the German official Calmeyer, involving an investigation of

9

ancestry by means of which one could present oneself as an "Aryan". And there were all kinds of people, often trustworthy, but more often untrustworthy, who arranged methods of evasion, emigration, exemption on a very long-term basis and so on. It was possible to gain admission to these last lists, but never free of charge. People had to stand very firm at Westerbork if, in spite of the prospect of deportation, they were not to give way to temptation and buy a place on one or other of the lists, just as someone who is dangerously ill and at his wits' end will seek salvation from a charlatan. All the lists smashed sooner or later, or, in German, "*platzten*", a verb borrowed from the camp jargon and having strong overtones of self-ridicule and gloating. "A list is a collection of Jews who will one day be deported," said Mechanicus cynically, and that applied even to the reliable lists. Anyone who had let himself be put down on an unreliable one before coming to Westerbork and, when he had been fleeced as bare as possible, was passed over into the hands of the Germans, stayed only for a few days in the S-hut, the "punishment hut", and had to leave there on the first available train because he was perfect "transport material".

In this camp too the German authorities towards the end of the war did their best to wipe out every trace of their misdeeds. But in spite of all their thoroughness they did not entirely succeed in doing so. In addition to a number of papers that were saved, we even have at our disposal a film taken at Westerbork which, in spite of its many shortcomings, is an irreplaceable document. The Imperial Institute of War Documents in Amsterdam has also collected a large number of testimonies from camp inmates; of these the letters of Etty Hillesum, which are incomparable documents of their kind, have already appeared in more than one edition.

The reader must judge for himself the quality of these writings of Mechanicus and he may possibly be assisted by a few comments about the diary genre in general as a record of events. As such it can be placed under the same heading as memoirs and letters, documents in which, more than in any other, the ego reveals or . . . conceals itself. One should also make a rough distinction in the case of the diary between the external type, in which the writer notes down things observed, facts and external experiences, and the intimate type, which is filled mostly with speculations and reactions to the outside world. There are classic examples of both genres

10

in historical literature.

The writings of Mechanicus undoubtedly belong to the first category, although some features of the second are present too. By reading the diary one can gain a clearer insight into the special value of such a record, compared with memoirs and similar documents which record memories set down after the event. These, of course, are always based on reappraisals and are streamlined by one's subsequent knowledge and subsequent understanding of events. They introduce something which does not amount to falsification, but which may certainly misrepresent or twist the story to fit in with one's ultimate understanding of the unity of life and its essential coherence. All this is completely absent from the day to day account and this omission represents a gain for the historian in every way. The diary of this experienced reporter and journalist is a case in point—it is no mere coincidence that "journal" can mean both diary and newspaper. How grateful we must be to him for not wanting to be anything more than the man who goes about with his notebook, noting down events from day to day—in fact, a war correspondent setting down his record while his life was constantly in danger, although he hardly ever seemed to realize it.

But what of the man behind this "history in the first person"?

Philip Mechanicus, born on April 17th 1889 in Amsterdam, had, after leaving the primary school, a humble post in the despatch department, then on the administrative side of the daily paper *Het Volk*. But he managed to educate himself by studying on his own and he was "discovered" and came into journalism when he was still only in his seventeenth year. After doing his military service he worked for years in the east, in Medan on the *Sumatra Post*, later in Semarang on *De Locomotief*. In 1919 he returned to Holland and obtained in August 1920 a post on the overseas editorial staff of the *Algemeen Handelsblad*. The travel articles he wrote for that paper attracted particular attention. Those dealing with the Soviet Union (1929–1934) were published together under the title *Van Sikkel En Hamer* ("The Hammer and the Sickle"), also the articles dealing with Palestine (1933), entitled *Een Volk Bouwt Zijn Huis* ("A People Building Itself a Home").

Immediately after the occupation he was given to understand that his presence on the newspaper would not be toler-

11

ated by the Germans. He went on working for it at home for a little longer and wrote short articles under the pen-name of Père Celjénets, until the directors dismissed him by letter. On September 27th 1942 when he was standing without a star on the rear platform of a tram he was probably betrayed by a fellow-passenger and was arrested by a policeman. At the Amstelveenseweg he shared a cell with the former alderman of Amsterdam De Miranda who was murdered so cruelly at the Amersfoort camp shortly afterwards. On October 25th he was transferred to that camp and he arrived at Westerbork, grievously ill treated, on November 7th, naturally as an S-detainee. He was kept in the hospital till July 29th 1943, during which period he was able, as I have indicated above, to get rid of his S. On March 8th 1944 he was taken to the Bergen-Belsen camp and on October 9th with a group of 120 persons from that so-called "special" camp to Auschwitz-Birkenau. From a couple of statements made by survivors it can be concluded that three days later, i.e., on October 12th 1944, he was shot there with his whole group.

J. PRESSER.

YEAR
OF
FEAR

Friday May 28th 1943: Got a new male nurse today who introduced himself to all the hundred patients in the ward and
shook hands with them. Very unusual at Westerbork, where
the nurses come and go without any fuss. Obviously a decent
fellow. And a professional—you can see that. Newly arrived.
He looks immaculate in a snowy white coat which shines and
glitters compared with the dirty, dingy coats in which most of
the other male nurses go bustling about. Lack of cleanliness.
Since yesterday we have had women cleaners in the ward instead of the men cleaners who have been deported. They are
under the direction of a leader, every inch a gentleman, tall,
aristocratic in build, very erect and with literary aspirations;
I have a play by him under my pillow to read. The *men
cleaners* used to make remarks, often annoying remarks, at the
patients' expense. Now it is the *patients* who are making remarks, often annoying ones, at the expense of the women
cleaners. What a feast for the eyes these pretty young women
are! They go about well dressed, one in slacks and the other
in a skirt. Roses in the desert! They bear themselves bravely.
They are not embittered, but have a grim sense of humour.
Their motto is: 'They'll never get us down—no, never!' They
sweep and scrub as if they had never done anything else. They
scrupulously shift every mess-tin, every pair of shoes, every
chair, every bundle of clothes so as not to leave a single speck
of dust or a single dry spot. You should have seen the male
scrubbers—just a lick and a promise! How long will the women
keep up their high standard of efficiency?

Paid a visit to the camp doctor v.d.R. He lives in a small
room measuring about sixteen cubic metres with his wife,
grown-up son and small daughter. He told me that he had had
a case of attempted suicide today—a mother and two children.
He intervened in time and used psychology on the woman.
Number of suicides high—on average, four per week. In my hut
six weeks or so ago a man of about seventy tried to take his own
life by hanging. The eighty-year-old mother of a friend of
mine committed suicide recently on arriving at Westerbork by
taking poison she had brought with her. Dr. v.d.R. was greatly
affected by the misery he witnesses daily and by the weekly

15

deportations. He held Britain partly responsible for the fate of the Jews and their annihilation because she did not take stronger measures with regard to Germany although she knew what was going on. She should flatten Berlin and, if necessary, use mustard gas—then the war would be over within six weeks. If Britain did not stop the annihilation of the Jews, then he would rather that Germany won the war as a punishment for Britain. The German people must be exterminated and sterilized. The doctor allowed himself to be carried away by his feelings and lost all sense of objectivity. Finally he burst out sobbing and brought his fist down on the table. He was overwrought. And no wonder.

But it is a remarkable fact that a very large percentage of uneducated Jews think along the same lines as the doctor—if they wanted, Britain and America could put an end to the war in a short time, but they don't want to because they are waiting for Germany and the Soviet Union to wear each other out. It is in the financial interest of the armament manufacturers that the war should go on. Britain does not care a scrap about the Jews. Britain prepared too late. Jews say: 'What can it matter to *me* who wins the war if *I* am not going to be there to see it?' Only the individual is willing to look beyond himself and examine according to objective standards the balance of power existing between Britain and America, Germany and Italy. This is not easy to do when you see several thousand Jews being herded week after week like cattle into a train that will take them to an unknown destination and has never brought back a single Jew to tell the tale. You automatically tend to look upon political friends who do not come to your aid in time as if they were your enemies. A narrow view of things.

Saturday May 29th: I feel as if I am an official reporter giving an account of a shipwreck. We are all together in a cyclone and feel the holed ship slowly sinking. We try to reach a harbour, but that harbour seems far away. The idea is gradually forming in my mind that I have not been brought here by my *persecutors*, but that I have gone on the journey *voluntarily* in order to do my work. I am busy all day long and am never bored for a single minute; sometimes the days actually seem too short. Duty is duty and work is ennobling. I write during a great part of the day. Sometimes I begin at half past five in the

16

morning and sometimes I am still busy in the evening after
bedtime, gathering my impressions or experiences for the day.
I play a few games of chess daily, read the newspapers carefully, chat with people, with doctors and nurses and patients,
pay visits in the camp in the afternoon and smoke my pipe in
between times. What more does a man need to fill in his time
in a gipsy camp like this?

Chief Rabbi Dasberg was sent back to Amsterdam today.
A friend of mine has received a letter from his wife dated
Wednesday afternoon in which she writes to say that she has
been a prisoner since Sunday afternoon in the Jewish Council
building on the N. Keizersgracht in Amsterdam. The children
have been left on their own all that time. Tonight a party of
about 450 arrived from Amsterdam.

The Commandant has decreed that Jews may no longer
walk along the middle of the main thoroughfare, the Boulevard
des Misères, during working hours; they may only walk along
the sides—quickly. When the Commandant was on his bicycle
today and saw a Jew who was loading a train standing with his
rear towards him, he kicked him in that area to let him know
that he was showing a lack of respect. Not a very easy thing to
do.

Sunday May 30th: The Jews are living here at Westerbork like
Job on the dunghill—without possessions. A suit and some
underclothes to cover their miserable limbs in the daytime and
a blanket at night, a pair of shoes, a cap, a knife, fork and spoon
and a mug are their only belongings. Like Job the religious Jews
have not lost their trust in God and every Friday evening and
Saturday evening bear witness to their devotion to the Al-
mighty. The non-religious, i.e., those among them who are
strong, trust in the power of their own spirit and bow down
their heads before the religious traditions of their camp companions. The believers do not enquire about the reason for
what has befallen them, the reason for their degradation.
They accept it and endure it as something that cannot be
pushed aside or avoided—in the firm conviction that their God
will help them through it all, as He helped their forefathers to
undergo trials of a similar nature. An unshakable trust in God
underlies their whole attitude.

The thinking Jew who does not have this trust asks the question: 'Why have I been placed in this degrading and dis-

17

honouring position?' There must surely be a *more fundamental* reason for his being so sorely afflicted. The mere fact that he is a *Jew* cannot be a satisfactory reason for his misery, his dispossession, his isolation, his banishment. This is an oversimplification, not allowing for other factors. It contains no lesson for life, no incentive to examine and take stock of his moral, spiritual or social attributes. He asks himself: 'Am I personally guilty or must I atone for the guilt that others have brought upon themselves?' He is prepared to acknowledge his guilt in advance although that guilt has not been revealed to him. He may have puffed himself up with pride or been unjust, quite unwittingly, and according to the karmic principle of communal guilt he is prepared to *join* in atoning for the guilt of others. He is prepared to look upon his banishment as a period of purification, humiliation and cleansing. But why purification? Must one leave this to the Mystery, the Godhead, Providence and not ask?

How many times in history has not the Jew been plunged into damnation and forced to purify himself! It began with his expulsion from Egypt; it continued with his exile and bondage in Babylon, his cruel dispersal over all the countries of the world, his expulsion from Spain, his tortures in the lands of eastern Europe. His fate was *perhaps* not quite as hard and his future perhaps not quite as precarious then as now. Is he compelled to purify himself *for evermore?* Is this the *specific* form that his *ever recurring* purification takes? Is this an expiatory offering for the survival of peoples and civilizations that have been ruthlessly annihilated or have perished? Then, generally speaking, his purification will involve, primarily, natural selection, extermination of the weak and survival of the strong. A spiritual tempering process, the will to live, endurance to the bitter end.

The will to live is present in the majority of Jews. They believe that unless they are killed and unless the war goes on for a long time they will see it through. They are full of life and, being materialists, they cling to life so hard that they will use their last atom of physical strength and their last atom of spiritual strength to prolong it—and survive. The spiritual strength revealed by their behaviour in the concentration camps bears witness to this. Many victims have fallen, but the majority have shown rugged will power which has helped them through the sorest of trials and has hardened them for what lies in store. Jews have been brought into Westerbork from the concentration camps at Amersfoort, Ommen and Ellecom, injured. Injured so seriously and in such a state of physical exhaustion that people were amazed at how they stood up to their sufferings in those camps, sometimes for months on end. As a rule it is the strong, the spiritually strong, who have carried on the fight against every attempt to undermine their nerves and their bodies. The spiritually weak have lost the fight and in so doing have forfeited their lives.

As may be supposed, the many periods of purification to which the Jews have had to subject themselves in the course of history have hardened them and have bred tough specimens. But in this most recent period of purification something more is being required and demanded of the Jews than merely the urge and the will to safeguard their ill-fated lives.

In this crowded and richly variegated community many signs of degeneration can be observed. The older generation profess an orthodox religion in keeping with the laws. This religion is often merely outward convention and tradition and is alien to real life; it has not been renewed and has, as a result, become rigid and petrified. The prescribed ritual is carried out and every deviation from it is harshly condemned, even here. But, spiritually, that generation are like children, morally they are simple and, from the point of view of hygiene, backward and out of date. Socially they are badly orientated and conservative. The younger generation still have their roots largely in the traditions and customs of the ghetto. They have, it is true, cast overboard the orthodoxy of the Talmud, but they have not acquired any other spiritual values to replace it and live purely materialistic lives—often downright materialistic and selfish through and through. A large group of Jews who are liberally minded are in an intermediate position between the old Jewish dogma and laws and the spirit of the modern age. They still hold fast to a final remnant of the old faith, as they have not the courage to sever their link with the past, but they have never taken the trouble to enter into the culture and religion of the environment in which they live. They are spiritual hermaphrodites.

The younger generation show clear signs of regeneration. What the old, and also old-fashioned, generation profess orally by tradition once a year—their desire for the coming of the Messiah who will lead the Jews back to Palestine—is for them

19

a living aspiration, every day and in every breath they draw. They have remained true to the old faith, but are striving to achieve a synthesis between the laws and regulations of the Talmud and the pressing demands of modern life. These young people are striving towards a state of their own, a society of their own, where they can make this synthesis a reality— Palestine. They have left the narrow, constricting ghetto and have made themselves familiar with new ideas. They are spiritually developed, although this development is often one-sided. They have a more firmly grounded moral sense, they are socially better able to cope, they are keen on sport and physically well developed. In Palestine itself you can find the best specimens—there, on horseback, with their guns upon their shoulders, they take it in turn to patrol their territories as *shoumerines*. Imbued with a strong spiritual awareness and physically strong and powerful, and brave too, they are the leaders of the new generation which has gathered here at Westerbork—members of the Hashera who receive favourable treatment from the Commandant. Young farmers who are preparing to leave for Palestine, often educated young men who have come from secondary schools. It is cheering to see how the younger generation are pushing the older generation into the background. The older generation, often not able to cope with the abrupt transition from their self-sufficient ghetto to this rough and callous community, are visibly losing ground; the younger generation coming from a hard school can hold their own here splendidly; if they were soft, they have the opportunity of building themselves up here. If they get a reasonable chance in Poland, the general picture will be the same there too.

In contrast to the great mass of the Jews, the old and old-fashioned, the young and liberal-minded, and the nationalistic, there is a small group, the so-called baptized Jews, who have become assimilated. They have alienated themselves from Jewish society and have become partly absorbed into the Dutch people from a spiritual and cultural point of view and they mean to return to their own firesides. And in between the groups are the unbaptized partners of mixed marriages, most of whom have a foot in both camps, but are now obliged to live in the Jewish camp or are being forced back into it. If they have any clear awareness of what is happening to them, they find themselves faced with a difficult choice. The idea of "purification" is perhaps more real to them than to any other group of Jews. Whilst *the others* have already defined their position and must merely keep an internal check upon themselves, *they* have to take definite steps and determine where they actually stand, that is, if they are given a chance to.

The Jews here are sitting destitute on a dunghill, like Job. It is a hard fate, but there is one thing still left to them—the realization that, after all that is being inflicted on them now, those who are spared will rise up again more mature and with a greater awareness—purified. This purification process involves cutting down the weak and those who do not come up to the desired standard. The strong who survive must carry out their own purification, as individuals or as a community, according to the spiritual and moral position they wish to occupy in the world in time to come.

In the name of the Commandant, Gemmeker, a typed notice was issued yesterday to the baptized Jews assembled in hut 72. Its contents were as follows: 'By virtue of the agreement concluded between the *Reichskommissar* and the representatives of the Evangelical Church you will not be deported to the east.' *Deported!* One Jew baptized before January 1st 1941 has gone home. One can see in this an indication that they will all be going shortly.

Yesterday three Aryans were shut up in hut 67, the S-hut or punishment hut, equipped with Jewish stars and S-bands. One of them had come to bring his Jewish wife a parcel and got through into the camp with two of his friends. They are to be deported to the east as Jewish sympathizers. A spicy detail in the story—one of them is an NSB man, i.e., a member of the National Socialist party; he had his badge on. A report from Amsterdam that the centre is *clear of Jews* and that all Jews are forbidden to enter the central area on penalty of being deported as S-detainees. American stock exchange quotations higher than they have been for three months. At supper time delousing of a patient and spraying of his bed, also those of his nearest neighbours. Was at a football match attended by many Jews on the parade ground. A good game. Filthy stench from the latrines on the moor, wafted over by the wind—very nasty. Had a whole cucumber today.

Monday May 31st: A good friend of mine who arrived here this week on one of the large transports from Amsterdam and

21

visited me today said with a sigh: 'I just couldn't stand it in Amsterdam any longer.' He was thinner and looked worn out. He thought I looked fit and flourishing. And he is not the only one to heave a sigh about life in Amsterdam. There are many who do so.

People's nerves are at breaking-point. It is a relief, even at Westerbork, to escape from the nervous strain for a moment and break the tension. You soon hear complaints about the huts. They are filled to overflowing with people and furniture. Night-time is sheer hell. There is perpetual restlessness and coughing and the sound of people walking and shuffling about on their way to the toilet. Daytime is hell too and full of petty annoyances. There are people who shout and shove and push, arrogant commands from the hut leaders, children whimpering and all kinds of minor vexations.

For those who move from a large living hut to one of the special huts, the hut for baptized Jews (72) or the one for the elderly (56), the change comes as a blessing. They fail to notice the poorness and meanness of their new abode and are aware only of the greater space available, although even there it is meted out very sparingly. Married couples who are allocated a small house no bigger than a doll's house (at present there are three married couples with families in one small house, each one with a little room of their own) look upon it as a blessing from heaven. At least they have a little privacy. People who come to Westerbork via the camp at Vught consider themselves very lucky; they are overjoyed at the prospect of being free at last from the strict and ruthless control of the SS and coming under the much more flexible control of Jews (directed and supervised by the German Commandant and his assistants behind the scenes). Everything is relative. The Jew who used to live in a spacious and richly furnished flat in south Amsterdam is grateful if he is allowed to move into a shoddily furnished little room in a nasty little house. Those are the conditions under which many doctors live here with their families.

How fortunate were the Jews who came from the concentration camps at Amersfoort, Ellecom and later Vught and found a refuge here. The rejoicing of those who were accommodated in the exemption huts was only short-lived. They were usually sent on to the east after a day or two. But people with haemorrhages or with internal or external injuries or those who were suffering from debility or mental strain and were admitted to

22

the hospital huts said it was like paradise. This was no exaggeration—like paradise. How many of them burst out sobbing when they saw the maternal care lavished on them by the women when they arrived. How many, to begin with, lay in rapture in the simple hospital beds under a pile of soft blankets with hotwater bottles, and how many cried out with pain and joy at one and the same time, until finally a doctor came to dress their suppurating wounds with fatherly solicitude and kindly words. And how many grasped the nurses' hands in gratitude. At Amersfoort, Ellecom and Vught the doctors spurned Jews suffering from injuries or fevers or diseases, telling them they could rot or die, for all they cared. 'Die, you Jew!' Women here out of the kindness of their hearts came, one after the other, to bring them bread or butter or bowls of milk or hot food or fruit, saying that it was for the Amersfoorters or the Ellecommers or the people from Vught. Everyone made way for them. From morning till night they were spoiled and pampered. Those folk from Amersfoort and Ellecom and Vught who had been starving, sometimes for months on end, did not eat in the ordinary way—they devoured and gobbled and guzzled the things set before them. They were insatiable. They were made a fuss of, as befitted men who had managed to escape death and the grave—martyrs of their race. In the hospital huts they got an extra ration of bread and butter and gruel and meat and were fussed over. Friends coming to visit them pointed them out to others as someone from Amersfoort —or Ellecom—or Vught. And the visitors thrilled with compassion and something like awe. Those who had come from concentration camps would argue about which had been worse: Amersfoort or Ellecom. The public took part. Amersfoort was recognized as representing the peak of human misery. The people from Vught who came later, but had lived at Amersfoort first, confirmed this. For many Vught had meant an easing of the misery, although Vught was bad enough. And after Vught Westerbork brought further relief. Yes, it was a paradise. While the Amersfoorters gradually disappeared from the hospital after months of treatment and, with a few exceptions, were sent away on transports, many of the Vught folk who came after them still lie in the hospital huts.

The Commandant has gradually become more lenient towards people who have come from concentration camps. The order referring to the first transport from Amersfoort in November was that the whole crowd should be sent on to. . . . But where? No one as yet knows. It should be obvious that they were sent on to a punishment camp in Germany, but some people hold the view that they were sent by *ordinary* transport to Poland. Mevr. Landau, for example, received a letter from her husband a month or two ago from Poland through a third party. He had been sent as an S-detainee with the above-mentioned transport and wrote to say that he was getting on well, but was in need of food (sent through a third party). If he had been put in a concentration camp, it was hardly conceivable that he could have sent a letter. It is assumed that, in view of the great need for labour in Germany, the S-detainees are simply absorbed into the so-called *Arbeitseinsatz*, or labour pool, but are given heavy work to do.

When the Commandant heard what had been going on at Amersfoort—practically all the new arrivals had been sent here with bandaged wounds—his heart melted. Some German National Socialists have soft hearts. It was thought that he looked upon what had happened at Amersfoort as a disgrace to the regime. And it is said that the Commandant was brought up in a good home. It is a definite fact that after that particular transport Amersfoort and Ellecom people came streaming into the hospital huts by the dozen. The Ellecommers still had priority. Amersfoort was a recognized prison camp. But Ellecom was not—it was a plaything of the Dutch SS. Men who were officially earmarked for the special labour camps in Amsterdam, Rotterdam and The Hague, aimed at increasing the volume of employment, and were not certain if they really had to go there were taken off to Ellecom under false pretences. The Ellecommers looked dreadful, every bit as dreadful as the Amersfoorters, but most of them had a longer period of suffering behind them. They were given an assurance in the name of the Commandant that they would *not* be sent on to the east, but that promise was finally broken and many of them were indeed sent there. The Vught people too, when they arrived at Westerbork, went streaming into the hospital huts by the score, mainly because they were undernourished and were infested with lice. There were many Vught people who had *not* been to Amersfoort and had been sent straight here from the Amstelveenseweg. A great proportion of these have in the meantime been sent away to the east. There are perhaps still

24

thirty to forty of them in hut 82. And there are a number of them in other huts too. The folk from Amersfoort, Ellecom and Vught still find the hospital a paradise. They would be glad if they could remain in this "paradise" till the end of the war.

The professional male nurse who was so bright and resplendent has disappeared. He has been sent to hut 83 on night duty. A pity, he was a fine man. Before the patients went to sleep, he would come and ask: 'Are you lying comfortably?' They could not believe their ears.

The wagons for tomorrow's transport are standing ready once more—forty-eight of them. A mood of depression. Glorious summer evening with a soft breeze. Had a tomato and an egg today.

Tuesday June 1st: A quiet morning. Drizzling. Not the usual grim Tuesday procession. Altogether four people from my hut have been put down for deportation out of the thirty being sent from the hospital huts. The announcement was made quietly and discreetly to them at six o'clock by one of the young doctors. No wild scenes. Yet the transport quota for today once again amounts to 3,000. The question is: Why are there so few invalids going this time? There is a rumour that they intend to keep on the doctors and nursing staff as long as possible because of the plan to turn the camp into a military hospital for the Germans. That does not sound very likely. A more likely explanation is that it is due to the influence of Dr. Spanier who is in the Commandant's good books.

The transports are as loathsome as ever. The wagons used were originally intended for carrying horses. The deportees no longer lie on straw, but on the bare floor in the midst of their food supplies and small baggage, and this applies even to the invalids who only last week got a mattress. They are assembled at the hut exits at about seven o'clock by OD men, the men of the Camp Security Police, and are taken to the train in lines of three, to the Boulevard des Misères in the middle of the camp. The train is like a long mangy snake, dividing the camp in two and made up of filthy old wagons. The Boulevard is a desolate spot, barred by OD men to keep away interested members of the public.

The exiles have a bag of bread which is tied to their shoulder with a tape and dangles over their hips, and a rolled up blanket fastened to the other shoulder with string and hanging down

25

their backs. Shabby emigrants who own nothing more than what they have on and what is hanging from them. Quiet men with tense faces and women bursting into frequent sobs. Elderly folk, hobbling along, stumbling over the poor road surface under their load and sometimes going through pools of muddy water. Invalids on stretchers carried by OD men. On the platform the Commandant with his retinue, the "Green Police", Dr. Spanier, the Medical Superintendent, in a plain grey civilian suit, bareheaded and very dark, with his retinue, Schlesinger, the head of the Registration Department, in riding breeches and jackboots, a nasty face and straw-coloured hair with a flat cap on it. Alongside the train doctors holding themselves in readiness in case the invalids need assistance.

The deportees approaching the train in batches are surrounded by OD men standing there in readiness (now NB men also, i.e., men from the Emergency Squad), to prevent any escapes. They are counted off a list brought from the hut and go straight into the train. Any who dawdle or hesitate are assisted. They are driven into the train, or pushed, or struck, or pummelled, or persuaded with a boot, and kicked on board, both by the "Green Police" who are escorting the train and by OD men. Noise and nervous outbursts are not allowed, but they do occur. Short work is made of such behaviour—a few slaps suffice. Some of the OD men, Germans and Dutchmen, have been recruited from the dregs of Jewish society, rough, coarse fellows, without refinement, human feelings or compassion; they just live for their cigarettes and for an easy affair with women like themselves. Like the "Green Police", they wear green uniforms and high jackboots. They base their uncouth behaviour on that of their German colleagues who are lavish in the use of their fists and inflict quick, hard punishment with their boots. The Jews in the camp refer to them as the Jewish SS. They are hated like the plague and people would gladly flay many of them alive if they dared.

Men and women, old and young, sick and healthy, together with children and babies, are all packed together into the same wagon. Healthy men and women are put in amongst others who suffer from the complaints associated with old age and are in need of constant care, men and women who have lost control over certain primary physical functions, cripples, the deaf, the blind, folk with stomach disorders, imbeciles, lunatics. They all go on the bare floor, in amongst the baggage and on

26

top of it, crammed tightly together. There is a barrel, just one small barrel for all these people, in the corner of the wagon where they can relieve themselves publicly. One small barrel that is not large enough for so many people. With a bag of sand beside it, from which each person can pick up a handful to cover the excrement. In another corner there is a can of water with a tap for those who want to quench their thirst.

The agents of Lippmann, Rosenthal & Co., following on the heels of the exiles, board the train and wrest their final small possessions from them, banknotes of low denominations, fountain pens, watches, by means of slaps and intimidation. Anyone who has not presented his few remaining possessions to friends and acquaintances in the huts or given them into their safekeeping tries to get them out of the train, if the opportunity arises, sometimes wrapped in rags. Jewish Gestapo men who have been lined up to act as spies beside the train go along the track after the train has departed like hyenas in search of coins and banknotes.

When the wagons are full and the prescribed quota of deportees has been delivered, they are closed up. The Commandant gives the signal for departure—with a wave of his hand. The whistle shrills, usually at about eleven o'clock, and the sound goes right through everyone in the camp, to the very core of their being. So the mangy-looking snake crawls away with its full load. Schlesinger and his retinue jump up on the footboard and ride along for a little bit for the sake of convenience, otherwise they would have to walk back. That would wear out their soles. The Commandant saunters contentedly away. Dr. Spanier, his hands behind his back and his head bent forward in worried concentration, walks back to his consulting room.

Everyone in the camp makes a kind of vomiting noise when he speaks about the transport. Three thousand and fifty people were taken away today. The mood in the camp is absolutely foul. In the night it was found that a further three hundred people were needed; they were taken from the work sections and offices. [. . .]

Saw the teams who work on the moor come back at half past six today—young men and women escorted by guards. They are healthy folk. Bareheaded. Tanned by the sun. Walking at a brisk marching pace in boots or clogs. No one would have thought they had a ten-hour day behind them.

27

Wednesday June 2nd: A few weeks ago I was given a letter signed by my house physician and Dr. Spanier, entitling me to pay sick visits to living huts outside the hospital area which is separated from the rest of the camp by barbed wire. So I can take a general look at the camp and find out about different things and meet all kinds of people. This will explain how I am able to note certain things in my diary.

A number of Jews who were baptized before January 1st 1941 and are at the same time partners in mixed marriages were sent back to Amsterdam this morning. Persons baptized after January 1st 1941 were deported to the east yesterday.

Aus der Fünten* is here again. The result—a tightening of discipline. He thought Westerbork seemed too much like a holiday resort. It was supposed to be a labour camp. From now on the Jews in the living huts must get up at half past five. The men up to fifty years of age and also those from fifty to sixty must in future be treated *militairement*. They have to march to work in lines of three, keeping a proper distance apart. Women from seventeen to thirty-five years are being enrolled in the teams going out to the moor to pull heather. Those over thirty-five have been or are to be enrolled in the women's work team who sit packed together in the Central Kitchen peeling potatoes from eight to twelve and from two to five. Everyone has to work and there must be no idleness. Children from ten to seventeen years old who have not been assigned to other duties have to scrape stones from now on. All must work.

For the time being camp inmates are forbidden to send their laundry home. It is feared that they will send spare garments home as the people on the transports are not allowed to take their rucksacks into the wagons with them and they have to be left behind.

As time goes on, the mood in the camp is getting gloomier and gloomier. Mistrust and fear are growing as far as Poland is concerned because of the vile and despicable way in which the Jews are being sent away. The few intellectuals who have been in the camp so far are firmly of the opinion that Poland means the end of everything and that the Jews will not be able to last out if the war goes on much longer. There are even Jews who

* The much-feared head of the Amsterdam *Zentralstelle für Jüdische Auswanderung*, who played an important part in the deportation of Jews from the Netherlands.

are doubtful whether Germany will in fact lose the war and there will be an Allied victory. They feel the want of physical training which would give them confidence in their ability to hold out. The workmen and tradesfolk who are used to heavy physical work and have strong muscles are more self-confident. But even amongst them there has been a decline in optimism recently. This is presumably connected also with the way in which the deportation tempo has been speeded up. Everyone is going around with a long face—there is no longer any laughter to relieve the tension.

A big spring-cleaning operation again today. *Stabsarzt* Mayer, the Senior Medical Officer, is expected to carry out yet another inspection. All the boxes stored on the benches have to be reduced to one box and they have to be neatly arranged. The beds are all being straightened, papers tidied away, hats taken from the walls, walking sticks hidden away. But the floor is as black as soot (because it hardly ever sees any hot water or soap). Breakfast and spring-cleaning coincide. The blankets smell of dust (because they are never aired or beaten), the pillow cases are grimy (because they are not renewed often enough), the window panes are like opaque glass (because they are hardly ever wiped) and we, the patients, stink (because we get too few changes of clothing and are not washed often enough), just like the male nurses (because they do not change their coats often enough). The façade is all that matters.

In the large living huts the leaders have ordered the women who have not been allocated to the daily potato-peeling team to take a box of potato peelings on their laps and pretend they are peeling potatoes, should the high-ranking dignitaries happen to come along. All a façade. Anyone who is idle and does not work will be sent away.

Thursday June 3rd: The other day a Dutch Jew and a German Jew had a disagreement about a seat on a bench. The Dutchman, who had been sitting there, stood up when a friend approached in order to say a word to him, and the German took this opportunity of sitting down on the seat. After his conversation the Dutchman turned to the German and said: 'Excuse me, but this seat is occupied.' Whereupon the German snorted: 'Occupied, occupied—who are occupied, the Germans or the Dutch?' This tactless remark, which quickly went

29

the rounds, was resented by the Dutch Jews, not because the joke was in bad taste, but because it expressed exactly what the German Jews *really* feel about the Dutch Jews in the camp. It is definitely a very tender point and is always approached with extreme care and diffidence.

There is something smouldering under the surface between these brothers of the same race—the fact that they cannot stand one another. The Germans despise their Dutch camp companions and the Dutch hate the German Jews, not as fiercely as they hate the German National Socialists, it is true, but they do hate them because they are *Germans—Prussians*. It is a complicated relationship. The German Jews here play the leader, just as the German Aryans are accustomed to playing the leader wherever they are. They think they have a right to do so. Many ask their Dutch fellow-Jews: 'What care and consideration have you ever given to us? What did you do to make our lot easier when we were flung in here by fate before you were ever subjected to the blight of the National Socialist regime?' They reproach them, saying: 'You have fallen short in your duty as human beings.' To what extent is not very clear.

In 1939 this camp was set up for Jews who were roaming about in Holland illegally or as stateless persons. Some of the Jews who had made fruitless attempts to get into the United States on the "St. Louis", which ostentatiously went on sailing to and fro off the American coast, also found a place at the camp. Likewise the Jews who had been accommodated in different labour camps in Holland. By means of fixed voluntary donations Jews made it possible for many other Jews to stay in Amsterdam and elsewhere. The so-called Special Emergency Committee defrayed the cost of admitting the Jews to Westerbork and maintaining them there. That was no small matter.

There are Germans who minimize this and say that the Dutch Jews should have done more, much more. That is one grievance. A second grievance is that the Dutch Jews did nothing to arrange for or encourage an outlet to America to be opened up for their German protégés who had come in perfectly legally. Either the money was not made available or they did not bring enough pressure to bear upon the Dutch government along these lines. Premier Colijn had held out a prospect of this being done, so, when they were put behind barbed wire in Holland, it came as a great disappointment to them.

That is the second point. It is a matter of esteem and respect. When someone feels embittered, and many Germans do feel embittered as a result of four years of camp life, he will demand the last drop from the barrel.

To explain and justify their dictatorial attitude the Germans say: 'We were in the camp long before the Dutch came. We have stood up to the miseries of the National Socialist regime since 1933 and have been hunted perhaps two or three times from our homes, but you only began to suffer those miseries in 1940.' The factors involved here are no longer esteem and respect, but strength of character and comradeship. If anyone wants to argue the point, he could say: 'Yes indeed, you *were* struck down by fate before the Dutch Jews and you *have* endured all these miseries over a longer period than they have, but when you arrived in Holland they came to your assistance at the very first call for help, although not exactly in the way a number of you would have wished. At any rate, you *enjoyed* the hospitality of the Dutch Jews. And you could have shown a similar spirit of camaraderie and brotherly love when they were finally put in beside you, overtaken by the same fate, and you could have divided up everything equally, even if only for the very reason that they were on their own home ground.'

The first Dutch Jews did not come to Westerbork until the summer of 1942, accompanied by part of the Jewish Council from Amsterdam. The German Registration Department remained in the hands of the German Jews under the direction of Schlesinger. When the Jewish Council had to plead for rights or obtain favours for the Dutch Jews, its members could apply to the supreme head of the German Jews with the requisite degree of humility. It is generally known that Schlesinger does not pay any heed to the Jewish Council and treats it as a *quantité négligeable* and it has very little authority. If a Dutch Jew wants to obtain anything, an exemption or a job, he prefers to apply direct to the German Jews in authority if he knows them or else through German friends.

That does not mean to say that the German Jews have left the Dutch Jews out of things—oh no! Up to a certain level they have brought them into the administration of the camp. Dutch doctors are in charge of hospital huts or assist in them, Jews, male and female, have become nurses or hut leaders and are employed in a fairly large number of subsidiary jobs, as stokers, window cleaners, hut cleaners, porters, or keep order in the camp or serve as members of the Flying Column. In view of the large number of Dutch Jews coming in regularly and in view also of the large number of Dutch invalids and elderly folk admitted to the hospital huts, the German Jews could not refuse to let the Dutch play a part in this way—indeed it was convenient for them to hand over certain jobs to the Dutch. But they held on resolutely to the key posts and more or less every one of the important jobs so that they could be in control of the whole organization and could give priority to the interests of German Jews.

The succession of German SS Commandants in the camp undoubtedly fostered the supremacy of the German Jews. Blood is, in short, thicker than water. When the transportation of Jews to Poland to join the *polizeilicher Arbeitseinsatz*, or Police Labour Pool, began in the summer of 1942, the German Commandant at that time, Deppner, promoted the 2,000 or so German Jews still remaining out of the original 3,000 to the status of Long-Term Residents, who were not liable for deportation. One can only guess whose influence was responsible for this mark of favour. It is said that the Commandant felt that the German Jews had suffered enough and that it was the turn of the Dutch now. But sentimentality of this kind or rather such sensitivity with regard to the just apportioning of all the violence and injustice inflicted on the Jews is *not*, as a rule, in keeping with the National Socialist regime.

One might venture to suppose that in settling Jewish affairs the Germans preferred to carry on discussions or negotiations or other business with German Jews rather than with Dutch. The example given by Amsterdam encourages this belief, namely, the *Expositur**, which is directed by a German (Austrian), Edwin Sluzker, who came originally from Bukovina. They are closer together and understand one another better, both psychologically and as far as language and ways of behaviour are concerned. Deppner's successor, Dischner, and Dischner's successor, Gemmeker, consistently maintained the position of preeminence of the German Jews. The last-mentioned even has a Jewish adjutant in the person of Herr Todtmann who forms the link between the Commandant and the Registration Department. The adjutant wears a service uniform. He, Gemmeker, has awarded the now famous red

* One of the most important sections of the Jewish Council in Amsterdam, which was authorized to submit applications to the Germans.

stamps to German Jews. These safeguard their position and, moreover, give them certain facilities, involving freedom of movement within the camp and other privileges. So the Germans have bound the German Jews to themselves to a certain degree and play them off against the Dutch Jews. Not all German Jews will accept this ugly role, but some— and these are not the morally strongest among them—do. They feel invulnerable.

The German Jews have undeniably abused their position of supremacy and continue to do so. They form, as it were, an almost exclusive association for the protection of the interests of German Jews. As individuals and acting together they do their best to save all Germans brought here from being deported and endeavour to keep them here. They have done this from the time that Dutch Jews began arriving at Westerbork. In this way they have, in point of fact, handed over the Dutch Jews to the Germans to suit their own convenience. Wherever possible, they have pushed the Germans into jobs and have kept the Germans here. The Registration Department with Schlesinger at its head has been able to do this. For example, during the seven months that I have been in the hospital, it has *nearly* always been Dutch Jews that have been deported. On one single occasion German Jews were sent too. The same complaint can be heard from the living huts. In the last few months the nursing staff has been considerably thinned out, and it is the best nurses who have in some preordained way disappeared—*Dutch* Jews. *German* Jews were *never* included. The same thing happens in the other huts—German Jews are seldom to be found among the deportees.

During the past five or six weeks Dutch Jews who had up till then been doing certain jobs have been systematically replaced by Germans—as hut leaders, porters and work leaders. Preference is given to the baptized. Among the Germans who have jobs to give out the baptized Jews get priority. They are a clan, the members of which keep passing the ball to one another. The male nurse Gottschalk takes the lead. I have heard of a recent case of a leading Dutch Jew who was recommended by an honest German because of his abilities for a position in the Information Service, but he was very politely, but quite improperly, sent packing and palmed off with fair words by the powers that be. The most annoying case recently has been the appointment of Herr Grünfeld as head of the

33

Jewish Council in place of the notary Spier who had moved to the "Jan van Schaffelaer" camp at Barneveld. It was said that the Commandant had more faith in a German Jew, but the German Jews accepted this as a matter of course. The Jewish Council has thus become a mere tool in their hands.

The German Jews do not only act as leaders by virtue of their official positions in the camp. They have evolved a certain measure of control in another respect which creates permanent tension as far as the relationship between German and Dutch Jews is concerned. They dictate and bawl and bark and snap and shriek and intimidate the others, often just like the National Socialists or Prussian soldiers. It is in their blood and without this they do not appear to thrive, they are not happy. This evil is to be found mainly in the subordinate staff, in hut leaders, porters, kitchen bosses, work leaders, people who, for the most part, have been given authority and a say in things for the first time in their lives. They have been given some power and they abuse it completely. The Dutch Jews, who are hard put to it in any case, do not "like" this tone of command, this throwing of their weight about, this self-importance—they hate it and the German *Jews* as well. Of course, the Dutch Jews are not all nice, and there is a good deal of riff-raff amongst them too, but they are used to different things. The German Jew, accustomed to *Tüchtigkeit* and *Gründlichkeit*, efficiency and thoroughness, cannot endure the lack of discipline or the touch of anarchy and individualism to be found in the Dutch Jews. *That* is why they do not "like" them. Also because of their matter-of-fact nature and their lack of enthusiasm for carrying out the measures laid down by the authorities. They despise them and show this openly. Leaving out of account the personal feelings of liking and friendship existing between German and Dutch Jews, and these are fairly common, there is a sharp emotional rift between the two communities. The Dutch say: 'Back to "Bocheland" with them, bag and baggage; they don't belong here with us.' The great question is how many even of the Dutch Jews will ever see their native land and their homes again. The future is certainly not rosy as far as the German Jews are concerned. A large proportion of them do not want to return to Germany which has given them such bitter experiences and such grim memories. But they cannot as yet see where they, as stateless persons, will be accommodated after

34

the war. This paralysing feeling makes them morally very vulnerable and, perhaps, over-sensitive.

Friday June 4th: Seven little girls deloused in hut 3.

A German Jew went for a sugar analysis to one of the camp doctors, a Dutchman. He produced medical certificates from which it would appear that from eight to ten per cent sugar normally occurred in his urine. The current examination showed one and a half per cent. The doctor informed the patient. The latter reacted as follows: 'I don't believe it.' The doctor: 'So I am lying to you.' The patient: 'I didn't mean that.' The doctor: 'But you did say so indirectly and that is a piece of impertinence.' The patient: 'I didn't mean it like that. You obviously don't know the niceties of the German language.' The doctor: 'But I am very well aware of the difference between impertinence and courtesy. Please go and see another doctor.' The patient: 'I shall go and see the Commandant and make a complaint about you. And you may be sure that you will be deported.' Just one instance of intimidation out of the many that occur here.

Met an old friend of well over seventy and completely blind who has come from Vught. The SS there took away his blankets, his topclothes and nearly all his underclothes. He arrived here wearing only a shirt. Thousands of others have had the same treatment. [. . .]

On Wednesday night a small transport of 300 persons arrived from Amsterdam. So far 71,000 Jews have been registered and sent on to eastern Europe. Had a tomato today.

Saturday June 5th: An independent surgical department has at last been opened at Westerbork. They had been working on it for months. The department was said to be intended for the German military hospital into which the Westerbork Camp would be converted after the last Jew had been sent away to the east. The visit paid to the camp by a number of high-ranking German officers from different branches of the armed forces lends support to this idea. The first operations on Jews have since been carried out there, operations which had been performed until then at the Academic Hospital in Groningen, where sick Jews were sent under guard. In the last few days there has been a rumour going about that Westerbork has

35

not been found suitable for use as a military hospital, so it will continue as a reception centre for Jews and Vught, which is larger and fitted out in a more up-to-date manner, will now be considered as a prospective military hospital.

So far the announcement made during the latest visit by Aus der Fünten to the effect that hut residents would have to rise at half past five and women over seventeen would have to pull heather and children from ten to seventeen years have to scrape stones has not been implemented. So everything is going on here as before. [. . .]

Sunday June 6th: Heavy rain. The male nurses bellow: 'Quiet there! The doctor is coming round.' But there is still a hubbub in the ward. The assistant appears in the doorway of the doctors' room and roars: 'Nurse v. E., if you can't get them to be quiet I'll fling you out, and the patients too.' Nurse van E.: 'You couldn't get it any quieter than that!' General merriment. That disposed of the assistant.

Every twenty minutes or so two patients behind me loudly sing the praises of haddock liver and roe, fillets of halibut, and smoked and fresh salmon. The neighbour on my left is philosophizing on another subject: 'When I think of the salt meat sandwich they used to serve at De Haas, and those rolls with two kinds of meat on them, my mouth fairly begins to water. It'll be the first thing I want when I get back to Amsterdam.' A third says: 'Oh, wouldn't you just fancy a slice of poppyseed loaf!' These are the subjects that recur daily.

Last night there was a general move from three of the large huts to others. They were vacated in less than ten minutes. People bustling laboriously about with beds and bedclothes, shabby tables and cases, rucksacks and stocks of provisions. Like a disturbed ant hill. Room has to be made for two large transports each of 1,600 people from Vught who will be sent on to the east on Tuesday. A large number of baptized Jews with dubious papers were also victims of the move. [. . .]

A surprise party in the doctors' room in the evening attended by a few doctors, a few male nurses and a few patients, *enfants chéris* who can enjoy certain privileges. Invective poured from the lips of the head nurse. Against the medical assistant who holds forth in learned fashion at lectures for the nurses, but omits to instil into them a love of their vocation. Against nurses who never miss a chance of shirking their duty and hide

36

in corners of the ward to have forty winks, or retreat into the washroom to smoke cigarettes—people who have no idea at all of service and discipline. The fault, he says, lies in the fact that the administration appoint "deferred" or baptized men and so on to do the nursing and send the qualified nurses out to Poland. Bridge and coffee. Off to bed at eleven.

Rumours that the last transport of 3,000 persons will be going to Poland on Tuesday and that Westerbork is becoming a labour camp. Great excitement. There is some talk of reclaiming a moorland area. A joker put this notice on his bench: 'Don't worry! Things will change.'

Monday June 7th: An emotional scene the like of which we have seldom seen. The women cleaners came sobbing into the ward this morning and the men snorted: 'That's about the foulest thing we've ever come across.' A mild description of all that people have experienced here in Westerbork alone. On such occasions language is inadequate. At about half past four in the morning a transport with 1,750 Jews arrived in cattle trucks. Except for about a hundred men, they were all wretched women with their infants and older children. Wives and families of the men who had been set to work at Moerdijk to dig earthworks and had been given an assurance by the German authorities that their wives would not be deported to the east. The women are in fact going on next Tuesday's transport to the east. They arrived as thin as rakes and worn out after a ten-hour journey. They spoke vehemently about their despicable treatment at Vught, the exhaustion and humiliation of it all. Up at four o'clock in the morning, roll-call at half past four, standing till six o'clock, at work at half past six, often with dogs at their heels. Until half past six in the evening, sometimes half past seven, with a meal break of one hour. Several of the babies are ill, with scarlet fever or measles. In my ward there is a baby, a curly-headed little thing not one year old, deposited amongst the other children. 'For the Police Labour Pool,' people say jeeringly. At Vught an average of four babies die every day. General interest and feeling evident.

For the last few days we have been hearing children's voices all night. They are often romping in their beds and have been nicknamed the "small predators section". Infant mortality is high—one child dies every day. Pneumonia, scarlet fever and intestinal complaints occur frequently. The climatic conditions

37

are harsh, the accommodation bad, the risk of infection great, the diet unsuitable. The care given by the doctors is excellent, but the surroundings are wretched, the nursing leaves much to be desired, especially as far as the babies are concerned, and the hygiene is appalling. The women are often without the help and support of their menfolk and the necessities of life.

Tuesday June 8th: On the dot of seven yesterday evening, when the gates of the hospital area were unlocked to let in the throngs of visitors, the whistle went for an alert. Astonishment —was this intended as an annoyance for the Vught folk to prevent them from visiting their relatives after the long period of separation? The fact that people think like this shows what we are used to here and what we consider a possibility. The gates were closed. Anyone already inside was firmly sent back and the patients were ordered to be confined to their beds. Until about eight o'clock, when the visiting time was over, the reason for the emergency remained a mystery. Then it was found out that one of the Vught people who had come yesterday, an S-detainee from hut 67, had escaped. The OD men were instructed to search for the fugitive in all the huts. Not until about ten o'clock was the all-clear given. So the Vught people did not see their relatives. Early this morning they were instructed to get ready for the transport to the east, and at eleven o'clock they departed in cattle trucks. There is sorrow gnawing at every heart as a result of the lack of pity shown.

Today I posed by request for the painter Madame Cohen-Bendiks who is doing a pencil portrait of me. A tiring business.

The tales of the Vught people are pitiful. Many more have been brought in infested with lice and have been deloused in the "circus tent". Women have had their heads shaved and have decked themselves out with headscarves to hide their baldness. All children under sixteen years of age from Vught have been or are going to be sent away. Only as a result of protesting have a large number of mothers managed to go with their children. But, in spite of this, young children are being sent alone. Vught is certainly one of the bitterest chapters in the persecution of the Jews in Holland. The men who are still working at Moerdijk and whose wives have just been sent on to Poland, behind their backs, via Westerbork, are in many cases the same men who laid the railway line from Hooghalen to Westerbork. Commandant Gemmeker had a particularly high appreciation of their work. He kept them from being deported to Poland and arranged for them to be supplied with extra food and when the time came for them to be sent to Vught he gave the impression that this was a mark of special distinction. There too they would be employed in laying a railway line and their wives would accompany them. In many cases their mistrust outweighed their enthusiasm; they had learnt from experience what the word of the Germans was worth. At Westerbork people knew where they stood; daily supervision was in the hands of guards, most of whom were friendly and lenient. At Vught supervision was in the hands of SS men who had been trained up in the German school. But, when the men and women finally went off together and were at last convinced that they would not be going on a transport to Poland, they rejoiced and wept like happy children. They were drunk with joy. Everyone knows the end of the story. The men were set to work digging tank traps and building bunkers at Moerdijk and the women, robbed of their clothing, were sent back to Westerbork with ailing children. A vile and despicable thing to do. Just as despicable was the fact that the German authorities lied to the men, saying that the women were taking the children to a children's home and would later be returning to Vught. When the women reached Westerbork, they cried at being separated from their husbands and at the fate of their children. They found their mistrust had been justified.

At half past two this morning a visit from Rosengarten, the hospital administrator. 'Your wife is on the list of people being sent away. Do you wish to go along with her voluntarily?' The man who had been wakened jumped up and gave a cry. There were beads of perspiration on his forehead. He burst out: 'Of course I'll go with her! I've got two children of three and a half and six and a half.' Rosengarten made a note on the list: 'Is going voluntarily.' Everyone was suddenly wide awake —tense and nauseated. Rosengarten went to another bed: 'Your wife is going on the transport in the morning. Do you wish to go along with her voluntarily?' 'Oh God, what am I to do? I've got a heart condition. I haven't discussed it with my wife. May I talk to a doctor about it first?' 'Of course, but you'll have to make up your mind. The doctor will be coming early enough in the morning for you to be able to speak to him.' The first man to the second: 'I'm shivering. Are you feeling as cold as I am?' Rosengarten: 'What are you going to do?'

39

'I don't know. I don't know. What should I do?' 'I'll just mark down that you're going. And you can have a word with the doctor about it.' 'My God, my God!' Male nurse: 'Go to sleep now. You have a few more hours and the journey will be long and tiring.' 'Don't make it any harder for me. Leave me in peace!' At half past five a letter came from the patient's wife: 'Stay where you are. I'm going alone. It's too much for you.' At six o'clock the man came from the Registration Department: 'I regret to have to tell you that your wife is going on the transport this morning. Do you want to go with her or not?' The patient jumped up: 'And yesterday I was assured that my wife would not be going.' 'I'm sorry, but it's got nothing to do with me. She is on the list and you'll have to come to a decision.' 'That's an easy enough thing to say! You just have to give the orders, but our whole lives are at stake!' 'Quietly, there's a good fellow. We'll be going too—a few trains later on.' 'I want to postpone my decision for a bit.' The man from the Registration Department pulled his watch out of his waistcoat pocket: 'I'll give you another five minutes to make up your mind.' Silence. The patient, vanquished: 'I'll go. I've got no choice.'

In the middle of the night the second transport came from Vught, about 1,300 people, men, women and children. Tired and worn out, filthy and ailing, some of them were simply transferred, amid snarling and shouting, beating and pummelling, from the dirty cattle and goods wagons they had come in to the dirty cattle and goods wagons that would take them to the east. The quota had to be complete. People here cannot see a single one of these trains without either cursing or sobbing or feeling revulsion. The train goes according to schedule and this is a torture and a torment. It is never late, it is never hit by a bomb. Why has Providence left us in the lurch? Several ailing children are being sent on the transport with their parents or just with their mothers who are being deported to the east. In my hut there is a man with TB. His wife and three children have been sent on. On the orders of SS officer Fischer, who is on a visit from Amsterdam, ten men were hauled out of the S-wagon of the train in connection with the escape of the prisoner from hut 67, a man called Hans Polak. These ten were taken away in the direction of the moor, near Assen.

An "Aryan" is now lying opposite me, a real Amsterdammer with bristling hair, a pointed turned-up nose, broad jaws and a Jordaan accent. He has come from the S-hut where he had been locked up with two friends because he tried to bring his Jewish wife a parcel. The Deputy Commandant informed him that he would shortly be allowed to go home. He was allowed to take off his Jewish star again. He is the only "goy", or Gentile, here and he occupies a position of honour. He feels completely at home with us, he says.

Sixteen Jews from the Frederiks List transferred to Barneveld, to the "Jan van Schaffelaer" camp. The last transport took place some months ago. People were not certain if another transport would indeed be going. A man marked on the list had to stay behind because his papers were not in order, a man called Boasson. The Commandant had not yet received the authorization for his transfer from Aus der Fünten in Amsterdam, but the Jewish Council had a copy of it in their possession. A ludicrous case; in Barneveld there are about fifteen men of the Boasson type, all of them men of the highest merit and essential to Holland. Most of them come from Middelburg, as does Frederiks himself. Barneveld has plenty of Boassons, but why not have the full complement? A pity that Boasson's papers were not in order. Had a piece of cheese today.

Wednesday June 9th: Officially only three had to go on the transport from my hut yesterday (out of over two hundred patients). Twenty-one actually went, i.e., eighteen ailing folk who went "voluntarily" as members of their families had been summoned to go, irrespective of whether they had relations in hospital. It has been semi-officially stated, on good authority, that in the next five weeks no more transports will be going. A sigh of relief has gone through the camp, but the mistrust with which the declarations and promises of the German authorities are usually received still lingers on in the background. The Commandant was busy conferring with Dr. Spanier yesterday.

The ten men who were hauled out of the S-wagon yesterday were taken by car to Assen, escorted by three members of the "Green Police", and were put back on the transport train. When the escape was reported to Commandant Gemmeker, he threatened that blood would flow. Obviously the authorities wanted to give the impression that these ten men were to be shot on the moor, thereby causing fear and dismay inside the camp, so that any desire to escape would be suppressed once and for all. The fugitive has not been found.

There has been much guesswork about the reasons for discontinuing the transports: 1. Railway stock is needed in connection with the coming Allied offensive. 2. The wagons are to be used for carrying Aryan workers to Germany. 3. It has been decided to keep 40,000 Jews in Holland. 4. The railway wagons are needed to carry French and Belgian Jews to Westerbork in transit to the east. [. . .]

A Jew, a man called Bonewit who had worked at Moerdijk, has been admitted to hospital hut 82. He had a shoulder injury and was brought back to Vught on the very day that his wife and child were being sent on the transport and he arranged to go with them to Westerbork. Lucky fellow! He told me all about Moerdijk. Ten weeks ago 500 strong men were allocated to Moerdijk and three weeks ago another 500 to the Gouda and Zwijndrecht area, to make tank traps and bunkers. They went off there in striped prison clothes. Work there goes on from half past six in the morning till half past six at night under the supervision of Dutch SS who stand guard in towers on a kind of conveyor belt system. The work consists of digging out heavy clay soil. Anyone who contravenes work discipline is reported and is condemned to a sound thrashing where he sits down. He has to do the counting himself; the times that he misses are not counted in. One of the worst cases was as follows: a Jew who could not stand the pace was ordered to wheel two barrows filled with clay up one of the bunkers. He fell and got a gaping wound in his head; in spite of this, he was beaten. As a punishment food may be withheld. The food consists of a third of a ration of bread per day with forty grams butter and forty grams sausage and a helping of thin beet or cabbage soup. The meal break lasts half an hour and during that time the men have to drink their soup in the midst of all the clay. In the evening after the roll-call they have to fetch their bread ration from the kitchen, and this sometimes takes until eight o'clock. One Sunday in four is free. Jews attend to the internal affairs of the camp and a Jewish doctor treats those who are injured at work. Injured and ailing men are sent back to Vught which has to see to the despatch of replacements at once. After supper the men go straight to bed of their own accord in order to recover from the heavy, fatiguing work and be able to keep going. [. . .]

Had a boiled egg today. It is reported from Amsterdam that there is virtually no butter, cheese, fruit or fish to be had.

Thursday June 10th: Close behind the barbed wire of the camp the purple lupins are majestically in bloom. A refreshing sight for the eyes of the thousands of battered men, women and children who can gaze at nature in the evening hours from the dry paths between the sepulchral huts or from the silent windows of the dirty washrooms. Rising amongst the lupins, at intervals of a few hundred metres, are the towers manned by guards with grim helmets over their red country faces and their terrifying muskets within arm's reach, who are there to prevent escapes. Guards with muskets on their sturdy shoulders patrol along the barbed wire. The lupins too are under strict guard; anyone who is not allowed to leave the camp to do outside work stays inside and does not stretch out a finger towards those decorative lupins. But the camp is full of lupins; on the rough wooden tables in the living huts they stand in old lustreless food tins, flaunting themselves in front of the windows. They lend some floral fragrance and colour to the dinginess of the tiers of beds and the stench of unwashed clothes and sweaty bodies. Towards evening the young men and women, in the full awareness of their unquenchable energy and vitality and covered in dust and sweat, come hurrying back into the camp from the moor, in marching step. They are decked out with bunches of lupins, the reward they have chosen for their daily stint of work. Under the escort of the guards, who maintain a strict check on discipline, but are glad to let the young men and women have the day's joy and consolation in the shape of those flowers, the symbol of their young lives which have been lopped off, but will not stop blooming. The moor is a mass of bloom, inside and outside the camp.

Scattered over the hospital huts are about fifty children who have come on the transports from Vught with scarlet fever, measles, pneumonia or mumps. Also two foundlings who were discovered at the Registration Department without any identifying marks.

As a result of the latest escape of an S-man from hut 67 the supervision of the S-men in the hospital huts, which had gradually been relaxed, has been tightened up again. They may only go about dressed in pyjamas and are not allowed to leave the huts. An OD man, a beast of a fellow, keeps guard at

43

the main entrance to the hospital part of the camp.

There is a rumour that the Frederiks Jews at Barneveld are coming to Westerbork today. No one believes this. Nevertheless there is some word of the Jews still in Holland being concentrated at Westerbork, so as to make it into a ghetto and change it from a reception camp to a labour camp. It would not really be so very strange if the Barneveld people did come here.

Saturday June 12th: Once again the partners of mixed marriages with children were all summoned to the Registration Department this morning—about 300 at a rough estimate. Gemmeker addressed them. They could either be sterilized and be sent back to Amsterdam without a star and with a distinctive type of J or face the possibility of being sent to Poland where they would collapse under an inhuman labour system. Those summoned to attend had to make known their decision by Monday. The whole episode has an ironical flavour. When the Germans started to discriminate against the Jews in our country, many Jews who had contracted mixed marriages had their marriages dissolved temporarily in order to safeguard their families and save their possessions. Until the Germans last year recognized mixed marriages and even dissolved mixed marriages with children, in the sense that the persons involved were exempted from deportation and the marriages were not broken up. Too bad for those who had got a separation from their Aryan better halves. But what the Germans gave with one hand they took away again with the other. First of all, the *dissolved* mixed marriages were flung on the scrapheap, then mixed marriages without children (unless they could show church membership or baptism before January 1st 1941) were broken up and recently partners of mixed marriages with children who wanted to escape the Polish hell were forced to let themselves be sterilized. Those who had their marriages dissolved to save their families no longer needed to have any regrets about this unless, in order to escape the threat of Poland, they had preferred to be sterilized. For men who had already given up married life in the true sense owing to impotence the choice given them by the Germans was not a particularly difficult one, but for young men in the full prime of life it was horrible. They have fallen into the clutches of Moloch who will not let them go.

Westerbork has become an apiary. A swarm of bees which

44

came flying into the camp was caught yesterday with the queen in a butter cask. The bees evidently have no objection to associating with Jews.

Today the morning roll-call came at six o'clock instead of half past, as had been the practice until now. The detainees who were transferred to Amersfoort four weeks ago returned today and their return seemed just as pointless as their departure. They look well, thanks to the better diet and the more favourable climatic conditions at Amersfoort. They came back with the report that Amersfoort has become a concentration camp once more. 190 Aryans and ten Jews have been admitted. [. . .]

One boiled egg today.

Sunday June 13th: Whit Sunday. The Descent of the Holy Ghost.

The sterilization problem has entered a new phase; a member of the Jewish Council went along the beds this morning to bring a message from the Commandant to Jews married to Aryan wives and having no children, asking if they were prepared to let themselves be sterilized *voluntarily*. A kind way of putting it! The messenger forgot to mention that anyone who was not voluntarily prepared to do so exposed himself to the danger of deportation to Poland, like those from mixed marriages with children. But he did add that those who were prepared to submit to the operation had to sign a contract— the *voluntary* nature of this business had to be clearly laid down—for the benefit of history.

For many the problem is a hard one. Opposite me are two men who had contracted mixed marriages, one of them with and the other without children, the first an Austrian of about sixty and the other an Amsterdammer in his thirties. The first man made up his mind. 'I'll let myself be sterilized. I have lived my life,' he reasoned with himself, 'and I can't give my wife any children now. So why not?' Later he reconsidered his decision. 'Until now,' he argued, 'sterilization has only been carried out sporadically on mental defectives to prevent them from reproducing themselves, but it hasn't yet been done on healthy individuals. It's not known whether an operation of this kind will cause mental illness later on.' So he refused and accepted the possible consequence of his refusal—Poland. The other argued: 'I know that sterilization is contrary to nature

45

and ethically wrong, but I'll get it done all the same and return to Mokum (Amsterdam). My wife mustn't do work that I could be doing. I must support her.'

The problem varies according to the individual. In all the huts there are serious discussions about what ought to be done; the young men and women in particular are faced with a dilemma. They feel they are between the devil and the deep blue sea. One is just as bad as the other, whichever they choose. Opinions are even divided among the doctors. They naturally agree that sterilization may produce unpleasant psychological reactions, but I have heard the view stated that anyone who allows himself to be sterilized is not entirely finished. After the war medical science will certainly find a means of undoing sterilization. But about one thing there is complete agreement: this measure marks the very peak of barbarity. Hitler has declared more than once that God gives His blessing to what he does. Of course he does not know what blasphemy means.

In the large hall of the Registration Department we had a first-rate symphony orchestra yesterday evening—the same hall where the transport people are brought, where men sigh and women and children weep and every week the walls resound to the entreaties of those who want to escape the awful calamity of being sent to Poland. In the front row in civilian clothes was Commandant Gemmeker with his wife, close behind him his Jewish adjutant Todtmann, Schlesinger, the head of the Registration Department, Dr. Ottenstein, the head of the Applications Office, and other Jewish notables. The audience was made up of 500 Jews, all nicely turned out, the women in dresses that they had obtained from the Welfare Department.

Thirty-five players, artistes and dilettantes on the platform with deadly serious faces. A meagre little group with stringed and wind instruments. They stood out like cut-out paper figures against the white background. A man called Neuberger conducted Aryan music in a grey lounge-suit: Weber's "Oberon", Schubert's "Unfinished Symphony", the "Valse Triste" of Sibelius. All the *tempi* were too slow. The soloists were: Erna Weiss with songs by Schubert, accompanied on a tinny piano; the Polish *hazzan* Rokach with an aria from "Pagliacci" in German, with the orchestra. At the Commandant's request Liszt's "Hungarian Rhapsody" as an encore. Pathetic. Wild

46

applause only for the songs and for "Pagliacci". A bouquet for the conductor. In the interval the Commandant smoked a cigarette with Neuberger. Also conversed with mevrouw Dassy, the wife of the conductor, who was sitting next to him. That is how the Commandant of Westerbork enjoys himself in company with his Jews and makes his life bearable. The Jews behaved very respectfully. When the Commandant came in, they all stood stiffly to attention, also when he left. They know how to conduct themselves.

Went for a long walk round the edge of the camp with an intelligent young girl who is here voluntarily. Enjoyed the magnificent view and the summer clouds piled up in the blue sky. Along the barbed wire is a trench about five metres deep which is well on the way to being completed. It is being dug by the Jews to make escape difficult. Depressing feeling.

Two ounces of sugar.

Monday June 14th: Five o'clock in the morning: time to wash. In the "small predators section" a pitiful yell went up for the umpteenth time that morning. A troublesome little boy who had come from Vught was wakened out of a deep sleep and bawled: 'I'm not going to be washed! I'm not!' The male nurse bellowed: 'At home you can do what you like. But you can't here. You've got to do what *we* like.' The boy screamed: 'I won't!' The nurse: 'If you won't, you'll be thrashed. Do you hear? Thrashed!' 'I won't even then!' 'You're provoking me.' Silence for a moment. The nurse: 'If you put on a face, I'll put on a face too and then you'll see something!' The nurse won the day. He is considered to be the best and most civilized male nurse in the ward. The head nursing sister heard of the incident and in her day's report she made a note that it was advisable to treat the patients differently and not so strictly.

The New Testament has been brought into the hut by the women cleaners. They are partners in mixed marriages and include some who have been baptized. For the past day or so one of them has been reading out a few chapters of the New Testament to a blind patient in between jobs. This morning one of his neighbours was angry and incensed. 'If you don't mind,' he interrupted, 'I happen to be a Jew and this is a Jewish community and it annoys me that you should have parts of the New Testament read out to you.' Half an hour later the protester was summoned to the doctors' room. The

47

doctor (a baptized Protestant and formerly a member of a church council): 'Is it true that you have objected to the New Testament being read aloud?' 'I didn't object, but as a Jew I felt annoyed and I was irritated because I'm ill and I didn't sleep well. I would have been just as annoyed if the Torah had been read aloud. I'm not a practising Jew.' 'What exactly did you say?' 'That I felt annoyed.' 'Nothing more?' 'I've told you exactly what happened. I didn't say anything more.' 'Will you put it in black and white?' 'I'm not up before the magistrate. I'm in the habit of telling the truth.' 'I shall make an issue out of this.' 'I'm sorry if I have annoyed anyone. If I have, I'm willing to offer my apologies. I was only annoyed because I was feeling terrible.' 'In that case, we'll leave it at that.'

Tuesday June 15th: The partners of mixed marriages have been told that they can postpone their decision about sterilization until next Thursday. Before then two Jewish doctors will explain to them the significance and consequences of sterilization. Yesterday a typed notice to that effect was put up in the vestibule of the Registration Hall where the symphony orchestra gave its third concert before a packed audience. [. . .]

There is daily discussion about the length of the war. [. . .] People are still dissatisfied with the British and Americans who are not progressing fast enough to prevent all the Jews from being sent to Poland.

'Don't get all worked up about what will happen tomorrow! You didn't before the war. In those days you didn't even stop to think what the morrow would bring. And you could have been dead the next day without being worked up the day before. So why all the fuss now?' 'Oh yes, but there's a war on and what has Poland got in store for us? What news do we ever get from there? Hardly a thing.' 'You only die once and it doesn't make all that difference whether it's ten years sooner or ten years later. The best thing to do is to live for the day. There's no *point* in getting tensed up about tomorrow. The war may be over tomorrow and you might fall into a ditch and break your neck on the very same day. Do you know the story of the soldier who was four years at the front in the last war without a scratch and one hour after the ceasefire was shot in the head and died?' 'Just go on and make a joke of it.' 'That's the last thing I'd do. But you have to live a soldier's life when

48

you're placed in a situation like this.' 'To hell with your soldier's life! I'll only live once.'

The tiresome boy began to wail. 'I want some bread and jam,' he bawled, 'I want some bread and jam!' Voices: 'Wring his neck!' 'Give him a good shaking!' 'Throw him out of the window!' Male nurse: 'Eat up your gruel first.' 'I want some bread and jam.' Head nursing sister: 'Eat up your nice gruel first.' 'I want some bread and jam.' Male nurse: 'That's enough, damn you. Are you going to eat it or not, you little wretch?' Voices: 'The boy's been badly brought up. He's spoilt.' 'Put him in the washroom!' The boy squealed like a scraggy sucking-pig: 'Ee, ee, ee!' The whole ward squealed in unison: 'Ee, ee, ee! Oh, oh, oh!' Another boy called out: 'I want the toilet.' A band of working folk went past singing (to Chopin's "Funeral March"): 'Zo gaat Jantje naar de bliksem toe!' (So Johnny goes to hell!) Uncontrollable merriment.

Rumours about the arrest of Mussert who is supposed to have stood out against the idea of bringing back the Dutch army as prisoners-of-war.

Wednesday June 16th: The current joke: What is the comparative and superlative of "ster" (the Jewish star)? Answer: "ster", sterile, "ster"-off. [. . .]

A storm of criticism and indignation descended this morning after breakfast upon the young man who had decided to let himself be sterilized. 'You're a coward!' 'You've no strength of character.' 'No proper man would do that.' 'You just wait till you're faced with it yourself! I'm doing it for my wife.' 'Your wife shouldn't want that. Perhaps she doesn't. What a joke— a sterilized man!' 'Do you know for sure that you won't be sterilized as soon as you get to Poland? I don't. Better have it done right away here. And stay with my wife.' 'You should just wait and see what happens in Poland. And what does it matter if your wife does have to earn her own living? There are others doing the very same thing.' 'The fact of the matter is that you have no strength of character. And the awful thing is that Jews in general don't have a very strong character. It's a pity, but it's true.' 'You don't say so!' 'Oh yes. Forty years ago the Zionists warned the Jews in Europe. But nobody would listen. They were too well off in western Europe.' 'You could go right back to Egypt.' 'The great mistake is that the Jews have not learnt to think historically.' 'Just you try and teach

49

the masses to think historically. Have you ever found the masses wanting to think? First of all, they must want to think. You should take a look and see what the masses think about here. They certainly do have problems to think about, problems of their own. They think about salt meat sandwiches and loaves and *hallah kugel* with pears on Friday nights. But as for spiritual and moral problems—well, I ask you!' 'Don't Christians eat salt meat sandwiches?' 'Of course they do. But the Jews are beastly materialists. Instead of taking the situation as it is and accepting the fact that there are no tasty morsels for them to eat and that they should toughen themselves up in preparation for the future, they think of their stomachs and their strolls along the Kalverstraat and dates with the "birds". They ought to make sure they have something in their knapsacks and see that they train the young people for the work they have to do. The young people represent the future.' 'Exactly. And isn't that just what the Zionists do? Don't they try to reach the young people and prepare them for the future?' 'That is the very best thing they could do. But as for the masses —they've had it so good and they've led such happy-go-lucky lives, with the cinema, the radio, motor bikes, all the gifts of technical know-how. But all these things aren't exactly calculated to strengthen the character, which is what a people needs. The moral ingredient is lacking.' 'Gentlemen, please be a bit quieter. This is a hospital ward.' 'Just so—the moral ingredient is lacking. And, if you thought along moral lines, you wouldn't allow yourself to be sterilized, I'm telling you. You're a coward.' 'Well, so I'm a coward. But you'll pipe another tune one day.' 'Perhaps. But you're running away before you smell danger. You're acting as if you've lost the war. And I'd like to see *that* happen!' 'Quiet!' bellowed the nurse. 'The doctor is coming on his rounds.' The discussion was broken off.

A boiled egg today.

Thursday June 17th: Mortality among the children continues to be alarming. This week two children from one family died, one aged four and the other aged two, and the mother is carrying a third child. The family came from Vught. The deaths are at the moment put at fifteen children per week. This is an example of how sick children are treated. A small child with inflammation of the middle ear was taken to the Academic Hospital in Groningen in an open bus, not accompanied either by its father or its mother. The ear was lanced and the child was put on the bus for Westerbork straight after the operation and the father took charge of it again at the camp entrance. The child had been ill for six months, practically without a break, with influenza, quinsy, etc. Inflammation of the middle ear, sore throats and infection of different organs occur frequently. The climatic conditions are harsh and there is a great deal of dust.

Yesterday afternoon a mild sensation occurred during the clandestine smoking break in the washroom. A corpulent, well-fed man with large blue eyes came shuffling along in a shirt and underpants, but without a collar. 'May I introduce myself? I'm Mr. So-and-so, judge at the court in R.' Great interest aroused. This was no small thing. A great acquisition for the Plutocrat Club and its supporters. Admitted without any vote being taken on it. The Plutocrat Club consists of a dentist, a number of businessmen and a journalist, all walking patients who have struck up a camp friendship. [. . .] We have some sympathy with the great man who once stood high above so many people and dispensed justice to them and now appears before us as an awkward and pathetic figure in underpants.

'You couldn't have imagined this would happen.' 'No, I thought they would leave me alone and not take me away. But they just came and fetched me from my home in the usual way.' 'You won't feel well disposed towards the Boches then? I could slit their throats.' 'Oh, you're up on your hobbyhorse again, are you? Will you never learn? You're just being child-ish.' 'Childish or not, if things begin to hot up and I get the chance, I'll be right in there with the best of them. I most certainly will. I'll string them up on ropes, damn it! You've got no blood in your veins!' 'If you can't rise above the scoundrels who are making you suffer, then you're not much better than they are. If you start up like that, you might as well get a lot of Jews out of the way, while you're about it. There are a lot of rogues among them too.' 'I don't care a damn, I must have my revenge.' 'That's your affair, but you will surely agree with me that anyone who wants to be *master* can't be a *roadsweeper* at the same time. In a revolution the dirty work has never been done by the masters. Even Hitler and his lackeys don't do the dirty work. By and by, when they've played their part, they themselves will be got rid of—by the angry mob and by the courts of justice. I for my part rely on justice being done. If you want to belong to the angry mob, go on and join it! What would you do as a judge?' 'The crowd will certainly want to vent their anger. But, of course, there will be special courts of justice to try traitors to their country. And they will no doubt be shot.' 'They should do exactly the same to them as they are doing to the Jews. Make them work in concentration camps till they drop. They've more than earned it.' The judge excused himself and withdrew. His underpants were coming down; the button had come off.

On an estimate, ninety per cent of men from mixed marriages have put their names down for sterilization. Implementation of this has been postponed indefinitely.

Had lettuce salad.

Friday June 18th: Morning conference between four sick lawyers on one of the beds: Mr. So-and-so, a criminal lawyer and two other legal men. Mr. So-and-so still does not feel very much in his element in this strange environment. 'I'm not bearing up well,' he said. 'I wasn't a real Jew any more and I had no dealings with Jews. Also I'm not a young man any more. And, to crown it all, my balance is affected. It's psychological, purely psychological. What am I to do about this whole business!' And there was such a good-natured look in his honest blue child's eyes, innocent and guileless, not like a real judge at all.

A hefty lad from a bed beside the criminal lawyer and opposite the two other legal men came sauntering up, looking more like a gorilla than a human being. He was fascinated by the company and asked if he might sit there. Mr. So-and-so: 'Yes, sit down.' The criminal lawyer: 'This isn't the first time you've "been sitting" (i.e., in gaol).' 'You mustn't insult me. I've done nothing. I'm a victim of the war.' 'I don't mean any harm. I've done time too.' Mr. So-and-so (aside): 'I know him. He is one of the court's regular customers.' To Mr. So-and-so: 'To me you're no more than a common street hawker.' Mr. So-and-so: 'I feel a bit like that here, I may say, quite a bit like that.' Opposition and malicious pleasure on the part of someone low in the social scale because fate has not struck at him alone. It has not spared the people higher up and at the top of the scale, the dignified, the proud. There is opposition to intellectual superiority and the snobbishness of those who have risen high in society. There is malicious pleasure at their downfall. 'Here,' he persists in saying, 'we are all equal!' The message in his voice and in his eyes: 'Contradict me if you can! You can be as smart as you like and as clever as you like, you can use the most scholarly words, you can have the grandest contacts in the world—but here you stand, just like me, naked against the wall and have no say in anything, none at all. Just try it and see. You have no more rights than I have—we're equal at last. True or false?' People from the lowest strata of society who have been given authority here bully, and often delight in bullying, those who at one time had authority in a free society. They ignore all lines of demarcation.

The intellectual and the snob and the *parvenu* will have nothing to do with this equality, this levelling process. Equal? Not at all—it only seems so. Cruel fate may have swept up poor and rich alike into a great dirty heap and made them both go along the same hard road, but that does not mean to say that there is no longer any difference. They discuss this amongst themselves. There are still natural differences, variety of aptitudes, differences in education and cultural background. The intellectuals and the snobs and the *parvenus* cling firmly on to these and from them forge a certain basis of spiritual solidarity. You see this in the last garments they have been able to save from the robbers, garments still possessing the old refinement. You hear it in their speech, which is educated and interspersed with unusual and difficult words and stands out against the bastard language of the great masses. Amongst themselves they maintain a certain degree of homogeneity and a community spirit. Inwardly they have withdrawn behind the bulwarks of upbringing, culture and refinement. Outwardly they have surrendered; they are too sensible not to realize that they are individuals lost against the background of the vast crowd and cannot openly maintain the privileges due to aptitude, upbringing, education and culture and create a recognized position of privilege for themselves here. What takes place behind the scenes is another matter and it is balanced and offset by what the other party is doing behind the scenes. [. . .]

A boiled egg.

Saturday June 19th: The *Untersturmführer* thrashed a Jew on the Boulevard des Misères—without any explanation. The Jew does not know why. He made the moor squad come back to do

53

digging on their free Saturday afternoon as a punishment because a number of Jews missed the roll-call in the morning after the rain had stopped.

A piece of cheese.

Sunday June 20th: Twenty members of the Flying Column and one hundred OD men were unexpectedly summoned at two o'clock in the morning and sent to Amsterdam. It is known that a raid took place in Amsterdam and that the purpose of this was once again to bring in a few thousand Jews. The immediate reason behind it is thought to be the heavy bombing of Düsseldorf. This means that furniture is needed for the stricken population.

In flaming red capital letters the following notice has appeared in the porter's lodge:

"F"

FÜRSORGE (i.e., Welfare)
WELFARE DEPARTMENT OPEN FOR
CONSULTATIONS DAILY
(EXCLUDING SUNDAYS)

In *German* only. In a hut where the majority of the people are *Dutch*. You can see a process of evolution in the treatment of language here. While German refugees were living in internment here before the war and even a considerable time after it started, they had to adapt themselves to a Dutch regime using Dutch as the vehicle of communication and not German. This was not difficult for many Germans. During their stay in Holland they had learned sufficient Dutch to understand the orders and also to make themselves understood. Dutch remained the official language till about four or five months ago. But, since the arrival of the Dutch Jews in July of last year, German and Dutch have been used side by side to indicate buildings, also for notices in the huts, depending on whether a German or a Dutchman was in charge. Linguistic rivalry. Many Dutchmen, however, were prepared to meet the Germans halfway in private conversations by using the German language. This often stemmed from vanity, sometimes from a desire to be hospitable. This still happens. Many Germans, often as a result of childish vanity or a desire to learn, showed a similar willingness to use Dutch when speaking to the Dutch. Both Dutch and German usually come off badly as a result: an abomination to sensitive ears. But there are many

Dutchmen who hold on tenaciously to their own language and there are even more Germans who will not abandon German under any circumstance and often have not taken the trouble to learn Dutch properly. When the occasion arises, they yap and snap at the Dutch in German as if German was the proper language for the purpose. [. . .]

Judge So-and-so could not stand the abrupt change in environment. He was moved today to hut 3 where people with mental disorders are sent for sleep treatment. Escape from reality.

At the end of a delightful summer day one of the last waves of Jews from Amsterdam was washed in here in the evening. Under the burning sun 2,000 men, women and children came into Westerbork in cattle trucks. Today it was stiflingly hot in the huts. In the hospital huts the patients lay half-naked on top of their blankets and the children were stripped to the waist. Those people who were "off duty" went for the good of their health to a vacant piece of moorland inside the fence on the eastern side of the camp. This stretch of moor has been transformed into a landscape of sand dunes. The sand dug out to make the trench about a metre or so from the barbed wire has been thrown up into heaps surrounding the camp grounds. On the camp side, immediately behind the huts, there are clumps of oak trees, but they are still thin and lanky. The imitation landscape would be ideal if it were not marred by a square in the middle with dirty and stinking old mattresses, their white covers partly burst open.

In this disfigured setting favoured folk seek respite from the heat of the camp. Men and women, boys and girls sit in pairs hidden among the clumps of trees, against the sloping sides of the dunes, facing towards the moor on the other side of the trench and with their backs turned to the barbed wire. Just as if they were among the sand dunes at the seaside, men and women, boys and girls exchange tokens of tenderness and affection, unconcerned and uninhibited and oblivious to the impending tragedy of the transport, true to the unchanging nature of mankind. Couples stroll along the trench as if they were strolling along the shore, the girl listening carefully for a fleeting word from the boy, moved by the ferment of love. Couples tan their bodies brown in the sun. As it is broad daylight everything is done in a decent and respectable manner under the watching and prying eyes of the guards in

55

their towers, armed with field glasses, and the guards patrolling along the barbed wire. Guards who look harsh and severe, but are gentle in their manner and show signs of pity towards the captive Jews and a dislike of the special duties forced upon them. And so life goes on.

While people here forget their own tragedy and consciously or unconsciously sublimate it in amorous fantasies or in an innocent "aside" with the sun, a new piece of tragedy is under way. Human beings wrenched from their native soil, robbed of their possessions, poor, degraded and humiliated, in cattle trucks. We all know the procedure, we know the scene—we have seen it here so often or know of it by hearsay. Again and again along the same road endless, disorderly processions of emigrants and gipsies have passed—men, women and children laden with luggage which they could only just carry. The tragic element has begun to wear off. It has lost its original grandeur and ruggedness. The first waves which rolled in here were of strong young men and women who had prepared themselves ideally for the unknown adventure. They came marching from Hooghalen and a tremor seemed to go through the camp, rather of admiration than of pity or horror, for this courageous and resolute advance guard of the Jews. Thereafter came the proletariat and the paupers, all mixed up together, with their many children and often poor clothing and humble possessions—a miserable procession that came slouching untidily along from Hooghalen, shabby and wretched, and rushed into the camp in an uproar. Pity, profound pity fills men's hearts at the sight of these battered creatures who have spent their whole lives on the very margin of existence and now, plundered and robbed, have been abandoned to the storm. Wave after wave of these humble folk and paupers have surged into the camp— always the same pattern of insignificance, faint-heartedness, poverty and misery. Without a pause, often as destitute as when they came, sometimes provided with rags hastily collected by others, they have gone on to Poland.

October 3rd marked the climax—still the blackest of black-letter days. 10,000 souls were crammed in here all at once, the men from the different labour camps, with their wives and children who had been picked up in a terrifying and fiendish raid. The road from Hooghalen to Westerbork groaned under the misery of the Jews and the callousness and shamelessness of their persecutors. A sea of dispirited, defeated human beings

56

—among them children and yet more children, who pushed and stumbled over one another in the throng. In the camp there was a shortage of living space—the huts overfilled, men and women all mixed up together; on the parade ground thousands had to spend the night under the open sky. Still mainly the proletariat from the populous districts of the large towns. Little by little the throng was transported to the east. Afterwards from all over the country came the elderly folk from the rest homes, the seriously ill patients from the hospitals.

The first transports came by train only as far as Hooghalen; from there those who were still able to put down one foot in front of the other came stumbling along to Westerbork, panting and puffing. The rest came by ambulance. A macabre procession of lame, blind and decrepit men and women jogging along into the camp, supported by members of the OD. It was heartbreaking for those who watched—the tragedy of lives lived out to their end and almost finished, accentuated by those signs of helplessness and powerlessness. Later on the train brought them right into the heart of the camp. These old uprooted folk died off like rats. Their remains were burned in the crematorium as if they were less than rags. After this the transports came via the camp at Vught. Men, women and children literally clad only in shirts were brought into the camp in cattle trucks, often thick with lice, first of all men and women together, later only the women separated from the men. One individual tragedy in the midst of universal tragedy. This was followed by wholesale transportation in cattle trucks, with forty, fifty or sixty persons in one truck, in amongst the luggage and on top of all the dirt—to Poland. The end was almost in sight—the Jews still remaining in Amsterdam were brought into the camp on successive transports of about 2,000 per train, also in cattle trucks—the last remnants of the proletariat and the lower middle class and a large proportion of the Jewish intellectuals.

The arrival of today's transports did not make the same tragic impact as previous transports had done—they were mostly well-built and well-dressed men and women provided with good blankets and equipment as if they had come to spend a holiday here. They were evidently used to travelling. A single invalid was carried away unobtrusively to the hospital on a stretcher. Nor did the public react as if they were going through yet another tragic episode in their tragic lives. All they

57

did was to look around for relatives, friends and acquaintances as if they were on holiday at the seaside and were joyfully welcoming new guests. There was none of the silent grief or the wordless compassion of people who see their brothers and sisters setting foot in a prison or on some sinister spot, but noisy shrieks of recognition and greeting. Westerbork-le-Bain, as a witty man has called the camp.

Monday June 21st: Yesterday was a bright day with warm sunshine. Today there is a nasty drizzle. In the night two more trains came in, each with about 2,000 Jews, also in cattle trucks, while everyone was asleep. The tragedy of the darkness pierced by the ominous glare of searchlights. Early this morning the thousands of cases, bags and bundles which the Jews had taken from their homes and which had been loaded into a separate truck were deposited by lorries on the ground between the huts where they are quartered—on the dusty ground, in the rain. The rain turned into mud. Thousands of men and women got their luggage back all muddy after a long and tiring wait.

They were driven into the huts in dense crowds, three, four and sometimes five persons to two beds, with their luggage. The beds are arranged in three tiers, separated by passages half a metre wide at most, without a single table or bench or chair. Up to 1,000 or 1,100 people in one hut, without elbow-room, without proper storage space for their clothes, all jumbled up together. They move like ants over and past one another, like small, insignificant ants. The human bodies all piled on top of one another send out heat like a furnace. They give off fumes like a burning torch. They sleep tightly packed together, restlessly, tossing about, often on the steel frame of the bedstead, sometimes on the floor. A great stream of people trudge to the WC.

They are about again early—at three o'clock in the morning, in order to have a chance to wash properly. Like bees from an overcrowded hive they gather in the daytime in swarms in and around the entrance to the huts. They swarm about between and around the huts or stand together in groups as if they were at a fair or a market. A continual shuffling and buzzing, just as there is inside the huts—running and trotting to the Jewish Council, to influential or supposedly influential men in order to obtain a *Zurückstellung*, or deferment, or, in hopes of this, a job to do. Those who formerly occupied important posts on the Jewish Council and therefore had special stamps go around here with anxious faces and now turn to the people whom they themselves once helped for help and assistance. They are bewildered by the sudden change in their fortunes; the last here are not the first—they belong once more to the huge grey crowd to which they belonged before. It's all rather tragic—the downfall of the little man who was once the obedient servant of the hangman's assistant.

Tuesday June 22nd: You can live like a lord here in the hospital hut. At least for some of the time. And I am indeed living like a lord. You can even do that in pyjamas when you are a prisoner of Hitler and his men. From my notes it is obvious that we invalids get an egg regularly, also perhaps a piece of cheese of the best quality, sugar and jam. The Military Commandant could have refused us this if he had wanted to, but he did not want to. People are always searching for the reasons why he doesn't. There are some who think that, although he wants to get the Jews out of western Europe, he has nothing personal against them and does not want to do them any harm. That is perfectly possible; even caddishness has its limits. So there are people who say: 'We are not as spiteful as you would think. After the war we shall not hang him up on an iron wire, but on a velvet cord.' That is one way of looking at things.

But, be this as it may, you really do feel you are living like a lord. This morning for example. First of all, after breakfast in bed, the barber came at about nine o'clock. 'Will you have a shave, sir?' 'Yes, please.' 'You weren't shaved yesterday, were you?' 'No, the day before yesterday.' 'That's all right then, sir. Will you lie down?' So I lay there stretched out at my ease. 'Razor all right, sir?' 'Excellent.' The razor flew over my face till it was as smooth as a mirror. You can even manage to be a little bit more of a gentleman. Like my neighbour—he owns an electric razor which he plugs in at a point just beside his bed and he shaves the stubble off his face noiselessly, without any soap. I am envious of him. Others are too. What a plutocrat!

While I was being shaved, the chiropodist was waiting for me, with instruments in a warm cloth. For the first time in my life I was having a pedicure. 'The left foot first.' I carefully followed the deft turns of the pincers and tweezers and lay watching in amazement what an expert could do to a foot.

59

Then the right leg. The same detailed treatment. In private life I never had time for this. I did it myself, as best I could. I was proud of having well tended feet. 'There you are, sir. I'll be back to see you in five weeks.' 'Thank you, mevrouw.'

In the meantime I got a signal from Heinz, the male nurse: 'Your hot water is ready. Shall I put it in the washroom?' Not indeed a first-class bath, but, bearing in mind the circumstances, a fairly good clean and freshen-up. Then I crawled back into my bed and started my work for the day. With the uplifting feeling: I have had a good time this morning and my most primitive human needs have been attended to.

Have I said too much about being able to live like a lord or at least feel like one? When attending to my bath I was guilty of a small error. I was standing there stark naked when one of the boys came rushing into the washroom from the ward. One of the head male nurses who witnessed this bellowed at me: 'That's disgraceful, thoroughly disgraceful. Nobody stands around naked where there are children present.' The nurse appeared not to notice three adult men sitting side by side relieving themselves in the presence of children. I was perplexed; I could not agree to the idea that it was so disgraceful. At that moment the house physician nipped into the washroom from the road side. 'It isn't very disgraceful, is it, Doctor, to stand about naked where there are children about?' 'I must forbid you to have a bath in the presence of children on medical grounds.' I was still perplexed. Having just finished the ritual, I dressed and disappeared into the ward. When I came inside, Mr. So-and-so was standing practically naked right opposite the line of children's beds, getting a support for his hernia. I was perplexed. During the day both nurses and patients told a number of doubtful stories in the hearing of children. That is how things are here.

A piece of cheese. The best type. Two old men passed away during the night.

Wednesday June 23rd: A member of the Jewish Council was in the hospital hut visiting a little old man who had asked for assistance. As shrivelled as an old yellow apple, with glowing red cheeks. A fairly advanced stage of senility. Eye-sight pretty bad. 'Miss, look here, I would like to make my will.' Laughter among the patients lying near him. 'His will! Tell me, am I going to be in it? I could be doing with something.' The little old man, sulky and half-crying: 'Can't it be done? I'll tell you the whole story. I'm so old now that it's only proper for me to think of dying. You see, my wife died in Utrecht last year and I would like when I die to have the urn with my ashes placed next to my wife's. I would like to have that put in my will. It will be all right, won't it?' 'He's quite round the bend.' 'And, miss, I would like you to bring me a notary and have it all set down properly. You will do that for me, won't you?' Laughter. 'What about sending a written request to the *Führer*?' The woman shouted in the man's ear: 'Of course I'll do it for you. Just have a nice sleep now. It will all be attended to.' The little old man nodded his little old head and smiled—happy that it was all being attended to.

Thursday June 24th: The young men who have just arrived have been enrolled in the moor squad and the young women have been given the task of pulling heather and wheeling barrowfuls of sand and turf. All day long processions of women walk along the Boulevard des Misères, taking the sand and the turf to a building site. A new element which is giving the Westerbork labour organization a kind of local colour. The whole thing is more like a masquerade or a scene from an opera rather than slavery or forced labour. Women in bunches of fifty or a hundred, under the supervision of the OD. In twos they carry tubs half filled with sand on a pole inserted under the handles, or each one of them separately carries a piece of turf from the moor under her arm like a little girl going to school with her slate. Not at a fast working tempo, but sauntering, like people walking along a beach boulevard. Not in working overalls, but in street clothes. In a suit, or a dress, or a blouse and skirt, with a raincoat and headscarf and walking shoes, often with high heels, and red nail varnish and lipstick and perms. Waving to right and left to relatives or friends along the Boulevard. The women are just playing at working in a labour camp. A musical comedy.

Cabaret this evening in one wing of the hut. Crammed with people. *Café chantant* songs accompanied on a harmonica. An Italian aria for two baritones. Yiddish humour. With the ever recurring refrain:

"We're weary of the war,
To Mokum we will go.
Oh, I miss my Kremjelish,

61

And I miss my Shabbestisch."

Cabaret mood in the ward. A lot of applause. Contentment. A glimpse of old Amsterdam, the Rembrandtsplein.

At the same time in a corner of the other wing of the hut a religious service was going on. Old men with grey beards, learned in the Mosaic Law and decked out in sober parchment-coloured praying shawls reaching almost to the ground, with black diagonal stripes. Men who are averse to frivolity and levity and here more than ever withdraw into prayer and bow down again and again and again, appealing to the Lord God of Israel to deliver them from misery and slavery. No babbling voices, empty and uninhibited, but the almost inaudible mumbling of words from the Talmud. Two worlds absolutely foreign to each other, separated by a small doorway.

Of the partners of mixed marriages confronted with the choice of being sterilized and returning to Amsterdam, or going to Poland, an estimated ninety per cent have opted for sterilization. A fierce debate. 'So much for the character and determination of the Jews! They're ready to let themselves be sterilized, although they have free will and the chance to refuse.' 'Do you call it free will when you've got a pistol pointing at your chest? Is Poland all fun and games?' 'No, it certainly isn't, but, all the same, it's cowardly to give in to the pistol in a matter like this. After all, several people have refused to give in and they've accepted the risk of going to Poland. They just won't lend themselves to the immorality that's demanded from them in exchange for freedom that isn't real freedom at all. These men have dared to cast aside their fears and they mean to keep their self-respect, whatever happens. *They* certainly know what free will is!' 'Do you know what free will is? It means you can say yes or no, and that's all. The proposal they've made to us is immoral because it's all being done under duress and nobody can object if we give in. Our free will is only a sham.' 'If all the Jews had stood together and refused as one man, I'd like to have seen what the Germans did then.' 'If, if! That's exactly the point. But they didn't stand together. That's the awful thing. They never have stood together. Away at the start they just folded up like a jack-knife. We should never have said who our ancestors were and the Jewish Community should have burned the records, then things would never have got to this stage. We've never had any leaders who dared to do that. So now we're sitting in the trap and our only way out is to let ourselves be sterilized.' 'And yet, and I'm sticking to this, it's all a matter of having a strong character.' 'Then I'd rather not have a strong character.' 'You don't need to get angry about it. I'm just saying what I think.'

Saturday June 26th: It has become known that another transport will be going to the east next Tuesday. Once again people's nerves are on edge. It was to be expected, of course. Many of the huts are too full and the people are living like rats in a sewer, all close together. The beds serve as a place to sleep, lie and sit down on, and also as a kitchen table, a luggage store and a writing desk for everybody at the same time. Irritating and exhausting rows and friction are caused by this. Everywhere you hear the same complaint: 'I can't sleep, I can't stretch my legs properly.' Men and women crawl out of their beds as early as possible in the morning and seek out the vacant patch of moorland where they can catch up on their lost sleep. During the day old, worn-out folk lie sleeping or dozing among the oak trees. And now they are on the eve of being taken away to the east.

Patient: 'Oh, nurse. Do me a favour—I've dropped my collar stud. Would you pick it up for me?' 'What's that? A collar stud? Bloated plutocrat!' Laughter. The community life of these compulsory emigrants is poor in amenities. The members of that community have left everything behind. They did not even think of bringing the small objects of everyday life, or spares of this and that. Collar studs, clothes brushes, shoe brushes, shoe cream, buttons, soap and shoe laces are all rarities—a real nuisance. The other day one patient asked another to lend him a clothes brush. 'Yes, I'll certainly give it to you. But you'll have to remember that my neighbour has just cleaned his false teeth with it.'

The gilt was off the gingerbread. The neighbour in question is the dandy of the whole hospital hut. He is ninety years old and hale and hearty. He is as straight as a ramrod, but shuffles rather than walks. He has been "deferred" for some reason or other, but is not suitable for an ordinary hut as he gets in everybody's way. So he has to remain in the hospital hut. Every morning he appears spruce and dapper, in a frock coat and high stiff collar with a black tie. He has a broad black trilby, a pince-nez on a black cord and a black walking-stick with a silver knob. He is our oldest walking patient, or rather—shuffl-

63

ing patient. And he shuffles about all day long from early in the morning till late at night, stiff and straight, like a living tombstone, along the narrow lane between the beds, setting down one foot in front of the other. With his large faded eyes staring into nothingness. He causes traffic jams all the time. Nurses and patients have to follow behind him at the same senile tempo, waiting till the dandy chooses to turn off along a side lane and so allow the traffic to move on freely. There is no grumbling, no impatience. He has the privilege of slowing down the traffic as often as he chooses. A few times every day he leaves the ward and goes to the washroom. In the morning to wash his face as far as the edge of his shirt—nurses do the rest in due course; and one of the other times to sit in full array, complete with walking-stick, in a certain well-known place, in full view of everyone who chances to come along. He is our archaic tourist attraction—a dandy outside, but a mummy inside. He walks about like his own ghost.

The darling of the hut died the day before yesterday— another ninety-year-old, Grandpa Knorringa. Months ago he was brought in with an old man's complaint. But in other respects he was still a stalwart fellow—a farmer from Uithuizer- meeden. He had a healthy round face without any trace of a Jewish nose, and looked like a true Aryan, with honest, guile- less blue eyes. A man with natural refinement, good manners and the disarming openness of a child. Typical dialect pleasing to the ear, and a voice that sputtered like a squib. He bravely accepted his fate and abandoned himself to the nurses, believing that he was in good and reliable hands. For every little atten- tion, including the chamber-pot, he displayed the gratitude of a dependent child. He thought he had been placed in a philan- thropic institution run by pure altruists. He expressed his gratitude with feeling: 'You are a public benefactor. God will reward you.' A chatter would go through the ward. The food he found "just A.1." And the whole ward found it "A.1." too. Grandpa had a good word for everyone, the word of a man who has grown wise through worry and sorrow and has kept his childlike faith and simplicity. When he was angry at inade- quacies or carelessness or a poor understanding of hygiene, his voice was aflame with noble indignation as if the whole of humanity had been insulted and scandalized. He himself had come to terms with life and looked forward to death calmly and quietly as a deliverance.

But he was worried about his grandson over whose head hung the threat of deportation. There were touching scenes when he visited him—the old man stroked the fresh face and the soft hands of the young man again and again as if he himself were Abraham and the young man Isaac. Anyone who watched these meetings was deeply moved. The caressing old fingers trembled with a longing to ward off the young man's fate, his awful fate. The young man clung hard to the grandfather as if to a guardian angel. But, in spite of the exorcising efforts of the grey-haired old man, fate was not warded off—the young man went along the hard road that so many had had to go before him. The death-blow fell. The healthy old man began to pine, his mental powers soon ebbed and his heart refused to function. The death mask revealed a human soul that was good and pure and whole. Old as he was, he had been looked upon as the "Benjamin" of the hut. This time there was none of the cold cynicism normally awakened in spectators by the unbroken succession of deaths, but sincere pity. The darling of them all was no more. [. . .]

Today the *Untersturmführer* thrashed a Jew on the road because he did not greet him submissively enough.

Sunday June 27th: Celebration this morning of a sixtieth wedding anniversary. A little old gentleman, healthy, but a little senile, with a red rambler rose in the buttonhole of his crumpled jacket. Visit from his bent little wife who, like him, is safely lodged in a hospital hut. He is the father of one of the doctors employed here who "has been able to do something for his father." Speech by the medical assistant: 'They have had a lot of joy and sorrow together. May they have many more years of wedded bliss, at home!' Sympathetic interest shown by their neighbours. They are terribly happy together, positively radiant, and they thank Heaven that they can still be together in this place of anxious waiting. He is to be allowed to visit her in her hut for supper until ten o'clock. What a gay celebration here in this bare and sinister place! In the afternoon a death occurred in the same hut. Yet another old man has passed away. The gloomy *sheimetz*, or death prayer, followed close upon the anniversary speech.

A comical incident in the evening. A crazy eighty-year-old who should be in a rest home became a nuisance and wanted to get out of bed. He is not fit to be with normal people. The nurse alerted the doctor who came with a syringe. Nervous tension among the patients. This sort of thing usually occurs only when there are transports, when people marked down for deportation get beside themselves and have to be given a sedative. The doctor looked for a suitable spot on the arm for the injection. His comment: 'Not a particle of flesh—all bone.' The eighty-year-old: 'It could be cement, Doctor.' Uproarious laughter.

The head nursing sister's programme is beginning to bear fruit. From time to time the blankets are beaten, the mattresses are turned regularly and the windows have been wiped once. She has an eye for these small details. She is endeavouring to create order out of the day to day chaos.

A new regulation this morning—no more communal visits to the washroom in the morning. From now on the men will wash from seven o'clock till half past, the boys from seven thirty till eight. The nurses called all walking patients out of bed at seven o'clock. Conflict with reality. At the moment there are a hundred and twenty in the ward, including about twenty boys. So a hundred men must wash in half an hour at twenty-six taps. The result: congestion, friction, rows, revolt. A regulation that could not be carried out. It has fallen into disuse already, like so many other regulations which are in conflict with practical reality. So far there has been no regulation preventing adult men and boys from visiting the toilet at the same time. [. . .]

Monday June 28th: For the past few days teams of men, three abreast and with spades over their shoulders, have been going past my hut singing in the early morning in the direction of the moor. An imitation labour force. The front lines of men in overalls and high boots or heavy shoes of Hungarian leather; the rest dressed in the clothes in which they were brought here, with caps or hats or bareheaded. The men in front march and sing: "Van je hela, hola, houd er de moed maar in" (Be of good courage, hallo, holla!). The men behind them make an effort to march and sing too and those who come behind that, the older men of forty or fifty, trudge along with miserable faces. The marching and singing are voluntary, and there is no law against trudging along and having a miserable face. On the return trip from the moor exactly the same song. They do indeed work long hours, eleven hours per day, but not hard. The complaints are not against the work, but against the food. The work in the open air uses up so much energy that the portion of bread and the helping of hot food doled out to them every day are far below their bodily requirements. The members of the moor squad go round begging when they get the chance.

Hunger has been more evident of late amongst the camp residents. There are several patients lying near me who have had no relatives living in Amsterdam or elsewhere for a considerable time and, as a result, they are not receiving any more parcels, so they and their relatives have to go hungry. They are not ashamed to accept the bread offered to them by others. Some of them ask openly, especially for their children's sake. [. . .]

At present there are seven women cleaning the ward in the mornings. They coax the bread out of the patients' mouths by the look in their eyes and eagerly accept the sliced bread that the better-off patients offer them as a treat. These women come from the ordinary living huts and regularly complain of feeling hungry. They look ill and some of them have gone a grey, dark colour, perhaps not caused entirely by hunger, but certainly by suffering. They were brought in here from Amsterdam with this eloquent colouring and their present environment with its annoying and nerve-racking problems of every possible kind is calculated to darken their faces still further. Many women here live on the verge of a nervous breakdown—many collapse altogether and are admitted to the hospital to be put right. For how long?

This morning Mr. Weinreb,* the man who is connected with the Weinreb List and is a patient in hut 82, was summoned to the office of Gemmeker, the Commandant. A captain of the German *Wehrmacht* and a high-ranking SS officer had come from The Hague to fetch him. The Commandant offered Weinreb a cigar and asked how he was getting on in the hospital. 'Very well,' he replied. The Commandant expressed his satisfaction with the way in which Dr. Spanier ran the hospital. Weinreb was given instructions to be ready in half an hour's time to follow the officers in their car to The Hague. Later he was ordered not to be ready for the journey till the following morning. The officers had heard that the Jewish Symphony

* A Jewish economist, who managed to trick the Germans by devising a special list which offered some temporary protection to those Jews who were mentioned on it.

Orchestra would be giving a performance this evening and they wanted to take advantage of this. As an official in the Department for Economic Affairs Weinreb had done meritorious service, supplying both Germany and Holland with food. As a token of recognition, the German authorities offered to give him the opportunity of emigrating to America. He asked them to allow a number of Dutch Jews to accompany him. The German authorities agreed to this request. So Mr. Weinreb compiled a list of thirty persons who were to benefit from this concession, together with their families. The list grew until it included seventy persons. At a certain point the Germans declared that the list was no longer valid. Many of those who had appeared on the list were subsequently sent on to Poland. Weinreb himself was on the transport list a few times, but was later deleted from it. Weinreb assumed that his summons to go to The Hague had no connection with the services he had rendered in the matter of the food supplies, but was connected with a number of recent arrests. He thought he would be examined as a witness. People in the entourage of the visiting officers had hinted at this.

On an ordinary train with first and second class a number of Jewish women who were British subjects departed today on their way to England. They are being exchanged for German subjects in Britain.

Two tomatoes.

Tuesday June 29th: Today another transport with 2,200 persons departed for the east. The period of respite had lasted only three weeks. 300 sick people have gone on this transport and 150 S-detainees, people who had gone into hiding and arrived last night and were sent straight on, every single one of them, without any equipment.

Early this morning two men in my hut tried to commit suicide. Unsuccessfully. One of them cut his jugular vein and the knife was wrenched out of the hand of the other man before he could harm himself. The house physician did an excellent job. A mood of depression and great emotion.

Now that the transport is over once more and the atmosphere is normal again, it is like a raging sea that has grown calm after a fierce hurricane. The huts are still crammed full.

A Jew who asked to be put down on the Puttkammer List has been asked for 60,000 guilders for his "deferment", and another man for 50,000. Both are S-men. One of them refused the demand and is just letting things take their course, and the other is still considering what he ought to do.

Received today from a Christian in Amsterdam a box full of tomatoes and a covering note which said: 'There are hardly any tomatoes to be got. I have had three so far, but my sister's children have had none at all.' Touching solicitude and willing self-sacrifice.

Great excitement about the death of *Generalkommissar* Fritz Schmidt who is said to have suffered an accident while on an official trip to France. People remember with bitterness how he declared in his speeches that the Jews must work hard in Poland and that he would not rest till the last Jew had disappeared from Holland.

Wednesday June 30th: A chess contest started today. And a big cleaning operation at the same time. Early this morning after breakfast fifty beds from the double row in the middle were carried outside into the lane between two huts. Twenty-five beds on either side. In the gloriously bright sunshine. Barbed wire in the background. And behind that the moor. Wheelbarrows scattered about. All patients who could walk were in their jackets and trousers which had been taken out from under their pillows. The others stayed in bed. Life and movement in the lane as if it were full of twittering sparrows. Games of chess here and there. Sunbathers. Lunch in the open air—hotchpotch in gleaming mess-tins. Little groups of men talking politics in the middle of the lane.

A man with black hair plastered down and no star appeared unnoticed, a tanned, insignificant young man of just twenty or so with one arm and a flapping sleeve and dragging his leg a bit. He walked jerkily along the lane without a word, not looking to right or left. Consternation among the nurses. 'Come on—back to bed—that's the Deputy Platoon Leader, the *Unterscharführer*!' a young stripling of a nurse whispered anxiously. He had never been a nurse before, but an icecream man. Now he has thirty patients under his care. Adult men, including some tough characters. 'Back to bed?' snapped a patient of some note. 'You snarl at us as if we were new recruits, but you tremble like an aspen leaf at the first German you see. Your *Unterscharführer* doesn't worry us. We're fine where we are.' The young nurse looked put out. *Inside* the ward, when the patients were lying in bed, he had never met with any opposition and it was easy to give orders. But the sun and the light had given us back our feeling of freedom and made us brave. In our outdoor clothes we felt we were human beings again. [. . .]

The patients just stood calmly where they were and went on talking unconcernedly. 'Do you know that chap's story? He was on the eastern front and when he came back and became the *Unterscharführer* here he said: "You Jews will come back from Poland all right, but the damned Russians shot off my arm and I'll never get it back." ' We were sorry for the fellow because, in spite of his neat civilian suit, he looked a very poor specimen. 'I'll tell you something else. When the train's going, he pilfers what he can from the Jews with the one arm he's got left, the blighter. And when the train has gone he's as nice as pie to the Jews and the Jewish question just doesn't exist as far as he's concerned. A grand chap!' We took a look at him. Can a man do that? We know that he can. [. . .]

Thursday July 1st: The first half-year is over. Amazing—although I have been waiting here without reason or purpose, just waiting—or so it seems—the half-year has flown past. I ask myself every day, like everyone else: 'How long will it be now?' There is an art in waiting. I have no choice but to wait, but it demands talent nevertheless. The ability to exercise patience is a gift from God. It means not being afraid of what lies ahead. A man who has the courage to look life in the face must also have the courage to look death in the face. Contempt for death and the courage to live stand side by side. You can only die once. Everyone in Europe is now at the front or is standing by and may be called to the front. So people have to take death into account. That makes life bearable. It makes a man strong during the most difficult time in his life. Space and time have ceased to exist—man lives against a background of nothingness. If he dies, then he dies; if he escapes with his life, then he will be a stronger person in the future. This waiting period is a time of moral training and maturing, a time to realize that life is not something we hold in our own hands. We have been given it on loan and we must quietly give it back when it is demanded of us.

The waiting period is going fast. The community I belong to is richly variegated and fascinating. Human beings have been

70

assembled here from all parts of this country and from all over Europe, from all classes of society. They are, it is true, united by a common fate, but it is their own individual fate, their own story, their own experience, their own version of it. Each one in turn opens up the book of his life and reads out a few pages from it. Each one recounts in turn in his own language and in his own way how he came into the hands of his persecutors and, sometimes after passing through other places en route, now finds himself at Westerbork. Each one describes his own path of suffering, each one makes his own accusation. Each one gives a detailed account of the fate of his wife, his children, his father, his mother, his brothers, his sisters. Each one points out how his family have been torn asunder, how he has been robbed of his possessions and humiliated. All these are tragic variations of one and the same fate, but they always claim your attention.

The hospital organization, the relations of the doctors and nurses to the patients in their daily lives, often bearing some personal stamp, keep your attention occupied the whole time, as do the newspapers with the events on the different war fronts. The regular transports of Jews from the country outside to Westerbork and from Westerbork to Poland create constant tension. The daily visits of relatives to the patients give a certain touch of warmth and intimacy to hospital life. The daily distribution of parcels from relatives and friends outside and regular correspondence with relatives and friends keep up your contact with the outside world. Party games tend to tone down the hospital atmosphere. All these aspects of life help to fill the days and they lend colour and variety to our existence, so that the days and the weeks and the months seem to fly past.

Our stay here reminds me of a patient waiting in a doctor's waiting room. The patient is in pain and he is frightened of the operation or treatment, but while he is waiting he can keep himself occupied in turn with the gruesome accounts he finds in detective novels or with lovely travel tales or pictures in photograph albums. Everyone is summoned in turn to have his operation or his treatment, but he has an opportunity of combating boredom till the time comes.

A hard boiled egg today.

Friday July 2nd: Hordes of flies.

The latest transport to the east had rather a sharp edge to it. Among those deported was a distinguished member of the Jewish Council in Amsterdam who had only just arrived, together with his wife and two children. He had counted on staying here, but had incurred the enmity of the Long-Term Residents. They looked upon him as one of those responsible for their being interned under wretched conditions at Westerbork. So it is said that Schlesinger, the supreme leader, personally requested Gemmeker to have him deported. A proper hullabaloo! Some Dutch Jews think it is disgraceful, especially as his wife is not very strong and his children not too fit. Others are glad because he had shown them a not very pleasant side to his character. That is what happens sometimes up at the top among men whose names have never been famous and who were once honest small-time solicitors and commercial travellers and can now indulge in the luxury of bearing malice. The lust for power reigns supreme among men in high positions and arrogance positively oozes from the eyes of many of them. When the time comes, this lust for power and arrogance, and sometimes the idleness that those in high places can presume to indulge in, are punished. But, quite apart from this, why should high-ranking members of the Jewish Council who were only bent on saving their own skins be exempted from deportation to Poland, while so many thousands, mostly ordinary members of the community, have been sent away, with their cooperation or knowledge? [. . .]

The Commandant has laid down that the Symphony Orchestra may not play any more classical music. It is too tiring for men and women who work all day long. From now on the orchestra is to play light music with a popular appeal.

The Commandant made an attempt to get the members of the NB accustomed to the tempo of military music when marching. It was a flop. So the Commandant resigned himself to this and the military music just has to adapt itself to the marching tempo of the NB.

Today a number of Jews who have four Jewish grandparents and are not partners in mixed marriages or baptized have been sent back to Amsterdam because, as we have reason to believe, the German *Wehrmacht* or industry requires them. Among them is one Jew who was at the concentration camp of Vught and came here as an S-detainee and was kept for four weeks in S-hut 67. He was allowed to take his father back to

72

Amsterdam, but not his mother. Other S-prisoners have endeavoured for months on end to get rid of their S, but in vain. The German *Wehrmacht* and industry are not interested in them.

Saturday July 3rd: Last night a transport consisting of 1,600 people arrived from Vught, 1,100 from the camp and 500 from Moerdijk. On arrival thirty of them were admitted to hospital. The transport arrived without any luggage, just with the clothes they stood up in, like tramps. The men from Moerdijk were the ones whose wives had been sent on to Poland a few weeks before. They say: 'We were able to manage at Moerdijk, although we had to work hard, and if we are sent on to Poland we'll be able to last out the few remaining months of the war.' Many do not look well.

The sterilization business has taken an unexpected turn. The Jewish Council has been officially informed that *all* partners of mixed marriages, either with or without children, are being sent back to Amsterdam, even those who refused to submit to the sterilization operation. People are wondering what is behind it all.

Friday evening is a time of religious dedication for the Jews and occasionally a time of friction between the orthodox and devout and the liberally minded young people. Bent rabbis with shaggy beards from all parts of Europe who have found refuge in humanist Holland, old Dutch Jews with their black skull caps, swearing by the Jewish laws, find themselves living like brothers with young, clean-shaven Jews, Socialists and men who have become assimilated. They do indeed live together, or rather alongside one another, but their lives have proceeded along divergent paths and their horizons are different. On Friday evenings there is outward fraternization—the Jews who have remained faithful to the laws and those who still have memories of their parents' home and normally keep the old Jewish traditions only on the great feast-days unite in the Shabbat prayer.

As darkness is falling and the Sabbath begins, candles are lit and a precentor comes forward and, together with the congregation who have gathered round him, he stands with prayer-book open and entones a prayer with a well marked flowing rhythm that sings of the joys of the Sabbath. A fine aria from a good opera. Patients in their beds join in if they know the words or just sing the easy tune. The candles, lit while it is still day and sending out a pale glimmering light, begin to glow when darkness falls and create a bright and joyous atmosphere. As it proceeds, the prayer acquires a more marked rhythm and finally a lightness which makes all earthly cares disappear. Throughout the week the melody goes resounding through the hut.

After the service everybody returns to his daily routine. The rabbis and the pious old men return to their beds to converse about the Talmud and the liberally minded younger men assemble in the washroom to comment on the latest political or military news, usually smoking a cigarette or a pipe. Criticism behind their backs from the devout. Yesterday evening there was an outburst for the umpteenth time: 'You should be ashamed to smoke on the Shabbat. First *oren*, first you say your prayers, and then you smoke—that's unheard of.' 'Why do you interfere? It's surely my own affair.' 'Ugh! You are a Jew and you should keep to the law. You know perfectly well that you ought not to handle fire on the Sabbath.' 'You yourself don't smoke cigarettes then, but to blazes with all your piety! Just tell me what smoking a cigarette has to do with religion.' 'You young whipper-snapper, I'm old enough to be your father. You have no respect for old age—or for the Torah. It is you who have brought disaster upon us. Hitler is a tool in the hand of God to punish people like you. Just think that over!' 'It's easy enough for you to say that, but you were the first people who stopped living up to your own laws. It's all very well for you to pray, but that's not the only thing. For example, speaking of observance, what do you do about your laws of cleansing and purification? What sign do we ever see of that? You're mortally afraid of eating milk and meat together. But your bodies stink. In the washroom the water only gets as far as your faces and your clothes never leave your bodies and you spit all over the place. Is there nothing about that in the Torah? And yet you go on at me about a stupid cigarette.' 'You must not be unreasonable. All that has nothing to do with it. You should respect the traditions of others. If they are shocked because you go against them, then stop doing so. There is no need to smoke on Friday evenings. I don't do it although I would sometimes like to. We *are* living in a Jewish community here, after all.' 'Do they ever ask if I mind them saying their prayers? Not that I've got anything against that—

74

it's a Jewish custom. But they must let me be free to smoke whenever I want to. It's a private matter. Anyone who doesn't want to see me doing it won't see. Just as I don't hear what I don't want to hear. Have I made myself clear?'

The debate petered out, as it always does when the subject of cigarettes comes up. It is an everlasting source of annoyance to the faithful, an attack upon their most sacred feelings. The younger generation are so keen on their cigarettes, which are the great luxury here, that they are deaf to all the repeated protests.

Sunday July 4th: The transport list is coming round once again and once again a shudder is going through all hearts. Little groups form in all the nooks and corners and there is whispering once again. We have heard that this time the hospital must hand over 200 patients who have no deferment and that for every patient less three members of the nursing staff will be deported. The last time 400 patients were demanded and only 257 were handed over. The writer of this diary has also been notified semi-officially that he will be appearing on the transport list. An extremely unpleasant piece of news. Only yesterday I heard from Amsterdam that attempts were being made to place me on the Puttkammer List and so I would get a red stamp. It is touch and go for me.

Today is O's birthday. Played a game of chess with Dr. Bloch this afternoon which I thought I would win outright, but I lost. Annoying.

Monday July 5th: In the night a small child kept crying for its mummy and daddy. The patients lay there protesting and cursing. The piping little voice is so penetrating in the stillness of the night. The child has been crying for its mother and father every night for a whole week and the patients have been shouting and cursing every night. Even during the day the child cries for its parents, but then the piping little voice becomes lost in the general hum of heavier voices belonging to the adult patients. There is no sympathy shown to small children here— everyone is too much taken up with his own silent worries. There would also be little point in feeling any sympathy, as sympathy can achieve so little here. Nobody can bring back the child's mother and father, and certainly not at the times when the child is crying for them. It is in the wrong company—

it should be amongst other small children who do not protest or curse and do not realize that the crying child is deprived of something in its little life. One of the many small children of whom people say here: 'He thinks he'll win the war with the likes of these.'

The Jewish Council was dissolved today. Some of its members were sent back to Amsterdam this morning, sixty with their families. The others, also sixty in number, have been issued with a red Z (deferment) stamp. They are remaining here and now have the same status as the Long-Term Residents who have lived in the camp for four and a half years. Those who are staying on are nearly all men and women whose parents are also here. Both those who have remained here and those who have gone to Amsterdam were faced with a dilemma. Both groups have had the same sad experience. They have seen people with stamps who thought they were safe here being deported when the time came and people with stamps who thought themselves safe in Amsterdam being dragged from their homes one day and sent to Poland via Westerbork. For the present, however, the first group are inclined to look upon the privileges given them as a reward from the Commandant for the many services they have rendered to him as members of the Jewish Council. *Noblesse oblige.* It is in reality a fiendish tribute from the representatives of a regime which used Jews to catch Jews and hand over Jews and guard Jews. It was the desire to have a safe stamp, the longing to save their own skins that induced these Jews to perform the grisly services that their tormentors demanded and exacted from them. In the process they benefited their own friends by handing out jobs to them and saving them from being deported. Nobody is begrudging them the right to be deferred "until further notice" by means of a red stamp, in reality a *testimonium paupertatis*, but, now that they have a respite from the breathless chase and the evil frenzy, they should dig down into their consciences, if they have a conscience at all. A conscience is a plant that is rarely found. Those who have gone home will perhaps have bitter feelings about their good fortune. They had become acclimatized here and, thanks to their privileged jobs here, they also occupied the best places from a social point of view—and the best accommodation here—*oggenebbish*, but the best nevertheless—and they had good relations with the kitchen staff and a certain freedom of movement, at Westerbork itself and between

76

Amsterdam and Westerbork, in short a lovely world of their own. In less than a year's time they got to know the camp inside out and they could move about with ease and they had also established firm contacts with the SS. Now they were coming home to an empty, dead city where unrest and fear hung between the houses like a thick haze. It affected them too because there might be a raid at any moment and they might be the victims. And what of their houses? Were they still standing? Would they not have been looted in the meantime? Where were they to live if they no longer had a house? In all probability in the new ghetto set up in the Transvaal district which would perhaps be fenced off from the city in a short space of time. There they would live in dismal isolation in spite of their stamps. All this, while their confederates at Westerbork were enjoying a fair degree of freedom within certain limits and could enjoy, through the barbed wire, the open expanse of moor and sky and could get happiness from these things. The Jewish Council has been dissolved. We anxiously await the next chapter. [. . .]

Tuesday July 6th: Weeping women. The cleaners are sobbing as they sweep, women are standing at the open windows all in tears. This morning brothers and sisters, fathers and mothers have gone on the transport. It is too much for the men—they gulp down their tears. The train whistles—and the venomous snake begins to crawl away. Two separate wagons with S-detainees. I myself escaped by the skin of my teeth. At four o'clock this morning I found out that my name had been deleted from the list. Congratulations from all sides—handshakes from my nearest neighbours. I received the expressions of sympathetic interest with a smile. Deep down inside I felt sorrow—everywhere around other men were being summoned out of their beds and told to prepare for the sinister transport. The congratulations must have been like a smack in the face for those who were going. [. . .]

On Sunday afternoon the house physician had a word with me: 'I must speak to you man to man. You are on the list for Tuesday.' 'Can nothing be done?' 'I can't do anything for you. The Registration Department have put you on the list.' (That meant that the house physician must have said that I was fit to travel.) 'But I am just telling you in good time so that you can take the necessary steps.'

I went to the office of Dr. Spanier, the all-powerful man in the hospital world. The porter was there at the door like Cerberus: 'You can't go in without a note.' Markus, the head porter, said: 'If it's to do with deportation, Dr. Spanier will not see anyone till Wednesday.' 'But the train goes on Tuesday.' 'I can't do anything about it. He's not seeing anyone.' Understandable—he would go mad if he had to listen to everyone who wanted to be taken off the list. Preparation for the transport was like a sort of merry-go-round. But I did make another attempt to get through to Dr. Spanier. Male nurse Gottschalk happened to come out: 'I see that you are on the list. I've drawn Dr. Spanier's attention to it. Just tell Markus to give you a note.' Markus went off to Dr. Spanier. Came back with the message that Spanier refused to see me.

I went to and fro seeing house physicians whom I know. They would consult with one another. Went to Heinemann of the Jewish Council—not in his office. Went to friends in huts 57 and 58 to lay hands on two letters which hinted at negotiations by "the successor of heer Wistik with a well-to-do gentleman" with a view to having me and two others, heer Rood and mej. Cirkel, put on the Puttkammer List. In luck—Rood accompanied me to the Registration Department where he has a nephew who is able to do a great deal and who gave him the assurance that he and the woman would not appear on the transport list during the next few weeks to give the Puttkammer affair scope to work itself out. The nephew showed an interest in my case. Rood said: 'A pity you didn't come sooner. I thought you were safe.' I shook my head. I had no deferment at all. I returned at half past four. A decision was then reached. I went back to my hut. Order from the head porter: on instructions from Dr. Spanier the discharge note was to be given back. Dr. Spanier was apparently angry. I handed over my note. It meant that my wings were clipped as far as attending to my own interests were concerned. A woman employee of the Jewish Council notified Rood and went with him at half past four to the Registration Department. Came back with the news that the matter was 75% settled. In the meantime he had got Heinemann into action and he had taken down my name. Heinemann is on the night contact committee, the members of which back their favourites. He has also penetrated into the circles closest to Schlesinger. The house physician came along: 'We've drilled the well and it will probably gush.' That was all.

I remained in a state of uncertainty.

A camp friend happened to appear on the scene, heer Schripperman, self-important, a drawing-room lion. 'I am on the list, mijnheer Schripperman.' 'On the list? And you've been here eight months,' he shouted in a hoarse voice. He pulled me over to a corner. Then he grabbed me by a button and whispered: 'You are not going on the transport, do you hear. I'll go at once to my father-in-law, Herr Trottel. He knows Schlesinger well and he has got two off the list today already. He always gets his own way.' He was bursting with vanity. I looked at him in speechless amazement. 'It's a fact.' Schripperman went straight off with the woman employee of the Jewish Council. After an hour she came back. 'It's 90% settled.' She was excited and completely taken up with the case. [. . .]

At seven o'clock Rood appeared, perspiring and agitated and upset: 'What a mess—I've been told that I'm going on the transport tomorrow.' I gave a start. 'On the transport? But I thought there was no chance of that for a fortnight.' 'That's what I thought too, but it's not like that at all. Juffrouw Cirkel is included too.' 'What about Puttkammer?' 'They won't wait. See if you can do something for me.' 'That's not so easy.' 'See if you can. I'll have to go now—I still have a lot to do.' And he raced off with the Puttkammer letters quivering in his hands.

A little old gentleman with a pointed beard appeared by my bed. 'I am Trottel.' He came and sat on my bed and began whispering: 'It's possible you may have to pack at four o'clock in the morning after all and go to the train. But just tell the orderly that there must be some mistake and that he must take you straight to Schlesinger. Give my name and say that I have discussed the matter with Frau Schlesinger and that you are waiting for a telegram from Puttkammer. That will settle the matter.' Schripperman appeared, drawn and haggard. Trottel: 'You are too late.' 'Yes, but just a minute.' Exit Trottel: 'So you understand how things are.' Schripperman explained the matter further. 'I have two friends. Can you do anything for them?' 'Out of the question—you're the only one. I'm doing it for you out of friendship.' A mysterious man. He disappeared as he still had things to do.

At eight o'clock a sturdy-looking man strolled past my bed, apparently for no reason. 'That's Schlesinger!' The Great Man himself! Was he there by chance or was it because of me? He lingered there. I sprang up from my bed. 'You are mijnheer Schlesinger? May I introduce myself? You know about me?' 'Yes, what can I tell the Commandant?' 'Puttkammer is under way.' 'That's no good. You've taken a long time to put your affairs in order. You've been in hospital for over three months.' 'Taken a long time? Well, first of all, I had my former mixed marriage, but that was no good after a time. I tried Barneveld, but that could not go through because of my political antecedents. Now Puttkammer is pending.' 'I'll see what I can do for you. You will be seeing me at the train tomorrow.' Exit Schlesinger. Everybody gazed after him in awe. The house physician came up to me: 'Was that Schlesinger?' 'Yes.' A pat on my shoulder. 'Then the matter is settled, old man.' He beamed with satisfaction. I remained sceptical. Tomorrow morning at four o'clock would come the dénouement.

At nine o'clock Trottel appeared as if he had risen out of the ground. He whispered: 'Everything in order then? I've spoken to all four of them. Now I'll have to go and settle your affair. Because there's another transport next week.' Who "all four" were I could only guess. From the woman employee of the Jewish Council I heard that Dr. Spanier had "given his consent." But he was displeased with me for doing so little for myself. I had to put my affairs in order. In the meantime Rood had been marked down for deportation. Mejuffrouw Cirkel has been spared for the time being because of a telegram from which it would appear that she is a citizen of Honduras. (Her passport will be sent on later.) [. . .]

Today 2,600 Jews were deported. A bitter note: among the deportees there was a male nurse who had been given permission by Dr. Spanier to sing a few songs in the hospital hut in the evening, but had laid on a whole cabaret show. For this excess he was punished by deportation. We must have discipline! In the night 290 Jews arrived from Amsterdam. 700 had been expected.

Wednesday July 7th: In the washroom this morning. 'It's a funny thing, but I had to come to Westerbork to meet my nephew for the first time.' 'And there are a lot of men who don't get to know their wives till they come here.' An allusion to the many cases of marital infidelity.

Did some washing after breakfast—a shirt and handkerchiefs. Sooty black with dust. There is a laundry here, but it is slow and it is a long time before you get your things back. If you get them back at all, because a lot of searching is necessary. So the best thing is to do it yourself, although the technical facilities leave a lot to be desired. Intellectuals, spoilt old men who never had to put a finger in water before, can sometimes be seen busy with their laundry in one of the washroom basins just like hardworking housewives. They have developed beyond what they were before. They have become good with their hands and realize that you're never too old to learn and that something learned is something gained. And so we educate ourselves here.

A sensational event was the unexpected deportation as an S-man of Han Hollander, the celebrated football commentator. It was because of a careless remark by his wife. A man ruined by a woman. Hollander had the most envied job in the whole camp. He was a sort of administrator in the so-called Moor Camp of the SS, halfway between Westerbork and Hooghalen. He had got the job because of his international reputation and because he was such a livewire. He was as free as a bird in the air and enjoyed many privileges. As a smart retort to the wife of a German Jew his wife had snapped: 'Times will change and then we'll make you filthy Boches pay for everything.' Many other Dutch people think like this, but they don't say so, at least not when German Jews are present. It led to denunciation by a Long-Term Resident and a report to the *Obersturmführer* who found that Hollander's wife had gone a bit too far. He had them both locked up in hut 51, the prison, a small square building, and put them down for deportation. [. . .] The incident reminds Jews to be humble amongst themselves. [. . .]

Visited Trottel. I made my entrance with fifteen cigarettes. He accepted them with the excuse that he himself had offered cigarettes on my behalf. But I must remember that he had intervened purely from altruistic motives. I had to accept this. Fifteen cigarettes is quite a substantial gift here; it works out at fifteen guilders, but that would be a paltry present. Money has no importance here! Trottel turned out to be a former courier at the German War Ministry and the holder of many distinctions. He told me he was one of the few at the camp who are received by the *Obersturmführer*. But he did not consider it an honour and criticized those who crawled in front of the

Obersturmführer. He consulted with me about the course I now had to follow in order to get myself "exempted". I needed an authentic confirmation that I had already been placed on the Puttkammer List or was being placed on it. I arranged for a telegram to be sent off at once through the Jewish Council to Mr. Planten, the director of the *"Algemeen Handelsblad"*, asking for this confirmation to be given as quickly as possible. A matter of waiting.

In the meantime the house physician promised that he would provisionally keep me on at the hospital till confirmation was received. Schripperman was also willing to accept a small quantity of cigarettes. He had, however, helped me purely as a friend. I had to accept this, as there was only a small number of cigarettes for him. But he is certainly an astute man. He thought it was not impossible that I might be of service to him on some later occasion. 'You never can tell.'

Thursday July 8th: In the night the little daughter of friends of mine dreamt that her doll had to go on the transport.

Telepathy in the hut. A female visitor prophesied the other day that the war would be over on August 16th. Pertinent. But it sounds almost impertinent after all the idle predictions that have been made since the war began by people claiming to have special insight. Every day she says: 'Remember August 16th—it will be a great day.' She is an odd woman. A sort of mermaid type with very blonde hair, a pair of large sea-green eyes and a face as red as a boiled lobster. Her speech is abrupt. She has read the palms of many of the patients and made gruesome prophecies. From the lines of my own she read two things: 'You wear a wedding ring, but I do not see a marriage.' Correct. 'You are not going on any transport.' Wait and see. Everybody is waiting anxiously for August 16th.

A new bombshell in the camp. Yesterday all holders of red and green Z (deferment) stamps have been freed from exemption. [. . .] The new basic nucleus is to be made up of at most 1,623 holders of red Z stamps, including only camp residents who really pull their weight in the work they are given to do. The group covers men and women of from fourteen to sixty-five years. The prospective 1,623 residents are to include 300 for the health service, 200 for the so-called outside work (digging) and 500 for industry. Children of from two to fourteen years will be accommodated in a kindergarten while their

82

parents are at work.

The blue Z stamps are not affected, i.e., the stamps awarded under a special dispensation to baptized Jews, Jews from mixed marriages, persons who are purely Portuguese, those who have opted for Palestine or Barneveld or the Puttkammer List and other privileged people, but the holders of these must perform the same duties as the holders of red Z stamps. Nevertheless the number of blue Z stamps has been reduced. The members of the Jewish Council have been told that they will lose their stamps unless the Central Office is prepared to renew them. There is, of course, no chance of that.

Schlesinger and Todtmann have been made responsible for carrying out the order. It means that a large number of camp residents will be available for deportation. Under present conditions there has been a lack of "transport material", as they say, but the intention is obviously to settle the Jewish question once and for all and only keep a restricted number of Jews at Westerbork who can perhaps be useful for carrying out specific duties. The baptized Jews and those from mixed marriages are already being sent home in small batches; what the future fate of the others will be is not yet clear. It would appear that Westerbork is becoming an *Arbeitslager*, or labour camp, of limited size. Perhaps with five or six thousand residents. Today the skilled workers, furriers and rag-sorters have been given the choice of going to Vught alone or being sent on to Poland with their wives. By far the greater proportion of them chose the latter. It is like the little game that was played with the workers at Moerdijk.

Once more Jews find their nerves are playing tricks on them. Many who thought they were safe because of their stamps see the danger of transportation suddenly looming up out of the deep abyss. The most recent transports caused great anxiety— many notable men could not be kept back any longer. Red stamp holders deprived of their rights are putting their stamps up for sale for the price of one cigarette! Real gallows humour! This is the tragi-comic stamp game that is also being played in Amsterdam—deportation by stages. Again and again the Jews let themselves be taken in and they hold on tightly to their stamps which, when the time comes, do not turn out to be gilt-edged securities after all.

Friday July 9th: Conference with Trottel in his hut. Crafty

83

through and through. He is full of stories about minor intrigues and the heroic role he has played in them. He has the eyes of a pike, yellowish, hidden away behind his eyelids. The cloven hoof has appeared. 'You must be sure to go to Schlesinger today and say that you have come from me. You must give him to understand that you will look after my interests and his interests and Stein's interests after the war. And give your word of honour. Later on we'll pay a visit to Stein. I'm completely behind you, but you must stand up for your interests yourself with Schlesinger. You will, of course, give him a copy of the telegram that you sent to Amsterdam about Puttkammer. That is necessary for your application which has, in fact, already been put in. Do nothing! Schlesinger can do it. Your affair is going well because I've got Schlesinger in the palm of my hand. You must let him see that you recognize his power. He was an ordinary little manufacturer and now he has tremendous power; he's well aware of that. And you must also make it clear to him that he will have some say in what you publish later on about Westerbork. Well, I leave matters in your hands. You're self-taught and you know something about life, I've no doubt. But you must go and see him this afternoon as the transport on Tuesday will also be dangerous for you and you must stay clear of it. You must leave Schripperman out of things. The fewer people brought in, the better.' I listened and was silent. [. . .]

The whole business intrigued me. I wanted to know more about Schlesinger; I wanted to see him and chat with him and probe him. [. . .]

On my return to the hospital hut the porter dashed towards me: 'Where have you been? You must go at once to the Registration Department, to Dr. Ottenstein. You ought to have been there at half past four.' Could this be news from Puttkammer? I went like lightning to see Ottenstein. I bumped into mejuffrouw Cirkel. 'I've got to go and see Ottenstein. I'm far too late already.' 'So have I.' It must be Puttkammer then. Mejuffrouw Cirkel was received first. Not by Dr. Ottenstein, but by Fräulein Slottke, an agent of the *Sicherheitsdienst*, or Security Service, and secretary to Rauter in The Hague. I watched mejuffrouw Cirkel over the counter—with a tense, drawn face. Then it was my turn. 'Are you mijnheer So-and-so?' 'Yes.' 'Married?' 'Divorced.' 'You were married to an Aryan woman?' 'Yes.' 'Had you a child?' 'Yes.' 'Any contact

84

now?' 'Yes, with the child.' 'Are you exempted?' 'No.' 'Why not?' 'I've been here for eight months and my summons envelope has been lost. Without it I can't get an exemption.' 'You were editor of the "*Algemeen Handelsblad*"?' 'Yes.' 'What did you write?' 'I did literary work in general.' 'Thank you.' That was all. I was careful not to say that I had written political articles. Safety first! What did they want with mejuffrouw Cirkel and me? I had a word with a former member of the Jewish Council. 'It will be for Theresienstadt. She deals with that.' Would there be a chance of us moving to Theresienstadt? Is that to be the result of Mr. Planten's activities? Oh dear, oh dear! We shall see soon enough. At any rate on returning to the hut I told the house physician what had occurred so as to convince him that he must keep me here whatever happened, to await developments. Today, it seems, my chances of remaining here for the present have improved.

Judge So-and-so who moved recently to hut 3 for a sedation treatment has returned to our hut. His psychological upset does not appear to have been cured. [. . .]

A Jew came to Samson, one of the influential bigwigs, to try and persuade him to save him from deportation. Samson surveyed the man from top to toe and said: 'What can you expect? You are ideal transport material.' Cold cynicism. The man indeed had nothing wrong with him and was not sick, so he was fit for transportation.

Blüth came into the ward. A patient drew Blüth's attention to the fact that he had a stomach disorder and was not suitable for being sent to Poland. Could Blüth not keep his name off the list? Blüth replied: 'It's all the better for you—you'll be dead all the sooner.' Cold cynicism.

Saturday July 10th: No reply from Schlesinger. Went in the afternoon to the Registration Department to find out from Dr. Ottenstein what the purpose of Fräulein Slottke's cross-questioning had been. Dr. Ottenstein was not there. He was asleep as he had been on the go last night. Bromet could give me no definite answer. Then to Trottel. We agreed to go to Schlesinger together. 'Must I say anything about help from Dr. Spanier?' 'That's not necessary. Schlesinger has seen to everything.' 'Did I tell you that the house physician is prepared to keep me there for the present?' 'Did you think he would do that without Schlesinger's approval?' This Schlesinger is a mighty man, I see! Trottel put on a solemn face when he heard of the interview with Fräulein Slottke. Schlesinger would know more about it.

Went to his office at half past five. We had to wait in the anteroom. [. . .] Schlesinger came at about a quarter to six— a heavily built, square fellow with a head as round as a ball, a tapering forehead with receding hair and a sensual face, red lips and phosphorescent eyes. A dictator type—he thrust his arm straight out in greeting. He shook hands with Trottel. He went into his office and came back a moment later to usher out Frau Schlesinger who had been waiting inside. His wife was as round as a barrel—she had lived well and fed well— a plump face like a moonfish, very dark, with gleaming white teeth, coquettish. Trottel first of all went into Schlesinger's room without me; it was better, he said, for him to meet Schlesinger alone first. [. . .] Five minutes later I was called in.

'Well, mijnheer So-and-so, how are you?' I placed my hand in his fleshy outstretched paw. 'First of all I want to thank you very warmly for your help last Tuesday. You showed yourself to be a real friend. And anyone who shows himself to be a friend is my friend for ever, you understand.' This was the lesson I had learned by heart. 'It was nothing. How are things going?' 'I was summoned unexpectedly to go and see Fräulein Slottke yesterday. She questioned me about my marital status and so on. Have you any idea what that can be for?' 'I don't know, although I have a pretty good idea.' Diplomatic expression; a long pull at his cigarette. 'There has been some word of Theresienstadt.' Schlesinger said nothing. 'Do you think that it's because of my newspaper? A colleague of mine was summoned too.' 'It's quite likely.' 'So it's a favourable sign?' 'I should think so.' It did not sound convincing. 'You know what? You must come and visit my wife and myself on Monday evening.' 'All right.' 'No, I've got another idea. You're an international journalist. You'll arrange to let me have a few lines about your career and your contacts abroad some time tomorrow.' 'So that's it'—the thought flashed through my mind. 'All right,' I said. 'I'll attend to that.' He stood up to take his leave of us. 'Don't you need to have a copy of my telegram to Amsterdam for Puttkammer?' 'You can keep it!' A mighty man! A firm handshake as we left.

Trottel said outside: 'It's all right—you'll be staying here. If you see to it that he gets those few lines about your career and your contacts. I've said I will vouch for you. I've got confidence in you.' Nice of Trottel! I see through you, you cunning little rascal. We'll see what we shall see. It's not as easy to catch me as all that.

At about seven o'clock I returned to my hut. Great excitement about the report, heard on the radio, that the British and Americans have landed in Sicily. Everybody is asking one another: 'Have you heard? Is that correct?' They are happy. The invasion is coming at last. It will free the Jews from oppression and bring their deliverance. That is the prevailing mood. A little moral uplift in the midst of all the wretchedness.

A transport consisting of 250 arrived from Amsterdam yesterday.

Sunday July 11th: The chess contest has broken down completely and been forgotten, firstly because people taking part had to go on the transports and secondly because people's minds were very much taken up with the cancellation of exemptions and the results of this as far as deportation was concerned.

Last week the father of a woman-friend of mine was brought into the hospital hut. A learned man, perfectly healthy, but completely unfitted for society, an eccentric. He lives quite off at a tangent from his environment and does nothing but read, holding his book close to his bad eyes. All his life he has been well cared for and spoiled and he is completely unfitted for this type of community life. The family thought that he and the other members of it could be saved from deportation. But this is the fate hanging over their heads nevertheless. They are in great danger of being made to go on the long journey on Tuesday. The wife says sadly: 'It would be best for me to go on the journey alone. With him it's impossible. I wouldn't know what to do with him.' The husband says with childlike optimism: 'It won't be as bad as we think—one must just take things as they come.' The daughter (who is herself exempted) says: 'It's terrible. My brother who is allowed to stay on here wants to go with my parents of his own accord and he isn't completely normal. The strain is unbearable. We're hoping that there will be no transport leaving on Tuesday. But then there'll be a whole week of fresh strain, and perhaps another after that, and in the end they *will* go. I'd like to ask: "Lord, make it soon!" ' [. . .]

The hospital hut with its 250 beds or so is the daily setting for family reunions. All the members of the family, the wife and the children, gather round the sick or the pseudo-sick. The father sits with his uprooted children on his knee and fondles them. Men and women sit close together, hand in hand. Women sit crying, overwrought by their soul-destroying life in the living huts, or frightened at the prospect of deportation. Families sit together looking at family portraits, sometimes the only possession they managed to bring with them from their homes, apart from personal linen. Others sit together eating their evening meal from the mess-tin that the wife has prepared in her own hut and has brought along for her husband to eat.

Understanding wives try to calm nervy or impatient husbands with words of comfort. It is like a colourful market where human tendernesses are exchanged—in an atmosphere of misery on the threshold between two worlds—the familiar and established milieu with its fixed values and the world of the pauper in endless space, indeterminate and unprotected.

Monday July 12th: During the visiting hour when visitors discussed with their relatives the chances of going on the transport the next day or, if they were certain that they were on the transport list, took their leave and offered a helping hand for the last time, I heard from the Commandant's Office that I had been deferred for the time being. Almost at the same moment I had a visit from mejuffrouw Cirkel who had been questioned by Fräulein Slottke at the same time as myself and came to inform me that she was going on the transport the next day. I did not know the reason for my temporary deferment. Is it because I have a child from a mixed marriage? Fräulein Slottke dwelt on this for a fairly long time during the cross-examination. Or are higher powers involved? I shall have to gather further information about this. Mejuffrouw Cirkel was very bright and was sure that we would meet again. [. . .]

Tuesday July 13th: The transport is over once more—this time Westerbork has had to give up over 2,000 Jews to the east. There was a great slaughter among the hospital staff—a large number of male and female nurses and administrative officials had to pack up, together with sixteen doctors. Male and female nurses who had worked here for many months have disappeared and they include some of the best ones, whilst others, who were among the worst, have remained. [. . .]

The so-called Parents List has been encroached upon, i.e., the list of parents of members of the *Expositur* staff, for whom Fischer in The Hague had granted special exemption; the majority of them were sent away on the transport. The *Obersturmführer* telephoned The Hague, saying that he was faced with a shortage of "transport material", and asked if he could encroach upon the Parents List. *Fiat.* The parents of the members of the Jewish Council who returned to Amsterdam last week, although previously exempted, were now sent away too. Only the parents of the members of the Jewish Council who have remained here and have been promoted to the status of Long-Term Residents are still exempt. [. . .] The Puttkammer List did not remain intact either—sixteen people from the list were deported, either because the sum of money to buy them off had not been paid in or because the funds had been blocked in Switzerland. [. . .]

This morning there were no dramatic *intermezzi* in my hut— they were all young chaps who set off for their unknown destination strong in the knowledge that their manly vigour was unimpaired. But OD men carried past the windows stretchers with men and women who could not put down one foot in front of the other. Recruits for the Police Labour Pool! Scenes that make you think of the Bastille and the French Revolution.

A cabaret show this evening in the Registration Hall! Westerbork has the best cabaret in Holland. National Socialist dignitaries come here to see it. Blood is thicker than water.

Yesterday I put my shoes in for repair. This morning I got them back, all finished and ready, well sewn and with a sole an inch thick. Service, sir, service!

Today the hut had to yield up one of its most outstanding patients—Flip, a cattle-dealer from the Rotterdam area who months and months ago had been brought in here in a bad way from the prison camp at Ommen and built up an exceptional position here for himself. A thickset figure, a bristling head on a bull neck, powerful biceps, a pair of iron hands, a face as grey as concrete, a voice like the rattle of a machine-gun, a pair of candid eyes of a faded blue. The man had "*Geltungstrieb*", the desire to dominate others. From the time that he was on his feet again he set himself up as the *maître de maison*. He was very good with his hands and did all kinds of small domestic jobs in the hut that would otherwise have been neglected. With his fantastic stories, juicily told, he gained an audience in the ward. He penetrated to the doctors' room where he did the daily tidying. He made the beds, did the washing, kept the whole show clean, tried his hand at cooking, scrounged things for the doctors' room and for himself, especially a tobacco supply. With his gnawed-off pipe between his teeth he pottered about all day long in blue overalls, going to and fro between the doctors' room and the hut and the washroom. [. . .] He felt he was indispensable and under the august protection of the house physician—invulnerable—exempt from deportation. He interfered with the way things were done in the hut itself, he criticized the work of the nurses and rebuked the patients. [. . .] Friction and rows were the result. The house physician left him alone and did not intervene in the bickering with the nurses and the patients—Flip was his factotum, his irreplaceable factotum. Especially when his wife and children were there—the service rendered was beyond price. Behind Flip's back intrigues went on all the time—envious or offended nurses or spies from outside brought about his downfall. The doctor had to dismiss him from the hospital hut. Flip moved to an ordinary living hut, but kept up his contact with the doctors' room—every morning he appeared in his old blue overalls, faithfully at his post, his pipe between his jaws, as if nothing had happened. He managed to go on like that for five more days. Then the all-powerful Registration Department put him on the transport list as a person available for deportation; no power in the world could prevent it.

This evening the dandy of the hut passed away. A violent attack of diarrhoea struck down the straight and stalwart body. For days he lay there with one staring eye like some prehistoric cyclops. Horrible.

Wednesday July 14th: First sign of the reduction of the hospital —this morning forty-two beds were taken out of my hut. The double row in the middle was made into a single row. There was more room to move about, the lane between the beds became a highway, ventilation was made easier and there was more space to breathe in.

Around noon there was great activity in the hut. The beds had to be put back in a hurry by order from above. The B wing of the hut had to be vacated. Some of the men are being transferred to the A wing where the writer of this diary lives.

90

The rest are going to hut 83. The B wing is being turned into a hut for women who have come from elsewhere. Everyone is busy. The doctors go along the beds giving permission to shift, the nurses labour with beds and mattresses, patients who are moving plead for good places for their beds, other patients take the opportunity of capturing better places for themselves. The small children stand up in their beds and shriek, driven wild by all the commotion, and they tumble about or have minor skirmishes. Patients tap their foreheads to show that they do not think very highly of the organizing ability at the top. It is a madhouse, a puppet show, a fairground, nobody knows exactly which.

The medical assistant delivers a vociferous speech in which he conveys to the men from the other wing the idea that the regime here is twice as strict as the regime there. [. . .] The assistant himself breaks the regulations more than once a day. He is like a puppy which jumps up and barks everywhere and knocks everything over. He goes through the ward bellowing all day long, he fights with the nurses and frolics with the patients, he smokes all day long, even while he is going on his rounds, he plays chess with the patients. Regulations and the enforcement of these regulations are two separate things. [. . .]

Today has been an amusing day.

Thursday July 15th: Changement de tableau—a change of scene. I have moved to a new bed, a top one in the farthest corner of the hut from where I can get an overall picture of the whole scene —the 130 occupied beds placed in four lines. I feel like a film director. I look straight out on a man who is a victim of shell shock and lies trembling and moaning for long periods on end, also a blind man. In the background there is a perfectly healthy rabbi with a snowy white beard, lying as if on a bed of state, flanked by two boys of nine or ten years old. Beside me lies a victim of the concentration camp at Vught, a man who has been in a weak condition for fifteen weeks and is still not entirely free from bouts of fever. A great proportion of the patients have the hut disease—diarrhoea. All day long there is a smell of faeces hanging about the hut. Strange to say, I am hardened to it. The nurses who toil all day long with bed pans are hardened to it. Why should I not be hardened to it? Under difficult conditions you get used to many things that would be disgusting in normal life. Here you forget what disgust is.

91

In an order out today the *Obersturmführer*—what a mouthful!
—has once more lashed out against the Jews. Anyone who does
not turn up for work or does not work hard enough is to be
sent away on an S-transport. Anyone who is deferred will be
reported to the higher authorities and by virtue of a special
provision will be sent away by S-transport and, until the provision comes through, will be enrolled in the punishment squad
at Westerbork. We really have become a labour camp. A
second order reminds us that we are forbidden in our correspondence to say anything about the transports or about internal matters in the camp. Any hut where the order is found to
have been infringed will be deprived of writing facilities.

Have heard from the Administration that I have got a blue
Z stamp. This means that "until further notice" I am exempted
from transport to the east, I am entitled to a smoker's card, I
can apply to Lippmann & Rosenthal, I can have 250 guilders
in my pocket and I can write letter cards to my contacts and
friends to confirm the receipt of parcels. I have been moved
up a whole class. I do not know whom I have to thank for the
blue Z—or what it is for. That will no doubt emerge later.
Many people are finding themselves in just such a mysterious
position as myself—thanks to the bureaucratic powers of the
camp. The prediction of the woman with telepathic powers
who said that I would not be deported appears to be coming
true.

A hard boiled egg, plus half a cucumber. In the last few
days milk ad libitum.

Friday July 16th: A good day for civilization today. At the
request of a number of patients, a nurse has screened off the
WC's from the rest of the washroom with a few mats which he
attached to pieces of iron wire hanging from the ceiling. Three
men can now retire properly without too much embarrassment
simultaneously. People are full of praise for the nurse who has
shown such understanding of the need for these amenities.
[. . .]

Turmoil in the camp—at ten o'clock this evening 300 Jews
left for Amsterdam, some of them partners in mixed marriages
and the rest jewellers and diamond workers. A few of the
diamond workers were on the transport list only last week.
Those who were leaving have been walking on air. Patients
who belonged to this contingent and were fit for transport left

92

the hut amid applause.

At the Registration Department I heard that my blue Z stamp was not the outcome of my interview with Fräulein Slottke. So it has come from some other source—I probably owe it to Schlesinger's intervention. What will it be worth in the long run?

There are rumours that the Palestine List is on the verge of a smash. A transport of twenty-five has come in from Enschede —people who had been in hiding.

Saturday July 17th: Tuesday is approaching once more and there is a feeling of anxiety. It is practically certain that all those who still have green stamps and those who have no stamp at all will be deported. There is no reason to expect that fresh transports coming from Amsterdam or Vught will put off the evil hour. In the night a small contingent of Jews came in from Amsterdam and Vught, about 600 in all. Among these 600 there are a large number of exempted persons. The result is that the old faithfuls of Westerbork will have to make up the greater part of the impending transport. This morning there was also an indirect official announcement to the effect that the Palestine List no longer provided a guarantee against deportation for many people. All who had an application under way for that list must substantiate it today between 12 and 4 o'clock at the office of the Jewish Council, either by means of official documents from Geneva or Palestine, showing that they have been entered on the lists, or by means of a so-called Palestine certificate, or by documents showing that the husband or wife is resident in Palestine. This means that, on a rough estimate, ninety per cent of those who have put their names forward for the Palestine List will be unable to authenticate their application and so will be going on the transport next Tuesday. The purpose of the Palestine List is to exchange Jews for German citizens—five Germans, it is said, for one Jew. So one Jew is equivalent to five Germans! The *Obersturmführer* is making a clean sweep—it is said that this transport will be the last for the time being and, as far as possible, everyone who does not belong to the so-called permanent nucleus, which is thought to number 6,000 persons, will be leaving. At the moment conferences are going on at the Commandant's Office to settle the precise age ratio of these 6,000 persons. [. . .]

This afternoon a long line of Palestine Jews stood outside the

Jewish Council building. Gloomy faces, gloomy conversations. They were turned away in groups. [. . .]

Altogether about 1,200 Jews and their families shared the same fate.

Before supper a speech by Chief Rabbi De Vries about the fate of the Jews. A tall, straight, prophetic figure with a high forehead and noble features. a long white beard, slender hands, a clear voice. Comparison with the exodus from Egypt. God and Israel are inseparable. Jews may perish, but Israel is eternal, the Old Testament is imperishable; people may take the Jews' possessions from them, but if they manage to preserve their lives the Jews will be, not beaten dogs, but lions. A fine piece of rhetoric and aesthetics, but no guidance to Jews about how to live now and in the future, no guide as to their relationship with the society in which they live. A disappointment in that respect.

Sunday July 18th: Have heard that the German authorities have hinted to heer P., the director of the *"Algemeen Handelsblad"*, that he would do better not to exert himself on behalf of former editors of the paper in connection with the Puttkammer List. Heer P. did not answer a letter which I wrote asking him to give me a helping hand at this critical juncture. At whose instigation Fräulein Slottke came to deal with my case is still a mystery. In the meantime the conviction is growing here that the only purpose served by the Puttkammer List is to extort "black money" from the Jews by raising false hopes of permanent exemption from the Police Labour Pool in Poland. The currency used consists of diamonds and gold—paper money is of no value for this purpose—paper is not gold. Puttkammer is an employee of the Rotterdamse Bank and acts as a decoy. But we Jews grasp at every straw in order to avoid the journey to Poland. We are convinced that if the war goes on for a long time we shall all end up in Poland and we also know that no list in the world can prevent it. But we all try to spin things out in the hope that something will happen in the end and will put paid to the deportations once and for all. The handful of Jews still living here feel like the last of the Mohicans. They are fighting to the last, not just to escape the uncertainty of their destination, but so that they will be around when the great turning-point comes. Many women live with their nerves almost at breaking-point because the continual

94

uncertainty about their fate is so wearing—they are tired and drawn with bags under their eyes.

And yet everything is relative. This afternoon I spoke to a Jew who has just come back from Vught. At the roll-call at Vught men who had Portuguese ancestors were summoned specially under a pretence of sending them to Portugal. He turned up although he had nothing at all to do with the Portuguese—he wanted to get away from the hell of Vught. All day long came the shout: 'Get on! Get on!' with the stick and the musket in the offing, just like a concentration camp. He landed at Westerbork with partners from mixed marriages and baptized Jews. 'If I had to choose between Vught and Poland,' he declared, 'then I'd rather have Poland. Things surely can't be as bad in Poland as they are at Vught. It's hell, sheer hell!'

That was said in the porter's lodge which is now the clandestine smoking saloon since the B wing was closed to male patients. The washroom in wing A is a proper pig-sty and could not possibly be used as a smoking saloon. The porter: 'I'm optimistic about Poland too. Things are sure to come right there. I know men who have come back from Buchenwald and Dachau.' An ex-army captain from Austria: 'Do you think they are sending us to Poland just to dump us in a nice garden? If I could be an optimist, I would. The National Socialists are sadists. I was in Buchenwald myself for two hundred and twenty-seven days and it ruined my health. I was as strong as iron and now I'm finished. Jews do come back from Buchenwald and Dachau, but perhaps only three out of every hundred. The best chaps die off there. I know for certain that when I'm sent to Poland, and I'm going off on Tuesday, I won't survive it. I can't work any more and they certainly won't feed non-productive folk like me. That doesn't suit their game at all. They're sadists. I am *not* optimistic.' A thick vein stood out above the ex-captain's temple. His face was deeply furrowed. The doctor: 'There can't be any question of optimism. Anyone who calls himself an optimist is just being frivolous. He has learnt nothing from the hard facts. What news do we ever get from Poland? Hardly any. On one single occasion a letter comes through secretly, containing a few lines that tell us nothing and people cling on to that and use it to bolster up their optimism. We hear nothing of those who have died. No, optimism can't change the true situation at all. It's a ghastly business. Anyone who goes to Poland is written off.' The porter: 'I'm still optimistic.' The ex-captain was choked with a bout of asthma. We looked into one another's eyes like wounded beasts.

Monday July 19th: [. . .]

Was told semi-officially by Trottel that Fräulein Slottke had removed me from the list of applicants for Theresienstadt, so I must allow for the possibility of being deported to Poland. But I do not need to worry about the impending transport—Schlesinger will remove me from the transport list if I should happen to appear on it. [. . .] Trottel put his cards on the table. 'I'm looking at things from a selfish point of view. I said to Schlesinger: "After the war the German Jews will find themselves in a difficult position and it's vital for us to have Dutch Jews who will look after our interests." ' 'I'll be willing to do that in so far as I am able.' 'You must say that clearly to Schlesinger. I have a lot to do this morning, but I thought I would just come and tell you.' Now I know that Schlesinger was behind the Theresienstadt application as he wanted to gain time.

Rejections of applications are still streaming in today, especially for those who claim dual nationality—Jews born in Holland of British parents, Jews born in Holland, but married in Britain, and so on. Definition of a list: a collection of Jews who will one day be deported. [. . .]

Wednesday July 21st: Yesterday was doubly wretched. First there was the transport. At four o'clock in the morning in the brutal light of the electric lamps the medical assistant, accompanied by a few nurses, once again began his macabre round of the hut, waking up the victims from their sleep, one by one. The house physician, irritated for some unfathomable reason, shared in his assistant's task. He too had a list in his hand and followed behind the other man till he reached the middle of the ward where he read out in rapid succession in a hard, loud voice the names of twenty-seven patients who had been marked down for the journey east. What would normally have taken half an hour of going about and searching was thus done in less than a minute—a more strident and cynical way of doing things, but quicker and brisker. Like the lancet of a surgeon that is inserted into a sick body with a steady, resolute hand.

Once again a number of elderly people and invalids had been noted down for the journey into the sinister gloom of Poland inside the belly of the venomous snake. The blind man who lay opposite me got up, saying bravely: 'I can't see, but I know that the sun and the moon and the stars shine in Poland too.' A strong, determined face and a high, noble forehead the windows of which are blind, but with a life of its own inside.

Every week they say that it is a terrible transport. All transports are terrible. It is heart-rending, again and again, to see mothers and fathers, or mothers alone with their offspring, a yellow card on their chests, or bent elderly folk laden with their last meagre possessions, setting out on the journey callously ordained by a hater of mankind. But there is a crescendo in the feeling of horror—this time pregnant women in their seventh or eighth month and week-old infants with scarlet fever were taken, in cattle and goods trucks. [. . .] July 15th was the date on which Holland had to be virtually clear of Jews, *judenrein*. July 15th has come and the quota of 90,000 Jews demanded by Hitler has been handed over. In the transport there was also a man (an S-man) with his wife, who had just had a confinement, and a small ailing child. This transport was terrible too because of the large number of families with young children— mainly people who had pinned their hopes on Palestine, but whose papers had been turned down. It was terrible for these people because their hopes had been reduced to nothing. They included practically all the teachers who took classes at Wester- bork. It was terrible for the devout Jews because a number of well-known Dutch rabbis were included in the transport. It was terrible because it was stiflingly hot. From a psychological point of view, it was probably the most wretched transport that has ever left Westerbork for the east.

Once again the same absurdity—contrary to the order from the *Obersturmführer*, some of the most capable, industrious and knowledgeable male nurses were sent away, whilst incompetent and lazy individuals remained behind.

Immediately after the transport there was a shift from hut 82 to hut 83. Pandemonium. Doctors raging, nurses shouting and a horde of people on the move with blankets, clothes and boxes of provisions. [. . .]

Thursday July 22nd: The first conflict in our new hut. At half

97

past eight this morning a walking patient, a boxer, with the muscles of a gorilla, coolly wandered out past the porter to go for a little walk up and down outside the windows. After the style of hut 82. The porter, a German with a face like an iron mask, rushed outside. He jerked his thumb imperiously over his shoulder and barked: 'Inside—get inside the hut! Nobody gets out of here before eleven!' 'Will you tell me what the time is. I wasn't used to this in hut 82.' 'I'm telling you—inside, or else you're for it. Then you'll go out and stay out.' The patient grew angry: 'What is that you're saying? I would be more careful if I were you.' 'I'm not afraid of threats, I would have you know.' The patient rushed in a fury at the little porter fellow, raised a powerful arm and bellowed: 'You scum, if you don't watch out, I'll beat you to a jelly. Do you understand?' The little porter retreated, cowering and pale as death, into a corner of his lodge, mortally afraid of the heavy arm that had been raised against him. Administrative staff came rushing up in a state of alarm. The porter, feeling brave again all at once: 'He must go, or I'll make a report to the OD.' The patient: 'Go to the devil!' And he disappeared inside the hut. The porter bawled out: 'I'm going to tell the OD.' Member of the administrative staff: 'You're really too harsh. You look upon the patients as prisoners. This isn't a prison. They're human beings.' 'I have my orders and I'm sticking to them. He's going out of here.' 'You can have your orders and yet treat the patients humanely.' 'I'm a porter and I represent the police authorities. There's nothing you can do with the damned Dutch character. They've got to behave themselves properly. I've made my decision and I never go back on a decision.' 'It's a great mistake not to be able to do that. A sensible man goes back on a decision if it's too harsh.' The porter hesitated. 'If he apologizes properly, I'll think about it.' [. . .]

A big check today on the bed luggage—boxes must not be larger than 20 × 20 × 30 cm. One of the nurses inspected the contents of boxes and threw out the foodstuffs that he thought were superfluous. A little dictator, trained up in the school of the *Führer's* servant's servant. Yet most of the patients, adults and children, have not been properly washed for weeks and lie sweating in their beds in the burning heat. Elsewhere the patients are carried outside, but here not a single nurse lifts a finger on their behalf. There is a stink inside the hut and not a single doctor bothers about it. The patients are furious—

they lie there grumbling and fuming and cursing. And angrily hitting out at the flies that buzz in droves round the beds. Great scarcity of tobacco. People readily pay 22.50 guilders for a packet of cigarettes.

Friday July 23rd : The *Obersturmführer* is going around with plans. The rumours that Westerbork as it is at present is to be consolidated as a labour camp are taking a more concrete form. A certain number of huts situated close together have been allocated for industrial purposes, working with metal, sorting rags and making clothes. The remainder of the inhabitants are concentrated in a particular group of huts.

The Commandant has said that he thinks Jews who work all day long need relaxation. 'My Jews,' as he puts it. A short time ago he gave practical evidence of this—in the shape of a symphony orchestra, later changed into a cabaret show which still gives regular performances, the only point being that Aryan music which was allowed to begin with is now forbidden. Only Jewish music is permitted. Clearly a whim. [. . .] Now it is said that the Commandant intends to establish a *café chantant* for the grown-ups and a playground for the children to add to the social life. He would appear to have a kind heart. He has also been having more personal contact with his Jewish artistes of late. He is very fond of them and has given them separate houses to live in and has exempted them from deportation. Recently, after one of the performances, he sent them cognac and other luxuries. Last night he had Ehrlich and a few other artistes visiting him until far into the night and he chatted with them in a very friendly manner. The artistes are no ordinary people! So they are not ordinary Jews. Indeed is it not the *Führer* and his friends who decide who *is* a Jew? When asked whether the Commandant was anti-Semitic, Ehrlich replied: 'Oh yes, but not where you and I are concerned.' 'What makes the Commandant tick?' people ask. [. . .]

Saturday July 24th : There is a story going round the camp that I am writing a novel about Westerbork with the consent of the *Obersturmführer* and that I have to read out a chapter to him every day.

Yesterday it was announced semi-officially that for the time being there will be no more transports, from Westerbork to the east or from Amsterdam to Westerbork. This morning came the news, like a clap of thunder out of a clear sky, which is never very clear in any case—there is always a cloud in it—that another transport was on its way from Amsterdam. Yesterday there was in fact a rumour that there were Jews imprisoned once more in the *Hollandse Schouwburg*. At six o'clock this evening a transport of 450 Jews was brought in, many of them members of the *Expositur* staff, also (with a few exceptions) the sixty Jews who had been members of the Jewish Council at Westerbork and were sent back to Amsterdam last week with a special identity card as a kind of reward for good conduct. There is a wry touch of humour about the incident, as they included Jews who had returned to Amsterdam with all their goods and chattels—their pots and pans, their peas and beans, all nicely packed up. They had left Westerbork like misers. Now they came back with a single rucksack and a blanket, the man with a thick growth of stubble on his chin and the woman all crushed and crumpled looking. Amongst the crowd you could hear the remark: 'It serves them right!' or 'He might as well have spent his money!' and so on. Delight in their discomfiture.

The henchmen of the *Führer* play a cat and mouse game with the Jews—they chase them from one corner to the other and take pleasure in their fear and gradual exhaustion. The henchman at Westerbork mocks and derides them by laying on a cabaret with light and airy music as a change from the macabre Tuesday morning transports. And the Jews are not ashamed to go to the cabaret (apart from those who are officially obliged to attend). It only costs ten cents. [. . .]

A mother sat at supper with her small daughter. The daughter pulled a nasty face at the pudding. Mother: 'Listen to me. If you don't eat up your pudding, you'll go on the transport without mummy.' [. . .]

A hard boiled egg.

Sunday July 25th: An order from Dr. Pick, the head of the Quarantine Department. As flies carry infectious diseases, every camp resident is under an obligation to catch fifty flies per day and deliver them, wrapped in a piece of paper, to the Quarantine Station. [. . .]

Paid a private visit yesterday evening to an eminent Dutch Jewish doctor and his wife in his consulting room. Another doctor and his wife were visiting too. Discussion about conditions in the camp. I said: 'The Dutch Jews hate the guts of the German Jews.' The host: 'And vice versa. I've spoken a lot with the Germans and they're still furious about coming here and because of the hunger and cold and all they had to do without at the start. They're angry because the Dutch Jews left them in the lurch.' The visiting doctor's wife: 'That's just idle talk. The Dutch Jews helped the German Jews as much as they could. They sent them whole consignments of cocoa and coffee and cheese. The other day one of the Long-Term Residents said straight out in my hut that the Dutch Jews were not to blame for what happened to the German Jews. They have the wretched Prussian spirit—they're never satisfied and shift all the blame on to others and always want more. They bellow and bark all day long and blow up every little thing into something enormous and threaten to deport anyone who doesn't obey at once.' The hostess: 'The German Jews have no reason at all to complain of the Dutch Jews. There would be more point in complaining about their own Jewish compatriots. What did the rich German Jews who settled in Amsterdam-Zuid with all their wealth ever do for their poor fellow-countrymen? Not much. They didn't dip their hands into their pockets. Just see if anyone can contradict that!' 'How were you received by the German doctors here?' Host: 'They weren't very friendly. I was allowed to hold a few consultations every day to begin with and when I had two I was busy. But I wasn't allowed into the actual hospital. That didn't change till later. The relations between the doctors are good now. There's a fine esprit de corps.'

Monday July 26th: There is a feeling of elation—the news has come in, through the guards, that Mussolini has resigned. The BBC broadcast the news and the German radio also announced it. [. . .] All day long the name of Mussolini resounded through the camp. The general view is that the war will soon be over. Confirmed pessimists have been converted into optimists on the spot. Optimists believe that they will be back home in a month or two. [. . .]

Met a friend of mine who returned on the latest transport to Westerbork from Amsterdam. He was surprised to see me still here. 'How have you managed it?' 'Because of Schlesinger's protection.' 'He will be expecting something in return.' 'I think so. Anything I can do for him without compromising myself, I will do.' 'But surely you don't have to see that he isn't killed off?' 'Oh no, not that. But *à la guerre comme à la guerre*, one must take the rough with the smooth.'

By order from above the schoolchildren were sent out to the moor today to pick lupins. A scorching sun. They came back dog-tired, several of them with sunstroke.

On the most recent transport from Amsterdam there were a few sterilized men who were sent to Amsterdam from Wester-bork not long ago. A transport of fifty women and children who had been in hiding has arrived from Scheveningen. [. . .]

Tuesday July 27th: Last night after a restless day the hospital patients had just begun to settle down quietly and were lying comfortably in their beds with only the unbearable heat to contend with when the seventeen-year-old son of the house physician came in to say: 'The Italians laid down their arms at a quarter past three today.' The patients sat up with a jerk. 'Then it will soon be over.' 'We'll soon be going home.' One of them struck up the soldiers' song: "t Is nog mããār een poepie daaage. . .' (A few more days, only just a few. . . .). Others joined in. A hum of voices in the ward. The nurses forgot that, according to regulations, the patients should be quiet. It seemed an unlikely story.

This morning a new version—the Italians laid down their arms at two o'clock in the morning. It is supposed to be "official" and has come from the camp guards. The rejoicing is subdued owing to a tightening-up of the camp regime—the Commandant has proclaimed martial law in the camp. Gatherings of more than two persons are forbidden. Also there is a stricter check on the wearing of the Jewish star. People busy talking politics, but there was a warning from the porter: 'Don't discuss politics. There are spies going about in the camp —there is even one here in this hut. Be careful!' People now whisper cautiously only to their closest friends. Many are convinced that the war will soon be over. I cannot help thinking of my "telepathic" friend. August 16th was what she said. [. . .] In the course of the day six Jews were arrested for not wearing the star in public, but they were later released.

The *Obersturmführer* is offended by malicious gossip which has been spread about him. And he has issued an order making known his displeasure. 'Once again,' he said, 'irresponsible rumours are going about the camp in connection with rehearsals for cabaret and concert performances and rehearsals of artistes. As a punishment I therefore forbid the proposed programme of light music to take place on Sunday afternoons. I would also like to point out that, should further rumours arise, there will be a serious risk of artistic performances being discontinued altogether.' (The writer does not hold himself accountable for the translation of the order which was originally worded in German.) The noble Commandant—a victim of idle gossip! As if we care whether he treats us to light music or not or whether his unsavoury cabaret shows are allowed to continue! We are waiting for the regime to collapse. [. . .]

Wednesday July 28th: The trenches along the barbed wire are nearing completion. A large stretch of them is one-third full of water, stagnant water. After a few days it takes on the colour of mud. [. . .] They send off a stench which combines with the stench from the latrines. Nauseating. There are living huts along the trenches. [. . .] The stench rises from the earth on all sides. On the edge of the camp is a small market garden. It is manured with human excrement. [. . .] Nauseating. People are nauseating too. Their breath stinks—their tongue is steeped in the sexual filth that they are incessantly vomiting up. If a woman or a girl goes past, she is often the target of lewdness and jeering. Any remark that can give rise to jokes about sex does.

The German Jews are in a state of nerves. As the end of the war approaches they have a problem: Where will they go? Their rejoicing at the way things are turning out is tempered by this. They have lost their native land, they have been driven out and expatriated, they are stateless and cannot and will not go back. They also do not want to run the risk of becoming once again the victims of anti-Semitism which made the lives of Jews in Germany a misery even before the Nazi regime. They ask themselves: 'Can we stay on in Holland and live here as free citizens?' They do not feel the answer will be 'yes'. [. . .]

It seems as if the tension between the two groups of Jews has become more acute since the dramatic fall of Mussolini. Trottel whispered in my ear yesterday: 'Things are beginning

103

to get dangerous.' This means to say that many Germans who have behaved badly towards the Dutch Jews and have snapped rudely at them and flaunted their superiority are beginning to smell danger and fear vengeance. Even now the German Jews have learnt nothing—they still shout abuse, they still satisfy their lust for power. Only yesterday Frau Stein, the dictator at the Accommodation Office, showed this when dealing with a German rabbi who came to ask for a decision about moving him to other accommodation to be reconsidered. Frau Stein, a mannish-looking woman, said with glaring eyes: 'I have made my decision and it cannot be changed.' Short and sharp, hard, arrogant—enough to make you want to pour a basin of cold water over her fiery head and cool her down. It is this brutish and inhuman arrogance that has caused so much bad blood among the Dutch Jews. And not only among the Dutch Jews. Among German Jews too who, embittered by their years of isolation here, would gladly vent their pent-up fury on their own fellow-Jews and compatriots who have acted like little Hitlers and have raged and scolded and threatened and exacted vengeance. [. . .]

People are searching for something to hold on to, for protection. Who will give them something to hold on to, who will protect them? Who will protect the others if and when the fury of the people is unleashed in the camp? It is time to think about having some organization to keep the peace, a body which will stand above the various factions and prevent or oppose the murder and slaughter.

Thursday July 29th: Today I saw my brother off and went with him as far as the guards' barracks. He is married to an Aryan. He was in the hospital for nine weeks with multiple sclerosis. Like so many patients suffering from chronic disorders he has gone very far downhill owing to the lack of proper medicines and, even more so, the absence of a proper environment with kind and loving care and nursing. He was scarcely able to move his legs, even with assistance. I could easily have escaped. Without the guard noticing, I went with the two members of the OD taking my brother away as far as the lorry that was to carry him to the train at Assen. I was tempted for a moment, but I resisted the temptation. I did not want to involve my brother in danger or trouble on any account. And the thought flashed through my brain: 'It's not worth the trouble now.

The war will soon be over.' It is a strange feeling to be so near freedom and yet reject it. It is like turning away from an attractive woman.

And yet this freedom would only be a relative gain. Anyone who can hold out at Westerbork and evade the transports can do more with his positive captivity than the Jew in Amsterdam with his relative freedom or the Jew who has gone into hiding and sits between four walls and is every minute in terror of being picked up. Captivity means the barbed wire and the discipline of hut life, but with a little imagination and a sense of humour and a love of nature you can create a world of your own in which it is possible to forget the captivity of the material body. Both in your working hours, provided they are spent out of doors and do not go beyond your normal strength—something which does not happen at Westerbork— and also in your free hours which can be spent outside, you can enjoy the vastness of the sky and the moor and the birds. The sky is so delightful here and there is colour on the moor. The sunsets are enchanting. Flocks of seagulls with white bodies and black heads, perhaps a thousand of them together, spend their lives cavorting in the air. I can stand and look at the gulls for long periods on end—they are the symbol of true freedom. They take off from the ground whenever they want to, they glide upon the wind, they rise and fall, sometimes in orderly formation, sometimes capriciously and in no order at all, like a succession of random thoughts, but they are always graceful. [. . .]

A great change took place today—the house physician discharged me from the hospital hut, not because of my health, but because the hospital is being reduced still further and they are finding there is a continual shortage of space. I have for the first time been put in an ordinary living hut (85) after spending almost nine months in the hospital. A somewhat dramatic farewell to many men whom I had got to know, superficially at least. For the first time since being admitted I am sitting writing at a table, not a strong or handsome table, but a table nevertheless, with a bench for me to sit on. Until now I had always written sitting up in bed or, on one occasion, sitting in a wheelbarrow in my old lane. I feel rather more of a social being here in the company of the other men who are sitting at the table reading the paper. I have been released from the presence of ailing old men, from the gurgling breathing and

105

the death-rattle, from the stench and the regimentation of the hospital. The hut where I have been put has the reputation of being a good hut. It is reserved for families without small children (up to fourteen years of age). It gives an impression of quiet orderliness. The floor looks a bit cleaner than in the hospital huts, although these floors are swabbed every morning. It is situated on the easternmost edge of the camp and looks out over the moor as far as the horizon. The beds are close together, three tiers high, but with proper passages between them so that the hut is not overfull. Not yet—this may well happen. After being there for an hour I already feel I have settled in. The ability of human beings to adapt themselves is amazing. Everything here is done at a furious pace, if it is done at all, and people with healthy minds can cope just as quickly and as easily.

The things of life are as dramatic or tragic as you yourself want to make them. Here you learn to look upon the unimportant things as being unimportant and only the really big and essential things as being big and essential. As a phenomenon and a harsh reality this camp is monstrous, but the things that happen in it are so colourful and varied and humorous that you keep your eyes open and often forget the camp itself and see only the things that are happening there.

Friday July 30th: The regime has become more strict. As a result of the way things are going, militarily and politically. The Germans are nervy. [. . .] As a start, there has been a tightening-up of the censorship of incoming post. A few days ago the agents of Lippmann & Rosenthal, who virtually had nothing to do now that there were hardly any transports coming in, were put in charge of the censorship. Many times already camp residents have been called to account for remarks and information in letters to relatives. Checking of employment has also become more strict. Since yesterday SS men have been inspecting huts and anyone they find there in the daytime has to give an account of himself. If he cannot produce a suitable alibi, he is either enrolled in the labour organization or punished. [. . .]

Last night took my first evening walk through the camp in the dark. The Boulevard des Misères was like a kind of Kalverstraat—giggling girls going along arm in arm in the midst of more sedate promenaders who made a detour round them. In the middle of the camp is a mighty chimney extending upwards to the lilac sky. At one side of the camp little tea-parties, at the other side shadowy courting couples slinking over the moor like cats. In one of the lanes jazz music from the cabaret orchestra: "Bei mir bist du schön", strictly forbidden in Germany because of the Yiddish touch in it, but arousing the interest of hundreds of camp dwellers. It is just like an Indian settlement in Central America in the midst of the prairie where civilization is being introduced for the first time.

My luggage is a burden to me in my hut. I only have a bed now and I have to share it out between my body and my luggage. [. . .] I landed here with practically nothing—a pair of pyjamas, a shirt, a pair of trousers, a toothbrush. I did not feel the want of anything and I was happy in that destitute and unencumbered state. At last I had nothing at all! My family and friends sent me all sorts of things, clothes, books, canned goods, etc. I became reconciled to my new possessions and was happy to have them. And now here I am with these belongings all over me and I don't know what to do with them. For the time being I have deposited on an unoccupied bed a full rucksack, another bag with clothes, a small case with provisions, a pile of books, a winter coat, a raincoat, boxes of letters and a host of small items. All this is three tiers up, so I have to be clambering up all the time.

Today the order has come that I, and others like me, must vacate the unoccupied bed; it is going to be occupied. I don't really believe this, as there is an order from the authorities which says the same. The only purpose of it is to keep everything neat and tidy. [. . .]

Saturday July 31st: Sleeping in the residential hut is more difficult than I expected. There is late talking and the lights go on early for those who have to be at their work early. A matter of getting used to it.

This morning I went to say good-bye to Dr. Spanier, the head of the hospital. A charming chap. Good manners and conversation. 'I hardly dare to ask you how you are getting on. You always have an ironic answer.' Dr. Spanier smiled. The melancholy smile of the sceptic who knows life. 'I've come to express my gratitude to you for what you've done for me. You know, of course, that I've been discharged from hospital? I was there for nearly nine months. I've nothing to offer you but my

thanks. Perhaps I can manage something more later on.'
Dr. S.: 'Well, well, who took away your S?' 'I don't know for
sure, but I've strong reason to suppose that it was your doing.
So I must thank you once again for that.' Dr. S. made a
deprecating gesture. 'Don't bother!'

The *Untersturmführer* appeared unannounced. A small broad-
shouldered fellow with a brutal, defiant face and the bleary
eyes of a drinker. Dr. Spanier went up to him. I got up and
stood to attention as per instructions. A movement of the hand:
'Just remain seated.' A man in his position can afford to do
this. A brief conversation between Spanier and the *Untersturmführer* beside a divan on which were four bottles all packed up.
Drink. *Untersturmführer*: 'How can I take them with me?' Dr.
Spanier with a laugh: 'Why do you wear such wide trousers
then?' The *Ustuf* slipped the bottles one by one into his two
wide trouser pockets. 'Good day to you.' The *Ustuf* held out
his hand to Dr. Spanier. 'Have a good journey,' said the latter
politely. The *Ustuf* is going on leave to Berlin and so on to the
eastern front. 'Perhaps the war will soon be over.' 'Perhaps,'
replied the *Ustuf* indifferently. Exit.

'Does he believe the war will soon be over?' 'Yes, but he also
believes that Germany will win it.' Dr. Spanier gave a mocking
laugh. 'Another boy,' I said, 'who has a lot to learn.' 'Yes,
indeed—he's forty.' Myself: 'He looks about twenty.' 'He'll
never learn. And those are the people who rule over us.' Dr.
Spanier is going on holiday. But I shall be meeting him again.

New order: those who draw out money will in future receive
only seventy-five per cent of the amount of the money order.
The remaining twenty-five per cent will be used for the common good of the camp. The usual procedure, the usual high-
handed action. So easy—to look after the community at the
expense of others! Nobody wastes any words on it. Those who
for special reasons feel entitled to claim the whole sum can put
in a request accordingly.

Sunday August 1st: The hut has become full to overflowing all at
once. Yesterday a whole batch of Jews joined us. This hut
which until now had been looked on as an élite hut has suddenly become a completely ordinary one where people sit
crammed together and jostle one another. They lie side by side
in their beds, they are all jammed together at the tables and

they bump into one another in the washroom. My luggage has stayed where it was—the bed next to mine is still unoccupied.

At six o'clock this morning I heard the following as people were getting up: 'May I introduce myself? My name is Cohen.' 'And mine is Kartenspieler, doctor of philosophy. Where have you come from?' 'From Gronau.' 'Are you the father of the well-known painter?' 'Yes, I am. He's done some magnificent things.' 'Where is your son at present?' 'In Theresienstadt. I have another son in Barneveld. And another still who is working here with the Jewish Council.' 'Oh, really. I was in Amsterdam, writing about "Jüdisch-empfindsame Spaziergänge".' 'That's interesting.' 'What do you do?' 'I'm a textile dealer.' 'Amsterdam is a beautiful city. I lived in Oranje Nassaulaan. From there I had to move to Oost. And from there I was taken to this place.' 'My son who is a painter lived on the Titiaanstraat. A lovely house with a delightful view at the back.' A voice from up on top: 'Shut up, damn you—I want to sleep.'

This morning for the first time for nine months I had a shower in the bath-house in the centre of the camp. Waited a quarter of an hour. The bath itself was not allowed to take more than a bare ten minutes. A miserable little jet of water. Far too hot. But I enjoyed it. I felt as if it was the first shower I had ever had in my life. But my fingernails are as black as soot again. The fight against the fine black camp dust—a mixture of sand and coal-dust—is hopeless and people are at their wits' end. They work away at their nails all day long without ever getting them clean—torture for a woman with a pride in her appearance. Nail brushes are rare. In the evening our feet are covered in black. Our noses are a permanent refuge for dust; adults and children regularly pick their noses in order to fish out the dust. Black particles become lodged in the corners of our eyes. The dust penetrates into our clothes and forms a pattern of stains that look like a map. Brushes are scarce. A bath means that you are clean for just a moment. [. . .]

During the night an S-transport of 150 persons arrived from Scheveningen and they were put in S-hut 67.

Monday August 2nd: The unbearable heat has persisted for nearly a week. It is stifling inside the huts and roasting outside. [. . .] The breeze laden with fine sand which often makes life difficult outside the huts developed yesterday into a kind of sirocco which sent clouds of sand swirling up and made walking a blinding ordeal. The heat burst like fire out of the ground. [. . .]

Towards evening the entire population of Westerbork came outside, gasping for a breath of air. People gathered in the lanes between the huts and the clumps of trees were swarming with life. The moor was speckled with black. In front of the one-, two- or three-family houses people gathered for tea parties without tea and on the scorched patches of grass between the houses many rested their heavy limbs. In front of the communal houses for bachelors the young people who did outside work assembled in their hundreds round tables and chairs that had been brought outside. A violinist and a harmonica-player brought life to the camp with popular tunes. There was a mood of expectancy in the sultry summer air—was there going to be a summer fair? Would all these young men and women who are artificially kept apart from one another and live perpetually in a state of extreme tension be able to resist the temptation to dance? They listened with pleasure to the music and let it carry them away, but they restricted themselves to a quiet rendezvous—no man or boy grasped a girl round the waist. The mood was one of serious resignation.

The people stayed outside till late, and the musicians went on playing their tunes. Couples slipped away, past heaps of coal, past hundreds of stacked bedsteads, past objects piled up to right and left, towards the outside edge of the camp. Along the barbed wire there was a kind of "wireless" courtship between patrolling guards and Jewish girls who walked along with the guards. Towards eleven o'clock they slipped back again to their huts for the strict evening roll-call, past huts and look-out towers that looked as if they were made of cardboard. The atmosphere at Westerbork is like that in a film city—all imitation and artificial.

The sirocco blowing again this morning. The plague of flies is unbearable. The tables are covered with flies which attack the food in hordes. They make breakfast and lunch and supper a torment. They attach themselves to the rims of mugs and bottles. They swarm round the open WC's. [. . .] There is a lot of dysentery. It is euphemistically called diarrhoea. The cause is unknown, but there is a danger of infection everywhere. There is now a plague of fleas too. Many huts are alive with fleas. The camp has also been swarming with cats recently.

110

They just appeared out of the blue. Every house has adopted a pussy as a mascot. [. . .] Life has become a bit difficult, more difficult than usual. [. . .]

Tuesday August 3rd: No transport this morning. Peace and quiet. The world seems kind and merciful. Children thank God that their parents have escaped the executioner for another week and parents thank Heaven because their children are safe for the time being. Every week means one more week and every week may be the last. Perhaps the war will not be over quite as soon as we hoped, but the regime in Germany may collapse just like the regime in Italy and then, at any rate, the persecution of the Jews will be over. Every week now represents a double or a treble gain. People still know practically nothing about Poland. [. . .]

Went with Trottel to Schlesinger's office for a talk yesterday afternoon, but Schlesinger's wife informed us that this was not possible, as Schlesinger was having a long conference with Gemmeker. Trottel said that I was getting a responsible post immediately under Schlesinger. He had asked Trottel if I was able to keep order. I am curious to know what he intends to do with me. The purpose of the talk was to discuss the antagonism between German and Dutch Jews in the camp and study the steps that should be taken to prevent them from being at loggerheads. Do Schlesinger and Trottel think I am a miracle worker and can exorcise the hatred which the German Jews have brought down on their own heads? [. . .]

The complaint against Schlesinger is that he rides rough-shod over everyone. He looks that type too—self-assured, arrogant, uncouth and cold. He is an upstart who has the power to do what he likes with the Jews. [. . .] This place is swarming with upstarts, big and little men who were commercial travellers and small-time solicitors in ordinary life and have dealt here with important matters of policy connected with the depressing transport business and go around with their chests puffed out. [. . .] Circumstances have helped Schlesinger to rise, just as they have helped Sluzker. He is under the authority of Gemmeker, the king of the Jews, and is his deputy. He has enjoyed all the advantages of his position and continues to do so. He smiles with satisfaction and is fairly bursting with self-satisfaction. As a dictator he has sent away on the transports men and women who thought they had bought themselves a place at

111

Westerbork; others he exempted from deportation for reasons which it would be better not to investigate. He has cast aside and insulted and humiliated men and has shown favour to women. He is no more or less guilty than the little potentates who at a lower level have done exactly the same thing, but he stands high up—he is the henchman of Gemmeker. So he is all the more vulnerable to the slings and arrows which the folk who feel wronged, injured, insulted or aggrieved are holding in readiness for the moment when things start to happen.

The dictator Schlesinger is guilty because he has allowed power to be delegated to him by the henchman of the Grand Inquisitor, but the guilt is shared by every Jew who has benefited from the power of Schlesinger and from the influence of the miserable little petty potentates who bask in his shadow. For every man and every woman that Schlesinger has managed to pull clear on his own initiative or at the instigation of others, he has had to deliver up another man and another woman—that was no secret to the people who have escaped by the skin of their teeth. But Schlesinger is guiltier than anyone else. He has abused his power in order to obtain something that he could not otherwise have obtained. The executioner's servant's servant could not achieve this without compromising and disqualifying himself. And now this servant is seeking shelter from the storm that is about to break over his voluptuous head. And Trottel is busy reconnoitring and preparing the ground for this. I shall probably hear more about it this evening. [. . .]

A case of meningitis in hut 5. The victim is a woman who is expecting a baby any day. The part of the hut where she is lying has been divided off with barbed wire. People are terrified that the infection will spread.

A Jew sent a letter to the *Obersturmführer* in which he requested exemption from deportation to Poland because, as director of a large store in Amsterdam, he had arranged for eighty per cent of the stock to be delivered to the German *Wehrmacht*. Another Jew, living in the Waverstraat in Amsterdam, wrote a letter to the *Obersturmführer* in which he requested exemption from deportation because he had as a policeman denounced several Jews to the Gestapo. He was deported at once.

Wednesday August 4th: Visited Schlesinger at his office yesterday evening together with Trottel. Schlesinger (in a blue shirt) handed round cigars. He began to tell me that he had just won a great victory in his talks with the *Obersturmführer*. He was now eighty per cent certain that no more transports would be going. Westerbork would become a labour camp and the elderly people and children who were here would stay on. [. . .]

I explained my views to Schlesinger about what could be done to remove the tension between Dutch and German Jews. It looks as if when the war ends there will be murder and slaughter at Westerbork. The Jews must not indulge in such a thing. Outsiders believe that we are all suffering here together and are united in our misery. It would be shameful if they were to discover that we are no different from the SS. We must do nothing calculated to create resentment which will alienate German and Dutch Jews from one another after the war and will stand in the way of a suitable settlement of the Jewish question. The Jews must not be their own judges. The existing conflicts are no justification in most cases for the feuds that are being built up. A Dutch-German contact committee should be formed to spread the idea that Dutch and German Jews should bury their feuds and, if necessary, create an organization which in an emergency would prevent acts of violence from being committed. Haste was imperative as peace was on the way. Schlesinger agreed to these ideas and expressed the wish that I would bring together a number of Dutch Jews who shared my views and were willing to confer with him. This would be my function.

Trottel said he was afraid that, when he got wind of this movement, the *Obersturmführer* would not be pleased. He considered it necessary to inform the Commandant about the plan and ask for his consent. Moreover, the idea could not be implemented without force and people were not allowed to own weapons. Schlesinger: 'When I go with this to the *Obersturmführer*, he will ask me, "Who are the people who are going about with schemes for murder and revenge?" And he will deport them. And I do not want to deport anyone. The committee does not need to bear the name of "committee", nor does it need to be official. There must be a representative of the OD on the committee too.' Trottel grumbled and said: 'I won't say anything more.' He left the office spluttering. A firm farewell handshake from Schlesinger who shows his physical strength and determination in the way he shakes hands. [. . .]

Thursday August 5th: The day began with feeling tired. It was a restless night—the fleas bothered me. My body is covered with round pink spots with a red dot in the middle. [. . .]

Towards six o'clock there was quite a parade—the endless shuffling of about 300 men trudging heavily and sleepily to the washroom. Trudge, trudge! Clump, clump! Jostling and pushing round the three WC's. Jostling and pushing round the water taps above a long sink by men who have to shave and wash. Lack of space to put down their things and hang up their clothes and towels. A dirty, muddy floor with puddles of water. Squabbles. Men dressing on their beds because of lack of space. Ten or twelve men pushing and juggling round one small filthy table with their boxes and mugs and bottles. Incessant coming and going along the passages between the beds by the residents and their wives who live in the other wing of the hut.

At eight o'clock a shouted command—everybody out of the hut for cleaning! Chased out of their home! Anyone who has not been enrolled for work or is not ill has to kill two hours. The sun may be burning down or the dust swirling about or it may be raining—but that does not matter as far as the cleaning is concerned. So out everyone must go! People loafing aimlessly about beside the hut entrance. Anyone who can think of an errand to do does it. Anyone who can't goes round in a circle. With his companions he ruminates about the political speculations of the evening before for want of anything better to do. Or he tells some hackneyed old story. Or he complains that he has slept badly. And so on. We are all poor creatures—wandering about without a home.

About ten o'clock the door opens again and we step into a clean room with our filthy, dirt-covered boots and shoes. Just imagine it! The floor has certainly been swept, but is just as grimy as the platform of a tram. When it is swabbed, it becomes black with mud. Everything you touch is grimy and grubby and greasy—the tables, the benches, the beds. Everyone turns to his work or his hobby. [. . .]

It is not easy to work. A passer-by breaks in to say: 'Is there anything new? When do you think the war will be over?' Fifty come along every day and ask the same old questions. You get weary of being polite—it takes time. You can't say: 'Go to hell!' That would be rude and you would get a bad reputation. You learn to be polite here with the silliest, the

114

stupidest and the most self-opinionated of people. Another interruption: 'Are you writing a diary?' 'Are you writing a book about Westerbork?' A group of people come and sit down at the table—there is a lot of loud chatter and the rickety old table shakes violently to and fro. Writing is impossible. Where can I retire to, where can I find some privacy? This goes on all day long. [. . .]

The men come streaming back from their work for lunch with large appetites. They take out their ration cards and stand in a queue. In a large dish there is a minute portion of potatoes in their jackets with a dash of goulash prepared in the Dutch style. They have to be peeled. Result—a cold helping of potatoes dipped in cold goulash. Washing up in cold water. Pot, mess-tin, knife, fork, spoon—everything stays greasy. An afternoon nap. Just fancy. Not that I am officially entitled to an afternoon nap, but if anyone can take an afternoon nap he does so. The work is pointless, but the afternoon nap is not. You might equally well say that the afternoon nap is no more pointless than the work. But you never manage to take the forty winks you want to. Chatter on all sides—a woman who is still furious about a row she had yesterday or is starting a fresh row—two so-called invalids who keep up a shouted conversation from one bed to the other—a young man and his girl-friend who have climbed up to a bed and are lying there giggling—a group of people who are talking politics or playing cards or conducting a vehement post mortem on the game. Or there is someone busy knocking in nails somewhere. Or something else that makes a din. The din is unceasing.

In the afternoon women, relatives and friends come visiting —a cacophony of voices, like the chirruping of a host of crickets in a primaeval tropical forest, hard, strident, penetrating. When the men come home from work the noise reaches a crescendo—the throng reminds you of an oriental bazaar and the uproar reminds you of a line of parrot cages at the zoo. When the daily papers come in, political and military speculations break forth once more like an avalanche, unthinking, loud, tumultuous. Until ten or eleven o'clock. By the time the noise has died down and everyone is lying quietly and peacefully in bed it is half past eleven. The next morning the men get up listlessly, heavy with sleep.

Friday August 6th: An evening stroll with an intelligent young

115

woman. Rainy weather. At the edge of the camp talked about
the reaction of the Jews to community life here. The eternal
topic. A young Jew came up to us—a tall, gaunt fellow. He
pointed to the deep trench that the Jews had dug on either
side of the barbed wire to thwart their own impulse to escape:
'Isn't that like a mass-grave?' We looked at each other. What
did the man mean by using that depressing word? I thought
of trenches at the front with soldiers falling like flies under
murderous artillery fire. 'Yes,' said the man, 'if things don't
work out, the Germans will throw the Jews in here en masse,
don't you think? It wasn't for nothing that they made us dig
these trenches.' I had to laugh—it certainly seemed a bit far-
fetched. But in my subconscious mind I had the feeling: 'They
are wicked enough to do it.' The man said: 'Remember Katyn.
It was definitely the Germans who did it. They could do the
same here at the eleventh hour. A few machine-guns and that
would be that.' We did not believe it. Katyn was definitely the
work of the Bolshevists. And how would the Germans know
it was the eleventh hour? In any case they would have something better to do then. We looked together into the deep
trench in the sand with the spades still standing up in a line
in it. It was suitable for the purpose and the rogues would
shrink from nothing. 'Don't work yourself up about it,' I said
to the man. 'Things won't turn out like that, I'm sure.' The
man went away. 'That's typical of the mood of the Jews and
the anxiety they feel.' The rogues are quite capable of doing
it.

It was pouring. So we stood up against a hut under an over-
hang and went on talking. A window opened and a man's
head popped out. 'Come inside!' A camp friend had recognized our voices. With muddy shoes we clambered in through
the window. We found ourselves in the midst of baptized Jews,
the *geschmadden*. We were in a party with a balalaika. We made
friends. 'Are you the man at the hot water tap?' 'Yes.' 'Are
you the lady from the Jewish Council?' 'Yes.' 'Are you Russian?' 'Yes.' My companion, the daughter of a Russian
mother, felt her Russian blood stir within her, and she burst
out in Russian: 'Govoritye-li vwi paruski?' The two young
people sat jabbering there in Russian like a couple of twittering sparrows. 'Will you play a Russian song for me?'
A Russian song on the balalaika. Two, three, four Russian
songs. [. . .] A strange combination—a Jewish camp, a hut

116

with baptized Jews, a Russian colony, visited by full-blooded Dutch Jews—and yet there was a feeling of brotherhood at once. The man with the balalaika said to the young woman: 'I know you from the old days. You once spoke in Russian to my small daughter in the street in Amsterdam as I was walking along with her.' Fond farewells. How fortunate that there is something else in the world besides war, National Socialists, parcels and weariness. We returned to our huts in a good mood as if something big had happened in our lives.

Yesterday they began to shave the heads of the S-men in hut 67. They are getting prison clothing. [. . .]

Great show on in the camp. A visit today from one of the high-ups, the secretary of Rauter, a man called Harster. Plenty of gold pips. The usual hectic show put on. We had to make our beds properly. Before half past seven we had to be outside the door because of the extra cleaning in the hut. No afternoon naps. Invalids had to wear a star sewn firmly on to their pyjamas. Why everything should look so spick and span in a hut full of Jews whom the National Socialists think of as untidy gipsies is not clear. It normally does not look spick and span at all; an outsider would see that at a glance. The roadways are patrolled by double guards, made up of OD and NB men, the former in green and the latter in blue overalls, to see that the Jews do not stand about talking. Damn it all, the camp must give the impression of a beehive where work is done. That is what the *Obersturmführer* barked at his superior who was conducting the inspection.

Attended a boxing match between young Jews in the hall where during the day a few hundred women sit crammed together peeling potatoes with subdued faces. Somewhere in a corner tons of potatoes lay between boarding. Everything shipshape: a ring, boxing gloves, supporters. Supervision by an OD man. Sport is under the august patronage of the *Obersturmführer*. Somewhere else, out in the open field, Jews were practising basket-ball.

Saturday August 7th: Trottel called out to me on the road yesterday: 'Hey there! I'm not going on with the business. I'm getting out of my depth.' He could not be responsible for our attempts to ease the tension in the camp and prevent disaster if we did it all behind the Commandant's back. 'Then we must go and see Schlesinger.'

A conference in his office at half past six. A jovial greeting. But roguish eyes. Be careful! Door locked. A long and detailed story from Trottel: spies on the watch all the time. (His pike-eyes turned a shade yellower.) If the Commandant got wind of it, we were all in it together and he wouldn't take it lying down. Schlesinger must first have authorization from the Commandant. Schlesinger: 'Gentlemen, I believe I have solved the problem. I have a plan here that I shall put before the Commandant. It provides for the setting up of an arbitration committee on behalf of the work sections which are to be reorganized. It is still highly confidential, gentlemen, so be discreet. Everyone in the camp knows this. If the Commandant gives his approval, we can carry on with our work under this cloak.' Trottel: 'No, we must put our cards on the table. And I'm sure we can do it. I'm greatly indebted to the Commandant and I sincerely believe that he will give us the job of keeping the peace in the camp. He's also well aware of the fact that the Germans have lost the war and that when this actually happens his life will be in our hands.' Schlesinger: 'Then you don't know the Commandant. He's firmly convinced that Germany will win the war. He is too well disciplined to show anything and he is certainly not frightened. We would do better to operate under cover.' He pulled his jacket lapels together with both hands to show what he meant.

Trottel told all sorts of involved stories to show how great his successes had been in apparently hopeless cases, thanks to his supreme tact or personal influence. 'You see, I have managed to do all that.' A diplomat, a man who knows human nature, but very vain. Schlesinger was bored and listened with half-closed eyes to Trottel's bombast. When Trottel had finished speaking, Schlesinger gave me a sly wink. 'What is in fact your intention? To ask for the political leadership in the camp? Then we'll all be done for.' Trottel: 'I only want to point out that there is tension here and say we are willing to play our part in promoting peace.' A volte-face by Schlesinger: 'I have no objection. We can certainly do that. I don't believe there is any danger in that. So, Herr Trottel, go and see the Commandant.' Trottel smiled. He had won. He was a pusher. To me: 'My intention is that you should be chairman of the Arbitration Committee which will consist half of Dutch Jews and half of German Jews. If you need me, you can always come and see me.' 'In that way we can serve the interests of Dutch and German Jews equally. In what precise way we shall no doubt see in due course.' Farewell handshakes. It was like two wrestlers gauging each other's hand pressure.

Visited Dr. Neuburger of the Applications Office in the evening. A charlatan who makes love to all the women and is forever making puns in Dutch. He had apparently heard of the conferences; he tried to pump me, but without success. I mistrust that slippery eel.

The report of the fall of Orel and of Catania in Sicily has once again put the camp in a more light-hearted mood. But this morning there were women standing in the doorway of my hut—chased out because of the cleaning operations. They had their coat collars turned up and were whimpering with cold and wretchedness. Poor creatures who do not have the physical strength or spiritual powers of resistance to rise above the nastiness of life here.

Sunday August 8th: Everyone in the camp is complaining that he has been receiving hardly any letters recently. The agents of Lippmann & Rosenthal carry out the censorship. It is asserted that letters on which the address of the sender is not shown are simply burned. Hardly credible. I myself have only received two letters in the past fortnight, with the sender's address shown. Again and again people who receive letters are called to account by the agents because of some cryptic reference to money or to persons in hiding. In this way they help the German authorities to recover money from Jews or to find Jews. The greatest fanatic here is a man called Scheltens who threatens Jews with hell and damnation in his attempts to prize confidential information out of them. He is dreaded like the plague.

Yesterday night another small transport came in from Amsterdam, including about a hundred S-cases who had been in hiding. Their heads were shaved and they were given prison clothing. The agents of Lippmann & Rosenthal are also playing a new part in relation to these Jews. They pump them to find out the addresses where they have been in hiding. The Jews are behaving worse than shamefully—nearly all of them give the names and addresses of their hosts and benefactors quite readily. They will presumably have to answer for this in

119

due course.

An elderly lady who is highly cultured and educated stopped me yesterday afternoon in the road: 'Just imagine, I'm in quarantine now because I had lice on my head. I must have picked them up somewhere or other. It's dreadful, but I thank God that I'm getting some peace at last. I'm in the hut for the baptized and it's so full there that there's an infernal din all day long and all through the night and one just can't get any peace. It's awful. And now in the quarantine hut I have a bed all to myself with nobody above me. It's a pity that I've got to go back in a few days' time. I'm with children whose mothers aren't there, little boys, who are looked after by the older girls. They have no toys at all. It's heartbreaking and touching to see them.' On the same evening another visit to the quarantine hut—a loathsome place like a stable. In this stable a cultured elderly woman who once lived in a palatial house feels more at home than in a so-called living or residential hut occupied by people belonging more to her own faith.

Yesterday I was worn out with the din in my own hut. I slept for twelve hours on end. I was not feeling very fit as a result of my typhoid inoculation.

Monday August 9th: Went to "tea" yesterday afternoon with Dr. Wachtel. This tea party was intended as a blind for an attempt at reconciliation between German and Dutch Jews. It's in the air—all at once the German Jews feel a tremendous urge to be reconciled. I wonder if Dr. Wachtel has got wind of my own venture and begrudges me it because I am a Dutch Jew. People are like that. There were ten people present, five Germans and five Dutch. [. . .]

Dr. Wachtel gave a long preamble in which he tried to explain the position of the Jews in the camp and endeavoured to show that the attitude of the Dutch Jews towards the German Jews was unjustified. The old arrogance—as if all the guilt lay at the door of the Dutch Jews. Or short-sightedness. [. . .]

The debate centred round the idea that the message to be carried from this meeting to the huts and elsewhere was that it would be a bad thing for the future of the Jews if they became guilty of acts of violence. It was pointed out that the animosity was not only between German and Dutch, but also between Dutch Jews and other Dutch Jews. The hatred and resentment were very deep seated. To a large extent they arose out of the behaviour of the hut leaders and the fact also that practically all the hut leaders were Germans who did not know the Dutch character, did not speak the Dutch language and were not understood. There was a plea to replace German hut leaders by Dutch. There was also a plea for a committee to be formed to settle differences. It was complained that the position of the German Jews after the war was absolutely uncertain. It was assumed that the Dutch Jews would receive all the help and support they required from the Dutch Christians, but the German Jews had become stateless persons and could not rejoice in the friendship of the Dutch Christians. Germans who had visited Amsterdam recently had seen that the Christians were just as hostile to the German Jews as the Dutch Jews were. The great majority of the German Jews had no desire to return to Germany where they no longer had any family or possessions left, whereas the Dutch Jews were still Dutch citizens and could get back their possessions which were in Aryan keeping. The German Jews needed a certain amount of goodwill on the part of the Dutch Jews and so the differences between them should be cleared out of the way. On the other hand, it was observed that the Germans had been rather slow to realize this, but the Dutch Jews were willing to help their German brothers and there was indeed a good chance of help now that only a few thousand German Jews were involved. Before closing the meeting, Dr. Wachtel expressed the hope that everybody would help to bring about a reconciliation between German and Dutch Jews within his own circle. He would gladly place his quarters at the disposal of other groups so that this question could be discussed. [. . .]

A concert yesterday evening in the Registration Hall. Those invited were nearly all Germans. The Commandant was present with five ladies from his entourage. He remained quietly seated when the concert was over. He obviously expected an encore that did not come. He had to be tactfully told that the entertainment was over.

Tuesday August 10th: Spirits are rising. Early this morning the rumour spread through the camp like wildfire that Hitler had resigned and the command had been taken over by Göring, Dönitz and Keitel. A flood of conjecture—the war will soon be over now, there will be no more deportation of the Jews, they

121

will be going home shortly, and so on. Everywhere, on street corners, in the middle of the roadways, people are discussing the rumour and work has come to a standstill. Once more sighs of relief all round. Freedom for us first—that is the theme you hear on all sides—and then our relatives will be fetched back from Poland.

Since a week ago last Friday the censors, the agents of Lippmann & Rosenthal, have been holding on to practically all the letters. Only the odd letter has trickled through. Friends who were in the habit of receiving letters every day have had no news for a fortnight. I myself have had no news of my brother's arrival. This is unthinkable. He left for Amsterdam a fortnight ago tomorrow. Have not heard anything from other relatives either. The censorship has become stricter in another respect too—there is an order stating that from now on camp residents may only use one sheet of notepaper for their letters and write only on one side of it in the German or Dutch language in a clear hand. Not a word may be said about what happens in the camp, otherwise the whole hut will be punished. [. . .]

Wednesday August 11th: The big event of the day—the woman who is lying in hut 5 with meningitis gave birth to twins in the night, a boy and a girl. At the same time a girl of sixteen has had a child. Many children are born in the camp in spite of the definite intention of the National Socialists to prevent Jews from living together and begetting offspring. The camp is full of pregnant women of all ages. Men and women obviously still come into close contact with one another in spite of the poky rooms and partitions provided by the authorities and the closely knit community life. It would appear that births are encouraged by the fact that contraceptives are unobtainable here. On the other hand, the rate of mortality among babies is high—all young mothers whom one meets complain of the wretched condition of their young children and the doctors bear out the fact that many babies die as a result of bad feeding and living conditions. [. . .]

Yesterday morning came the order: all luggage under the beds, because there was to be spraying against fleas. Everyone toiling away. From one, two and three beds up, all cases, rucksacks, bundles, boxes, pots and mess-tins had to come down below. Not until late yesterday afternoon did the spraying

122

team appear and they could only get a part of the job done.

Early this morning came a cleaning order: all luggage out from under the beds and up on top of them again, because the hut had to be cleaned. Everyone toiling hard once more to get the cases, rucksacks, bundles, boxes, pots and mess-tins up on the first, second and third tier of beds. Presently they had to come down again for the spraying team. Poor organization. And so something comes along every day to add to our weariness.

A sign of the times: today a man bought a winter coat for the price of eight cigarettes. The transaction shows that money no longer plays a part here as a form of currency and that cigarettes have a high purchasing power. Indeed in many cases cigarettes take the place of money. People here are gasping for tobacco and anyone who has plenty of cigarettes can control the commodities market. [. . .]

Scene in Schlesinger's office. A hut leader came to complain. 'Why does hut leader Ströbel get leave and not me? He is the rottenest of the lot and ruins our reputation with the Dutch Jews. If he gets leave, I want to get leave too; I have a right to it.' Schlesinger (diplomatically): 'You're right, old man, but I can't do anything about it. It's all decided by the *Obersturmführer*. If he thinks that a hut leader is entitled to leave, then he gives him leave!' Everyone knows that Schlesinger is the boss and does exactly as he pleases.

Spirits have fallen—no confirmation of the rumour that Hitler has resigned. The war will be going on much longer and the Jews are once more in great danger.

Schlesinger has obtained the approval of the *Obersturmführer* regarding his proposal for the reorganization of work sections and the setting up of committees to settle differences. Trottel said: 'Now he has all the power in his hands.'

Trottel was received in audience by the *Obersturmführer* this afternoon. The latter offered Trottel an armchair, saying: 'Let's have a nice cosy chat.' Trottel told him that he had come to see him out of gratitude for all he (the *Ostu*) had done for him. He wanted to keep him informed about what was going on in the camp. The *Ostu* declared that he was, in fact, fully informed about everything, including the conference held last Sunday in Dr. Wachtel's room. He had ascertained how many Dutch and German Jews were in the camp, namely, 6,000 and 4,000. Trottel requested permission for Schlesinger to appoint committees to settle differences and the *Ostu* gave his consent. He also asked the *Ostu* to keep a weapon in reserve —he should point out that he was fully aware of the tensions in the camp. And he also asked for permission to visit the Commandant from time to time and keep him informed about how things were getting on. The Commandant granted him that permission. Before working out our plans in detail, Trottel and I agreed to wait until the *Obersturmführer* had told Schlesinger about the visit and had granted him the necessary authorization.

Thursday August 12th: Autumnal atmosphere. A crisp blue sky with a nip in the air. Another meeting in Dr. Wachtel's room yesterday evening. Two new groups. The discussion was mainly about whether a better atmosphere could not be created by replacing a number of German hut leaders by Dutch leaders, which might tone down the animosity. Dutch representatives reported various examples of rudeness on the part of German hut leaders. On the German side it was argued that where two peoples come together friction is unavoidable, but that the position of the Jews in Westerbork was very good, compared with that at other camps. It had been the express wish of the Commandants that Germans should be put in control. Moreover, there were good and bad German hut leaders, just as there had been good and bad Dutch leaders; there were shouting and barking Germans, just as there were shouting and barking Dutchmen. The idea was put forward that, if towards the end of the war the Dutch Jews felt like venting their hatred upon the Germans, the Germans would join together to prevent this. It was thought that the end of the war would instead arouse such a strong desire within the Dutch Jews to return home that they would forget their resentment. The feeling was pretty general among the Dutch Jews that it was too late now to bring about a reconciliation. That should have been started a year ago. They did not see much point in committees for settling differences, mainly because they could not believe that the Commandant would give his consent to such committees. It was interesting to note that here too the Germans tried to justify themselves by referring to history.

Friday August 13th: Had a note yesterday evening: 'Please come and see me at nine o'clock tomorrow morning. Schlesinger. Departmental Head. Department II. Administration.' Punctually at nine o'clock this morning the bull's head and Hitler moustache of Schlesinger appeared round the door. 'Good morning, gentlemen, come in.' A round table conference of six to seven men, departmental heads, also Trottel and the present chronicler.

'Gentlemen, I have asked you to come here in order to hear your views on the following plan—namely, the setting up of what we might call an Organizing Staff. For the present not a word must be breathed about this outside, otherwise we shall be in trouble. This staff will make proposals to me aimed at benefiting the various work sections, and they will undertake to settle any differences, personal or otherwise, occurring in the work sections. These sections must pay their way and the staff must examine the work projects and see if they are an economic proposition. The camp will see to the raw materials and the profit resulting from the work will be for the benefit of the camp. As well as the tailoring, mattress and metal sections, there will also be a toy section. Everyone in the camp will now have to justify his existence by taking an active part in these sections. Provision will have to be made for the invalids and the children. It cannot be termed industry as such, but work for a wage.'

There was a detailed discussion from which it emerged that people agreed in principle to the idea, but felt they would see where they were going once it had been put into practice. Some members of the Organizing Staff would be "arbitration officials". The members would get a separate office and would have to go about their work very discreetly and delicately. The office would only start to function gradually in order not to create a stir. The objection that the war would only last a short time was not a valid one. The Commandant should be allowed to continue in the mistaken belief that the war would go on for a long time. The workers should be urged to submit ideas for setting up new work sections. The making of pot-cleaners from heather was worth considering. The best labour in the huts must be recruited for the different sections.

Schlesinger concluded the conference by saying that he would be reconvening the members soon and he expressed the desire that members would visit him separately whenever they felt it necessary. Schlesinger did not touch on the actual purpose of the Organizing Staff, i.e., the promotion of reconciliation between German and Dutch Jews; we were aware of it in the background. Schlesinger's phosphorescent eyes said more than his glib tongue.

Since the order from the German authorities that camp residents who had diarrhoea were not to stay away from work unless they had a temperature of over 38.5° there are a lot more listless people going about. The Jewish doctors try to help the sick as much as possible by putting them to bed, but they have to be prepared for the Germans checking up at any time and so in many cases they send patients to work although they are unfit. Patients who are ill and do not move into the hospital are officially considered to be "off duty". Sick school-children are also considered to be "off duty".

In the past few days schoolchildren of all ages have been sent out in the afternoons to dig potatoes at farms in the vicinity under supervision of the women teachers. Many of the children have come back ill from over-exertion. [. . .]

Saturday August 14th: You can be ruined here in a single day. The following calamities befell one family yesterday—the master of the house had his shoes pinched, the only pair he had; the lady of the house broke her thermos flask; the son of the house lost a blanket. Yes, these are calamities here. The man who is middle-aged and is in hospital can no longer take his afternoon walk; the woman cannot bring her husband tea any more, and he is on a diet; and the son is cold at night. Where can you get a pair of new shoes, a new blanket and a new thermos flask? [. . .]

Yesterday was the tenth day of potatoes in their jackets for lunch. Potatoes in their jackets are terribly good for you because of the vitamin just under the skin. But there are potatoes and potatoes underneath that skin. If you get thirty small potatoes in your mess-tin instead of seven or eight large ones, and if they are hard and glassy into the bargain, instead of deliciously mealy, the whole fun of having the vitamin goes. Especially if they are nearly cold. Every day I bravely proceeded to peel my miserable little potatoes and dipped them, cold as they were by the time I reached the last ones, in some imitation goulash with a sliver of butter from my own store, and I chewed and swallowed them down bravely.

But yesterday my potatoes were smaller and unsightlier than

ever and tasted of soap, bad quality soap. I went on eating them for as long as I could and then I was so sick of the soapy taste and so fed up with the peeling that I simply threw the rest of them into the refuse bin. There now, at last I was rid of them. But what about the taste of soap—how was I to get rid of that? A plum, I thought, a real greengage, would surely be good for that. But the taste of soap was still there, it adhered to my palate and stuck to my teeth. A pear, I thought, a fine, juicy pear which had just arrived in a parcel. No good—the taste of soap was still there. I have had enough of potatoes—once and for all. I don't want to peel them any more, or eat them or see them. When I went past the Central Kitchen this morning hundreds of women were sitting there peeling potatoes, just as they had been doing yesterday and the day before. What in Heaven's name are all the women peeling potatoes for if I have to eat them in their jackets and they turn my stomach? Incomprehensible, just like so many other things at Westerbork.

You queue up for everything here, just as you queue up in a Communist society. In a certain sense this is a Communist society—everyone equal, the same rations, the Central Kitchen, everyone in a queue. For bread, butter, soup, beans, a bath, hot water, the barber, everything. And in the Central Kitchen, as in all central kitchens, a lot sticks to the fingers of those who work there. In many an individual house the soup, butter and bread are twice the normal amount, and meat and other commodities not intended for the masses end up in places where, according to the principle of equality, they do not belong.

Here you even stand in a queue for the laundry, not to get it back, but to hand it in. This morning a queue of fifty people were standing outside the laundry collection centre. Everyone who hands in his laundry may not be content with a straight-forward list of the items he is putting in. No, he might note down more items than he has actually handed over. A woman counted out one hundred and forty-five items to the official on duty, so many sheets, so many towels, so many pairs of knickers, which all had to pass his scrutiny. A grand little game. This community is poor in worldly goods. So everyone is obliged to open up his bundle of laundry and count out the items and show what he has brought. A cumbersome process which encourages queueing. And makes life wearisome. [. . .]

127

Sunday August 15th: A tête-à-tête with Schlesinger in his office yesterday afternoon. 'Do you play chess, Herr Schlesinger?' 'No, I have no time.' 'A pity, it's just the game for you. Chess is a subtle game of balance, for strong nerves. It's a war game.' 'Yes, I know, with the knives on the table. But I have too much to do.' 'I play it nearly every day. But since I left hospital it has lost some of its charms. Also, I'm playing against too feeble opponents.' 'I thought so. You are a man of war and you need to have strong opponents.' 'Correct.' 'I rise above everything here and the squalor of it all.' 'So do I. One can feel free here deep inside.' [. . .]

'Is it thanks to you that the camp is as it is nowadays?' 'That is thanks to Deppner. He has set his stamp on it. Dischner wanted to bring in the SS and he sent a telegram to that effect to The Hague. But I sent off a counter-telegram to The Hague. Dischner threatened to shoot me for that. He stood with a revolver in front of me. I said, "Go on and shoot."' 'Not like Asscher and Cohen. They gained their reputation in peacetime, but they did not have the courage to go and stand in front of their people in time of trouble.' 'No, leaders must have the guts to say "no" when the time comes. That is what they are there for.'

'What do you think about the immediate future?' 'Oh, we should set up arbitration committees everywhere in the huts and at the top of them will be the committee that you and Trottel will direct together, in conjunction with your men and mine. Then you can turn your experience to good account. The committee will also take control when the Jews are brought back from Poland. This must not be left in the hands of people who have made serious errors and have compromised themselves.' [. . .]

Yesterday evening a transport came in with barely 400 people from Amsterdam. A large contingent of sick people from the NIZ. Poor old men with hardly any luggage. Evoking horror and pity. [. . .]

For some days now three Jewish women have been locked up in prison; they had denounced other Jewish women to the Gestapo in Amsterdam. People are forbidden to sing or talk when sorting the beans. Since this order was announced, men and women have been seeking employment in this section. They are longing to be free from the eternal chatter which can be heard everywhere and which makes people feel tired and ill.

128

Monday August 16th: Today is the great day named by the blonde woman with telepathic powers as marking the end of the war. No signs of this as yet. Since yesterday there have been so-called IPA reports (Jewish Press Agency—the nickname for rumours) going round the camp, according to which there are mighty things afoot on the Allied side and the Russians are gaining decisive victories.

The sorrow of the individual is drowned in that of the masses. It no longer contrasts with happiness and as a result makes scarcely any impact. The sorrow of all the separate individuals has united like innumerable drops to form a sea of sorrow which is too much for normal human feelings and in which you drown if you venture out upon it. It is so great and so universal that not only is it impossible to describe, but you cannot pick out the main features in it. Universal suffering has become a normal state and those so afflicted have become resigned to it. Anyone who cannot bear his own suffering and that of the masses becomes slowly or rapidly submerged. Cases of mental disturbance occur in men and women who in normal society were known to be sturdy, resilient folk; they have had a shock.

But these are exceptions. The great multitude live on as they did at home, in the midst of all their suffering. They eat and drink and make love. The food is frugal, the drink is ersatz and the love is unnatural. There is music. An orchestra caters to the best of its ability for the musical needs of the camp. In the huts and the individual houses violinists and flautists reach for their instruments now and then and make music alone or together. The OD have their own radio for gay music. Artists, usually dilettantes, exercise their talent. They sketch huts and record human types on paper. Men and women play bridge together or skat as if their lives depended on it. In the hut for men and women over fifty-five and without children you hear the rustle and click of playing cards in the afternoons and on Sundays as they go flying over the tables. The men also play their game of chess or draughts or dominoes or patience. Families play party games, monopoly and so on, and solve crossword puzzles from the newspaper. Men and women go visiting, just as at home, and have tea with one another.

All this really happens, but in a minor key. There is always sorrow in the background—they speak again and again about members of their families who have been deported to Poland, about sons or fathers who have perished in concentration camps, about the injustice and despotism they have encountered, about the uncertainty of the future, the discomforts of camp life, their weariness and exhaustion. Life goes on. The daily suffering is greater and more oppressive, it is permanent, but it is a feature incorporated into life, just as a healthy man or woman incorporates some serious physical disability into his or her life. It is annoying and wearisome, but it does not put an end to life.

Tuesday August 17th: Today I set my heart on having fried potatoes without a row. I do not believe that any other camp resident has ever succeeded in this. It is certainly not easy. I peeled my batch of potatoes nicely and went on the dot of twelve to the washroom where the stove stands, right opposite the WC's. Everything is together for the sake of convenience.

The stove was absolutely full—a large pan of French beans, two pans of barley and a dish of potatoes put to brown. And there was a circle of men standing round about with mess-tins of potatoes or hotchpotch or slices of bread and butter. The potatoes had to be fried and the hotchpotch heated up and the bread and butter toasted. The prospect seemed hopeless. [. . .] I just listened and gazed straight ahead of me at the potatoes cooking there. They were beginning to change colour and there was some hope that one of us would soon be getting his turn. One of the men who had something to do with the barley came along once to have a look. He lifted the lid, tested it, poured in some more cold water and disappeared again. People secretly cursed him under their breath. Couldn't he have boiled up the barley in the morning? [. . .] Couldn't the fellow with the beans have cooked them in the morning too? [. . .] They only wanted to fry their potatoes till they were just brown or warm up their hotchpotch. The damned so-and-so's! [. . .] I kept my lips tightly closed. The potatoes were brown at last. [. . .] A pan of mash went on. The other men stayed there holding their mess-tins and went on waiting, with ironical comments to show how they felt. Those who had bread and butter pushed or twisted the slices into the open spaces between the mess-tins and burned their fingers in the attempt. 'Who do the damned beans belong to?' 'Can't they be taken off for a while?' [. . .] I kept my mouth tightly shut and would not take any part in the squabble. [. . .]

130

I was in luck—it was my turn! There were the spuds in their modest little dish next to the huge pan of French beans! It had taken nearly an hour. 'Damn it, I'll have to go! Can't that pan be taken off? Whose is it?' [. . .] I kept my mouth tightly closed. I only wanted fried potatoes and nothing else, however long it took me. Aha, the butter was spluttering merrily. They were beginning to cook nicely with a brown patch here and there. 'Your potatoes are beginning to get nice and brown.' I glanced surreptitiously at the speaker who was holding a pan of hotchpotch and I said nothing. [. . .] My potatoes were crackling away nicely—they were looking grand. A little salt on them—I had forgotten about it. 'Surely your potatoes can come off now. They're brown enough.'

I was drawn out of my silence: 'You're wrong. They aren't brown enough.' 'I think they are. You only need to fry them a little.' 'I don't think they are. They're not fried right through.' I had made up my mind not to get involved in a row, and there I was in the thick of one. [. . .] 'You have time and I haven't.' 'I don't want a row just for the sake of it. My potatoes aren't brown enough. But you are in a hurry and you have to go to your work. So I'll just have to take it that my potatoes *are* brown.' I went off with my potatoes. I had spent exactly one hour and a half on this stupid business. But they tasted good. [. . .] This is what happens at the stove all day and every day. [. . .]

Wednesday August 18th: Right is right. The other day a baby of nine months was brought in as an S-detainee and was admitted to the hospital. When a few days ago the children in the hospital were taken outside to enjoy the sunshine and the fresh air the baby of nine months had to stay inside. Because he was an S-case and might escape. Right is right. Safety first!

Thursday August 19th: There has been a fair amount of stealing in my hut in the past few days. [. . .]

A few days ago my fine map of Russia, torn out of a Russian Baedeker, was stolen. I was kind enough to show a group of interested people where Poltava was situated. It is said to have been taken by the Russians. Afterwards I stowed the map carefully away again in a school satchel where I keep a few curios. When I went to get the map out again, it was no longer there. What can one say or do? I unobtrusively informed the Admi-

131

nistration that I had lost a Russian map and a member of the administrative staff shouted out in a gruff voice a few times to say that someone had lost a map and asked for it to be returned. All in vain. Who knows if the administrator who was one of the group of people to whom I had shown the map did not himself take possession of it? [. . .]

There are quite a number of honest people living amongst us—not a morning goes by without some sleepy or absent-minded man leaving his soap or his comb or his shaving tackle in the washroom. These articles nearly always find their way back to their owners. But again and again pieces of soap disappear as if by magic from under the very noses of the men while they are washing. It happened this morning to the most respectable and well-bred man in the whole hut. Soap is a scarce and valuable commodity. [. . .]

Friday August 20th: A stifling hot day. No wind. Outside the men are going about with sunburnt faces and stripped to the waist behind tip-up carts in which they are wheeling sand—strong, healthy men who used to work at all kinds of trades. Old gentlemen sit on chairs in front of their huts, puffing away and wiping the sweat from their faded brows. Mothers wheel their babies through the camp in deep prams to let them have some sunshine. They murmur soft words of endearment, but their hearts are heavy and they are thinking of the husband who is not there, of the older children who are not there, of the brother and sister who are not there and about whom nothing is known. The mothers laugh to their babies who just will not grow or thrive. People ask why the babies are not thriving—the food is good and they can get what they need. And yet they do not thrive. Is it the climate? There are so many children who do thrive in spite of the sand and the dust, in spite of the way that people are all packed together—like roses in bloom. Is it the mind that is making the babies sick—the grieving and distraught minds of the mothers? They suckle their children, not with the joy of the mother whose child is going on to a secure future, but with a feeling of anxiety and sorrow. That is why the babies are not thriving, that is why they are going downhill.

There is a mood of nervous tension in the camp—next Tuesday another transport will be leaving, with 300 S-men and women, 400 ailing elderly folk with their families and all people suffering from tuberculosis. 1,020 in all—a margin of twenty to allow for those who collapse on the way. Gruesome, revolting. It had been hoped that there would be no more transports going.

The heat of the sun lingers warmly over the camp. The sun itself has gone, it has disappeared behind the horizon. We gasp for air. Along the trench with yellow water on the perimeter of the camp men and women on the sand hills try to get some respite from the oppressive atmosphere hanging over the lanes between the huts. They are sitting in a row on the pile of sand opposite the barbed wire. In front of them is the helmeted guard with his musket in the square look-out tower—a cuckoo clock with a man in it who appears at every whole, half and quarter hour. He leans stiffly and wearily over the balustrade, first to the left and then to the right, again and again and again. In the distance is an immense expanse of moorland like purple velvet which gladdens the eye and captivates the senses. A sky full of flames and streaks which grow fiercer with the coming of the darkness. The men and women feel they are on their summer holiday. They forget the trench with its yellow water and the rusty barbed wire—they forget the little man in the cuckoo clock, the huts and the barren field that stretch out behind them—they stare into the limitless distance where in the quivering twilight the purple heather merges with the flaming sky. A wearily hot day that has now come to its poetic close. People tear themselves away from the fascinating tableau of nature and make ready for the night and for reality. Behind them lurks the threat of deportation which weighs upon them and makes sleep a hell. [. . .]

A visit to "the store". In the store are stacks of crockery which the henchmen of the Gestapo have collected from the houses of Jews in the vicinity. Originally the store was managed by an Aryan who guarded everything like Cerberus. The old camp took things out of it as it wished. Suddenly this came to an end. A few days ago the store opened again and women queue up early in the morning to "do their shopping". Everyone may take a few items which he fancies—some plates, a vase, a pillow, etc. [. . .]

Countless Jews, including the cultured and educated ones, do not seem embarrassed when it comes to grabbing items which once belonged to other Jews, stolen goods which sometimes have blood sticking to them. [. . .]

133

Sunday August 21st: Six cases of diphtheria were diagnosed yesterday. [. . .]

This afternoon visited the S-hut where there are 550 men and women. All wear a band with a large red S on their arms. It is a hut like all the others, but there is far more litter about. As if in some oriental city men and women swarm along the narrow passages running up and down and across between the piled up beds. On the beams and hanging from the ceiling on nails is an endless variety of coloured draperies from their wardrobes, like stage properties in a garret. Along the barbed wire outside and in between the barbed wire is the gigantic multicoloured awning and bunting formed by the washing they have hung out to dry. Gipsies in the midst of their rags. Everyone knows that their fate is sealed—Poland. The younger folk are lighthearted, the older ones despondent.

Along the barbed wire stand men and women in their hundreds waiting to be admitted to the hut. They pass the green man of the OD in groups of fifty. Today is the last visiting day before Tuesday when the transport goes. Everyone is absorbed with the same idea—today I shall perhaps be seeing my friend for the last time; tomorrow night I may have to pack and go off with my husband or wife or fiancé into exile. Everyone in the hut knows that there is no escaping that exile. When they meet and when they part they read that same thought in one another's eyes: fate has decided it. [. . .]

In the hut I met a *fin de siècle* lady who is a painter. 'Do you think I'll be able to get out of it? My parents were British.' 'Have you any papers? Have you let the Applications Office know?' 'Yes, I have papers belonging to my father and mother. But I don't have my divorce papers yet.' 'You must see to it that you get them. You can perhaps be held here till your papers come.' 'They've promised to keep me here for the time being. Do you think I can rely on that?' 'I think so. If they've promised, then they'll do it.' 'Just to make sure, I'll write them another note and remind them.' 'You could do that. I think your chances aren't too bad. Now I'll have to go. I can only be here a quarter of an hour and I have to see someone else too.' 'That's a pity. I had one or two more things to ask.' 'You could do that out at the barbed wire afterwards.' 'I shan't be able to. I'm waiting for the sculptor So-and-so. He's going to do a picture of me.' 'First things first. Good-bye!' Vanity in the S-hut in spite of the impending transport.

134

There are swarms of flies. They come flying in their thousands through the hut. In their tens of thousands they settle in the evening on the ceilings of the huts, like locusts which have settled on a field of corn. When they are disturbed, they rise in clouds. At night you sleep with a handkerchief over your face. They sit in their hundreds on the beds and on the towels. There are more flies than people about.

An exhibition of toys made by schoolchildren and intended for industrial purposes—for Germany, so it is said. Very likely. A short time ago the photographic studio here which is directed by Jews processed photographs of Hitler intended for Germany. In Germany there have been no adequate facilities for this since the closing down of so many concerns not essential for the war effort. Wood carvings: horses, elephants, donkeys. Good work. The children sang today. This morning the *Obersturm-führer* graced the opening with his presence, surrounded by his retinue and by the Jewish departmental heads. First of all, the children sang a German song which the *Ostu* and his retinue warmly applauded, after that Hebrew songs which they were certainly willing to listen to, but did not applaud. They haven't got as far as that yet. In the afternoon the children sang Hebrew songs for the camp residents with the "Hatikvah" to finish off with. Zionist vitality in the service of the Germans, plus a touch of vanity. The *Ostu* is proud of "his" Jewish children who are so smart and industrious.

The *Obersturmführer* had a surprise in store yesterday afternoon for the Jews who had been sent to dig potatoes; a few hundred of them were allowed to go outside the camp, to Hooghalen, Beilen and Rolde, and pick blackberries, free from police supervision.

Yesterday afternoon there was a football match on the parade ground. At the same time running for the boxing team and training in a field on the perimeter.

The train for the transport has come in—twenty-seven wagons. The wagons look older and more weather-beaten than they did last time—from the sorrow and suffering they have witnessed. A group of schoolchildren who were going to the moor and are in the habit of singing every day as they walk along went past the train in silence at the instigation of one of the children who cried out: 'Boys, there's the plague train again. Don't sing, do you hear!'

Tuesday August 24th: Once again a great and gripping film. Yesterday evening, after the visiting hour, the men and women gathered together in the corners of the huts as if after some great disaster—a double murder and a suicide, or a burglary in broad daylight. But this was not after the disaster, it was before—a transport made up almost entirely of ailing elderly folk and S-detainees. [. . .]

There was a thrilling prelude to the film. Three of those condemned to deportation tried to avoid it by attempting to escape yesterday evening—three S-men, two from the S-hut and one from the hospital. [. . .] Like bloodhounds OD men in green uniforms and with police sticks—rather like table legs— were sent out after the fugitives. [. . .] One of them was discovered about half past eleven in the so-called quarantine tent. At once the warning signal, "OD, OD," went through the camp, and OD men came running up from all sides. They all proceeded to corner the S-man who tried to make off. He was seized and locked up in the prison. A second fugitive was apprehended in Beilen. The third is still at large.

The transport struck a special emotional chord in the camp. In addition to the S-cases intended for deportation, the *Obersturmführer* put down fifty more Jews who had to go along too as a punishment for the attempted escape, some of them from the S-hut and some from the hospital. The horror of the transport was, as a result, overshadowed by a feeling of indignation against those responsible for the punishment of the fifty S-men. Curiously enough, the indignation was not directed against the Commandant who had arbitrarily put down the names of fifty men for the S-transport for something they had had nothing to do with. Or against the OD men, Jews who had gone out after other Jews like wild dogs and had not allowed them to escape. The mental degeneration of many people here has advanced to such a degree that their indignation did not fall upon the executioner and his henchmen, but upon those who had attempted to escape from their clutches. These attempts have sometimes been childishly clumsy. But a prisoner has still a right to escape, even though the executioner threatens reprisals against those who do not. They know that they will be deported one day, but they cannot or will not offer any resistance; they merely go a little sooner. [. . .]

The public were already seething with indignation when the film itself came on the screen. The familiar procedure with a few variations. Outside the train, on the platform, or hanging out of the wagons of a third-class compartment were the Green Police in their olive green uniforms. A cigarette dangled from the red, unformed faces of country yokels with pigs' eyes— completely indifferent and insensitive to their surroundings. An occasional flicker of interest in a good-looking Jewish girl passing by or in a Jew with head held high or a strong or erect posture. [. . .] Under their scrutiny the OD men in moss green uniform carried out their duties—men with completely different faces, tanned, with black curly hair, often classical features and brutal, burning eyes. Two worlds that are diametrically opposed. They do not understand each other and gropingly size each other up. The OD men act as assistants to the Green Police. In an unbroken stream they went along carrying stretchers with broken, half-dead human beings whom they hoisted efficiently into the cattle trucks. In the hospital these people were just shoved into a few garments that had been hurriedly got together, while a strapping young S-man—amid the tears of patients and nurses—blessed his wife and two young children who were staying behind and was himself blessed by a rabbi, alongside aged Jews who were saying their own *sheimetz*, or dying prayer. Children at the windows of the little houses along the Boulevard des Misères repeated again and again: 'That's another sick man.' Other OD men chased the public away from the Boulevard with threats or entreaties. In amongst the stretchers there were little groups of S-men and women. They numbered 300 and were spread out over the train, with the stigma of the red S arm-band removed from their arms.

Everything was done under the direction of Pisk, the head of the OD, who looked like a sort of southern pirate, with a chunky face, thick jet-black eyebrows over coal-black flashing eyes and a jet-black toothbrush moustache under his nose. A face sketched in charcoal. Dr. Spanier appeared in his characteristic long waterproof, with his hands behind his back. He paused here and there and exchanged a brief word with someone, outwardly unmoved. The wagons were filling up. People "fit for transport" were standing or sitting in the entrance to the cattle trucks to watch the arrival of the others. Hardly any tears were shed. Just one woman who was not accompanying her husband on the transport and was seeing him off was dabbing her eyes with her handkerchief. Men were wheeling barrows with luggage and boxes of provisions. The members of the Green Police went on smoking their cigarettes, quite unmoved.

The *Obersturmführer* appeared in uniform. The commander of the men in green, a fat, greasy, well-nourished fellow, came up and saluted. He handed him the consignment note for the transport, then did a smart about turn. [. . .]

When the train was full and all that remained was to close the doors and give the signal for departure, Schlesinger came up in a black jerkin, with a few hairs standing straight up on his cropped head—a heroic figure, a lion-tamer. A fêted lion-tamer. A few handshakes here and there, a few words with this person and that. Not a studied performance. He went up quite naturally to the *Obersturmführer* who received him with a stern face. Still in a bad temper about the escapes. The tall, gaunt *Ostu* gave an impression of asceticism compared with the heavily built and well-fed leader of the Jews.

The wagons were shut tightly. The members of the Green Police took possession of the remaining paper mattresses of the patients and spread them out on the hard seats of their third-class compartments. The wearisome journey would take a long time. The train got under way. At the oblong ventilators high up in the wagons the heads of Jews and Jewesses appeared all in a line, as if at a puppet show. They went past like the pages of a book of living pictures. Bare, swaying arms and waving hands stuck out of the ventilators like independent living organs, like the limbs of buried human beings giving their last sign of life. Depressing. The silent film was at an end. [. . .]

A stencilled notice has been put up in the hut doorways. It is worded as follows:

Sport at Westerbork Camp

Light Athletics Contest

It is planned to hold contests for the following events on Sunday September 5th 1943:

100 metres race	4 × 100 metres relay race
200 ,, ,,	high jump
800 ,, ,,	long jump
1500 ,, ,,	putting the shot
	tug-of-war

Entries accepted up to Thursday August 26th 1943, every evening from 8 to 9 p.m. at the Secretary's Office, Potato Kitchen. [. . .]

Wednesday August 25th: Yesterday's transport had an ironic note. A few NSB men were sent along too. As baptized Jews they had been accommodated in hut 73. Rauter had sent them to Westerbork to operate as spies. But the *Obersturmführer* had sent his camp detective, Simon, out after them. The detective reported that the NSB men were operating against the Commandant who, in their opinion, was too kind to the Jews. As a result of this report the Commandant had them locked up in the prison and sent away on the S-transport. But first the guards beat up one or two of them.

A meeting on the road. A woman of about sixty-five—with a tired, worn-out face. 'May I stop you for a moment? You know that my husband and I are still in danger of being deported. Could you possibly do something for us so as to keep us here? If I were alone, it would not matter to me if I were sent away. But not with my husband. It's unthinkable. He's an academic man and he's completely unfitted for this life. They steal literally everything from him. His shoes have just been stolen again. And he doesn't wash because he can't. I've never thought of suicide in my whole life, but I've been thinking of it recently. He's a burden to me. We're exempted because we're on the Parents List, but I'm afraid it will smash, just as so many other lists have done. We had great hopes of our Palestine papers, but it was found they weren't valid. You know that I'm Russian. When I married I said I was a Jewess and that is what appears on my marriage lines, but it's not at all certain that I am Jewish. I'm not enrolled with the Jewish Community. It's very likely that I have several non-Jews in my family. It has been investigated and I've had a document drawn up which shows this. Do you advise me to do anything about it? You see, I can't square it with my conscience if I bring it up now. And of course my marriage lines say that I am Jewish. And I've opted for Palestine. I have a very gifted son who has a recommendation from one of the greatest men in the country. Could we be exempted on that account? I could never go on the journey with my husband. Could you put things right for us? Couldn't you point out to the powers that be that my husband is a great linguist and has done a great deal for the study of languages? Talk the matter over with my daughter, if you wish.' [. . .]

The daughter has a clear, perceptive mind. 'My mother is a very sweet woman and highly intelligent, but she fusses so.

She has always been like that. She gets on my father's nerves. He's a scholarly, introspective man who needs to be quiet. He is, in fact, far too proud to go about cadging favours from every Tom, Dick and Harry just so that he can stay here. He says, "If I am fated to be thrown on the dunghill in Poland, then in God's name, so be it!" My father was a great authority on his subject and also a man who could keep strict discipline. Here he is simply going on living in the same old way without bothering at all about his surroundings. That gets on my mother's nerves. I wish I could go to Poland instead of them, if they do have to go.' [. . .]

Friday August 27th: Received a letter yesterday from my youngest daughter, dated August 6th. [. . .]

Yesterday an arbitration committee was established in principle, consisting of Dr. Wachtel, Herr Hanf and the writer of this diary. The committee has been approved by the *Obersturmführer*. Schlesinger told us this in his office. Difficulties have arisen as far as the Dutch Jews are concerned—a second Dutch Jew has still to be appointed to the committee. Dr. Wolf has been put forward for this. He has reserved his decision—he does not want to have anything to do with Schlesinger; he has not given details as to why not. The Dutch, moreover, want a special committee on which both sides are equally represented to draw up measures for keeping the peace in the camp. They also want an equal ratio in the administrative staff for huts and work sections as a means of bringing reconciliation.

Saturday August 28th: An argument this morning on the ground in front of the S-hut between two sections of barbed wire. It involved four women and an OD man who was standing at his post, fiddling about with his stick. Woman of the people: 'I'd rather have the men in green any day. You know where you stand with them, at least.' 'They hit much harder than we do.' 'I'd rather have the men in green than you because you beat your own people.' 'We carry sticks, but we don't need to use them.' 'You do that all right. And even if you didn't hit anybody at all, I'd still rather have the men in green. We hate you more than we hate them. So now you know!' Applause from the other women.

Those who have been partners in mixed marriages and have

half-Aryan children have to report to the Applications Office tomorrow "in their own interest". People from mixed marriages who have put in an application because of that or have been deferred do not need to report. There is a rumour that they will be sent to Theresienstadt. I have been advised to wait and see which way the wind blows and not get in touch for the moment until their intentions have become quite clear. They do what they like with the people from mixed marriages, depending on the mood they are in. [. . .]

Sport has attacked the young people in the camp like an infectious disease. In the evening after supper there is boxing, ju-jitsu and gymnastics. Early in the morning young men do their training in light athletics and also run on the parade ground and are exempted from their duties because of this. [. . .]

Heard from the Dutch camp detective V.R. that heer D., one of the baptized Jews who were sent away on the most recent transport to Poland, had denounced altogether twenty-four Jews to the Gestapo. The detective force was on the trail of a fresh case of spying in the hut for the baptized, but did not yet have sufficient evidence available to bring in a charge.

Sunday August 29th: Visit to hut 73 where the baptized Jews live. Listened to a sermon by the parson Tabaksblatt who was originally a Russian, but became a naturalized Dutch citizen. The parson, in a blue jacket and a snowy white collar, used as his pulpit an empty bedstead three tiers up. There was luggage all round him—under him cases and boxes, along the walls rucksacks, garments, shoes. The congregation of men and women were spread out on benches in the narrow passages between the beds throughout the hut. The singing was accompanied by music on a harmonium. The parson flung the torch of battle into the Jewish camp. As the text for his sermon he took the words of St. John to the Laodiceans—choose to be cold or hot, not lukewarm, not colourless, not insipid. He exhorted his congregation not to hesitate between two ideas, but to go straight on, for example, if you were treated with contempt in the Potato Kitchen because you lived in hut 73. 'Stand firm, whenever people say scornfully of you: "A bad Jew has gone and a bad Christian has come in his place." ' As believing Christians all these baptized Jews received with eyes closed and head bowed the blessing of the Lord from the lips of the parson. He preached with the unctuousness almost of a

141

born parson.

I rubbed my eyes. Here in a camp for prospective Jewish slaves this great group of baptized Jews were united in prayer and the pastor had thrown out a challenge to the Jews who had retained their old belief and looked upon the baptized Jews as traitors, as an open sore in their midst. No other relationship between religious groups can be as grim as that between orthodox and baptized Jews. It is tragic to see such dissension in a period of ordeal. This dissension is indeed accentuated because the baptized are driven together into a group. But at the same time it is understandable in a world where an ancient belief clashes with a living belief that could not fail to appeal to the consciences and hearts of the Jews.

Spent an hour waiting in Schlesinger's outer office. Always a different entourage. Inside were Dr. Ottenstein and Pisk, the head of the OD. Two Jews who had to go on an official trip were waiting, self-satisfied, with the feeling that they were indispensable and irreplaceable. Magnificent ties on blue shirts. A fair-haired young woman with plucked eyebrows, her straw-yellow hair piled high and her club-shaped legs crossed coquettishly, was opening her bag every minute or so to get her mirror, and kept titivating her eyelashes and patting her hair all the time. Was she attempting a conquest of Schlesinger or was she trying to hold him? She seemed self-assured. The two camp detectives Van Rijn and Simon came in. Van Rijn, the Dutchman, was unassuming and Simon, the German, bustling, jovial and amusing. They had come to discuss a fresh case of Jewish NSB spying in hut 73. Work section leaders popped inside.

Frau Schlesinger, dressed in black, swept in like an actress about to step on the stage, or a fishing-boat sailing before the wind. She took a quick pull at a cigarette, haughtily exhaled the smoke, without greeting or seeing anyone, sped like an arrow from the bow to Schlesinger's door, opened the door without knocking and disappeared like a phantom.

Weinreb, the man connected with the Weinreb List, came walking in with heavy glasses, absent-minded. Nine or ten days ago he came back from Scheveningen where he had been in prison for weeks. He had to defend himself against the charge of underhand practices when he was putting the 700 people on his list. He succeeded in convincing the German authorities of his integrity and he was sent back to Westerbork minus his S.

142

But he must return to Scheveningen again today for a fresh hearing or a resumption of the previous one. Weinreb, a scholarly man, went and stood modestly in a corner.

Everyone was waiting and they all went up to Tom, the young porter, the handsomest boy in the camp and the darling of all the girls, to ask if Schlesinger would be receiving visitors and, if so, when. Tom diplomatically pretended ignorance—he did not know if or when Schlesinger could see anyone. [. . .]

A tall, slender and very dark bird came fluttering in—fashionably attired, a smart little hat, high heels, very much made up, bright red cheeks, a pair of currant eyes, ingenuous, as innocent as a dove, under high arched brows, a delicate nose which hardly projected beyond her cheeks at all. She is considered the most beautiful girl at Westerbork. Everyone looks after her and points after her. She is the protégée of the people at the top because she is so beautiful. 'Is Schlesinger in his office?' 'Yes, but he has visitors.' Tom recognized her as a regular customer. He knew that she had come to plead for her favourites. 'Give him this note then.' From her bag she produced a prepared note on which she had scribbled something in pencil in a steep backhand. 'Give him this and see what he says.' Tom disappeared and came back a moment later with the message: 'You can come in.' The most beautiful girl at Westerbork walked in self-confidently. A few minutes later she emerged and bustled out as if she had urgent business to attend to. The woman with the straw-yellow hair gazed after her with every appearance of extreme interest. We all looked after her with extreme interest. [. . .]

Pisk disappeared. Dr. Ottenstein disappeared. Schlesinger appeared in the open doorway like a juggler on the point of performing some amazing feat. The waiting people pressed forward. Schlesinger: 'Easy now, ladies and gentlemen, take it easy!' [. . .]

After an hour it was my turn to say something that perhaps took a little over half a minute. Schlesinger was charming as always, charming but to the point, a man who knows exactly what he wants and knows human nature. He must be very attractive to women. When I left the waiting room there were definitely about ten people still standing or sitting there, waiting to be admitted to the great man's presence.

Monday August 30th: Was stopped yesterday evening by members of the OD on the road. On the stroke of ten o'clock when the whistle went for the evening roll-call. That was not good enough. One ought to be inside by ten o'clock. [. . .] I had to show my Camp Card and was marked down in a notebook. The OD man whispered in my ear: 'I have to note you down because Pisk has just gone past and he has seen it all.' 'Well, write it down and then tear the page right out. And I'll see to it in future.'

This afternoon at two o'clock sharp—"punctually" it said in the summons—I had to appear in person before Pisk, the pirate, in the OD barracks. Horrible to have to appear before the supreme head of the Jewish section of the German Gestapo. But much easier than I had expected. I was not the only transgressor. Pisk, enthroned behind a desk in a large room, asked almost good-naturedly: 'Why were you not in on time?' I replied: 'Because I didn't hear the first warning whistle. I was sitting chatting in a friend's house.' Pisk tossed my Camp Card to his assistant who was beside him and motioned to me to go to him. [. . .]

When he had examined five or six law-breakers, he addressed us briefly in German: 'The Commandant wishes the regulations to be strictly observed. This time I shall merely give you a warning. Any person guilty of any further offence will have to deal with the *Obersturmführer* in person.' Turning to his adjutant: 'The next group.' I could go. Yet another scene reminiscent of a puppet show.

Persons who have been partners in mixed marriages and have children have been registered provisionally.

Tuesday August 31st: Birthday of Queen Wilhelmina. This morning another transport left for the east with over a thousand people. Every transport is like a shipwreck. Those who are put on the transport disappear into the depths and their belongings are left floating on the surface. People sent on a transport take only the barest essentials with them—a total of fifteen kilograms. The rest is left behind in the hut, on the beds, strewn on the floor, like traces of a living being who has been swallowed up. [. . .] You slowly see your last friends disappearing. [. . .]

There is something loathsome going on in the background when every transport leaves. This time, while the transport was being got ready and was moving off, people were dancing.

Actually dancing. Rehearsals have been going on for some time for a revue. As if Westerbork itself was not rather like a theatrical show. By order of the *Obersturmführer* two thousand guilders have been made available from the camp funds for costumes. The costume-makers had to work all through the night before the transport and on the morning of the transport the dancers had to rehearse for the ballet at an early hour to make sure the première of the revue was not a flop. The fun starts next Saturday evening. When the Commandant undertakes anything, he does it thoroughly and energetically and nothing and nobody can stand in his way. [. . .]

An illustration of the religious conflict in the camp. On the partition of one of the latrines the following has been written in pencil in large letters: 'Hut 73 will be set on fire after the war with all its contents. *Omyn* (Amen).' The baptized Jews live in 73.

The playground is ready: four seesaws, two horizontal bars and a sandpit. I now feel as if I am living in a rather primitive little hotel somewhere out in the wilds where they have made an effort to lay something on for the children too. Guards look out from their tower all day long at the sandpit and the children playing. Later on one of them is bound to write a book called: "The Jewish Children in the Sandpit and Me." [. . .]

Saturday September 4th: The fate of Westerbork Camp is sealed. Yesterday it was decided to close down the camp and send the Jews to the east, to Auschwitz, Theresienstadt and central Germany. The decision came from Rauter. The *Obersturmführer* fought to the last to keep the camp going as a labour camp, primarily in his own interest, it is assumed, to avoid going to the eastern front. It is said that the new decision made a great impression on him. A greater impression than the weekly transports of Jews. He sat for half an hour with his head in his hands when the decision was made known. He said to a leading Jew: 'I care more about many of the Jews than about most of my own SS men.'

The camp is full of this latest decision. Some say: 'Haven't I always told you so?' and wail: 'There is just no limit to our misfortunes.' The others say: 'Why should they keep this small group of Jews while the rest have been sent away?' and: 'We'll manage to get through this too.' The camp is like a

145

beehive; everyone is scurrying about to see everyone else and discuss the whole business. Resentment against the British and Americans is rising to the surface. They have indeed landed in Calabria, but not in Holland, so they are a long way from reaching Westerbork. Reproaches are heaped on those who predicted that the war would certainly be over before the last Jews were taken to Poland. This is still possible! The guards say: 'We don't see it happening yet.' The Jews encourage one another to use up their supplies and eat up their vitamins so that they will arrive in Poland or Germany or wherever it is feeling as fit as possible. [. . .]

Stamps no longer have any value, whether they are red, blue or green. Lists no longer have any value either. All Jews go the same way—they are removed from Dutch territory without any exceptions and without respect of persons and are deported to the east.

And in the meantime the show must go on. While the news was hurtling down into the camp like a bomb, like a direct hit, the departmental heads and the other people who had been invited were making their way to the dress rehearsal of the revue. [. . .] This evening is to be the première. I am going to see it. As a chronicler of the camp I must see, not what happens, but how it happens.

In the meantime the Commandant has ordered that no more operations may be performed without his prior consent. It appears that operations have taken place that could not be justified medically and were only performed to keep those concerned from being deported to Poland. That has also occurred in Amsterdam and elsewhere. We know of a tragic case in which a mother had an appendix operation performed on her only child and lost it as a result. [. . .]

I feel like a man who is on the eve of going on a long journey and is sauntering aimlessly through his house, severing his contact with it and full of what is about to happen. Will I escape and go into hiding or will I go on the long journey, along with the crowd? I must think about this.

Sunday September 5th: [. . .] The revue was a mixture of antiquated sketches and mild ridicule of the conditions and circumstances prevailing at the camp. Not a single sharp word, not a single harsh word, but a little gentle irony in the passing, avoiding the main issues. A compromise. [. . .]

A faultless performance put over very professionally. With the Jewish star on their chests, a splendid decoration—all members of one and the same company. A revue that has come off and with which the company might tour Holland with some guarantee of success. The (German) audience were in raptures and often joined in the tunes. The Commandant was enjoying himself like a schoolboy—blessed are the poor in spirit. One of the catch-phrases lingered in my mind when I went back to the hut: "If you sit up to your neck in dirt, what have you got to chirp about?" All of us here are sitting up to our necks in dirt and yet we go on chirping. A psychological mystery. Light music beside an open grave. It should have been classical music, with the stirring funeral march of Chopin to end up with. Or a dance of death like the "Pavane" of Ravel. We sound the retreat, cracking jokes as we do so. Ehrlich was delighted with his achievement. 'To think we have been able to put this on under such adverse conditions!' He positively glowed.

The brunette who paid a visit to Schlesinger on Sunday of last week in between two OD men is going about freely and openly without her S. Her visit was evidently a success.

Monday September 6th: The remaining camp residents have become reconciled to the idea that they will eventually have to travel to Poland or Germany before they are released. People are, in general, convinced that the end of the war is at hand and so they are not going about in fear of their lives any more. Also, those for whom the privileged position of the Long-Term Residents was a thorn in the flesh have become reconciled to their fate because they no longer feel that people are being measured with two different yardsticks. But for the Long-Term Residents the decision came as a bitter blow. They were still relying on being able to last out the war in this fairly comfortable camp and not be pushed yet again out of a kind of social relationship to which they had grown accustomed. The Dutch Jews have now lost a basis for their feelings of annoyance against the German Jews who are once again being flung, together with them, into the melting-pot. Annoyance of this kind finally becomes groundless when they take into account the fact that a group of Jews have been able to maintain themselves in a favoured position at Barneveld and also that the number of German Jews at Westerbork represents

147

only an insignificant fraction of the total number who once lived in Germany, most of whom, just like the Dutch Jews, have been sent to Poland, if they did not perish in concentration camps or die in some other way. There has been some talk of the Barnevelders being sent on to Germany too and coming here in transit. So the rest of the German and Dutch Jews will finally suffer the same fate and will be thrown on the great scrapheap after all, either at Auschwitz or Theresienstadt or in central Germany.

Tuesday September 7th: The eleventh month of my stay here has begun today. How long will it go on? I am bored to death on board this ship which has been listing for so long without sinking and without any help coming.

There was another transport this morning. The men and women who feared they would be deported packed yesterday evening with a resignation which could have been mistaken for courage, but was simply the resignation of human beings not familiar with the passion of indignation and opposition. It is the resignation of caged beasts who have lost their natural impulses and have got used to the cage. No word of protest, just calm preparation for the journey. [. . .]

People were excited about the Calmeyer List which had smashed and the T. List which had smashed and the red stamps which had smashed. [. . .] But the Calmeyer List had not smashed. Fräulein Slottke had merely rejected "applications" from Jews who wished to be considered for the list and had put down the applicants for deportation. Such is the power of Fräulein Slottke! [. . .]

Red stamps have smashed by the dozen. You could tell this even yesterday from the fact that people employed on "outside work", i.e., digging or work with farmers, suddenly had to stay inside the camp. It was no surprise this morning. It was also known that relatives, fathers and mothers, sisters and brothers, of Long-Term Residents were no longer "exempt" and would be deported. One surprise was that the Shoemakers List had smashed, i.e., a number of shoemakers had to go on the transport too, unexpectedly. Another surprise was that a transport which had been expected to arrive from Amsterdam and go straight on consisted, not of 280, but of 140 Jews, so a number had to be hurriedly taken out of the reserve here. That is presumably why the Shoemakers List smashed. Jews appearing on the Puttkammer List were put on the transport too. Not for the first time. Puttkammer is a shady business, if not a downright swindle. Puttkammer's price has risen continually and anyone who could not make up the deficiency in time lost his money (his diamonds and his gold) and was coolly deported. [. . .]

Each transport has its special tragic cases. The latest transport saw the disappearance of a young and gifted pianist called Mischa Hillesum who was under the august protection of Willem Mengelberg himself. The latter had written a letter to Rauter in which he drew attention to the fact that Hillesum was a brilliant student of Willem Andriessen and that it was important for the artistic life of Holland to keep the gifted young man here. Rauter offered the musician a place at Barneveld, but he said he preferred to follow his parents to Westerbork so that he could protect them to the best of his ability. He himself and his friends in Amsterdam did their utmost to ensure that they would remain together at Westerbork. The parents were, moreover, exempt because of their daughter who had gone voluntarily to Westerbork in the service of the Jewish Council and was given the rights of a Long-Term Resident.

On Monday the order came unexpectedly from The Hague that Mischa Hillesum was to be deported with his family. The Commandant took this to mean that the whole family had to go. There was nothing that could be done about it. The reasons behind this intervention by The Hague are not definitely known, but presumably the musician had, as people say here, "worked his case to death", like many people before him who have tried to consolidate their position by contacting The Hague. The people in The Hague do not know exactly what is happening at Westerbork, but are glad to intervene in certain cases that come to their notice or in which they become directly involved. It is quite likely that the authorities in The Hague felt sore because Mischa Hillesum turned down the privilege of going to Barneveld.

A great number of orphan children have been deported without anyone accompanying them.

Wednesday September 8th: Some of the sixty members of the Jewish Council who had come here "voluntarily" on July 15th of last year, were sent home a few months ago with a special

149

identity card to save them from being arrested by the Gestapo and were nevertheless arrested and brought back to Westerbork, were sent back to Amsterdam once again on Monday morning. The honour of the *Obersturmführer* was at stake. Out of gratitude for their voluntary service he did not want to send them on to Poland; he wanted to reward them by restoring them to their original status. The Gestapo in Amsterdam did not care one whit for the *Obersturmführer*. How long will the Jews who have been sent back to Amsterdam manage to last out this time? [. . .]

This morning a number of Jews who had bought the so-called 120,000 stamp for exorbitant sums (in diamonds) were sent back to Amsterdam. Almost at the same moment The Hague decreed that it was time Holland was clear of Jews. For diamonds the National Socialists are willing to compromise—even with Jews.

This morning all the members of the OD underwent a strict medical examination. The Commandant has given instructions that no (more) OD men are to go on the transports. They are to be equipped with truncheons. The view is held in OD circles that the OD will in future serve as guards for the prison camp into which they think Westerbork is going to be transformed.

The report of the unconditional surrender of Italy has been greeted with enthusiasm. The Jews congratulated and embraced one another indoors and on the public road and held fancy dress parties in some of the huts. [. . .]

The Commandant has called together the Aryan staff of the camp and ordered them not to associate with the Jews in the camp. In the past few months relations have been very friendly, as indeed they always have been. He portrayed Badoglio as a friend of the Jews and ascribed the defeat of the Italians to his treachery. His master's voice.

Thursday September 9th : The children's playground is complete— two horizontal bars and three high swings have been added. Young people are going up and down on the seesaws and swings till late in the evening. Some children were still playing there at half past nine tonight, in the bright moonlight.

The half-moon this evening was like a death mask, chalky white, standing out against the flaky black crape of the heavens. An Oscar Wilde atmosphere, reminiscent of "Salome". The sun had set like a blood-red balloon and sunk down into the endless moor, as if into a sea arched over by an endless deep blue sky. Dazzling and awe-inspiring. Later in the evening the western sky was covered with fiery red streaks, like flames from an unseen fire, as if the blood-red balloon had burst and its contents had been scattered. [. . .]

Young women and girls wheel barrows with stones through the camp. Supple, sun-tanned folk in blue overalls, bare-headed and with red scarves. Twenty, twenty-five—two by two. At a snail's pace. Ten or twelve stones in the barrow. After every hundred steps or so they set down the barrow and go and sit in it listlessly, or stretch themselves out in it lazily, as if in an armchair. They remain like that for ten minutes or a quarter of an hour or half an hour. And so they get through the long, dreary day. The work is pointless, useless, unexciting, stupid. The women and girls are lively and think that sitting in a wheelbarrow and looking around or dreaming is more agreeable than wheeling it, and certainly less tiring.

In the camp wheelbarrows are a substitute for seats. You find empty wheelbarrows everywhere, in front of the large huts and the small huts, in the clumps of trees, on the flat expanse of field, and men and women simply sit down in them to enjoy in comfort the fresh air or the lovely view. In place of seats of which there are none (except in the huts). Apart from a discoloured iron garden seat which has come to rest by mistake in the middle of a clump of trees and on which court-ing couples are wont to converse by day and in the evening.

The latest order is that 1,000 Jews will remain provisionally in the camp. [. . .] The Commandant has taken a random shot. He has instructed each of the departmental heads to nominate a certain number of "workers" for a prolonged stay in the camp. Long-Term Residents who had counted on getting privileged treatment have been left out of things. Dutch Jews have been given preference. Until now the Dutch Jews had been left out in the cold. It is said that the Commandant was disgusted at the haggling that was going on to get a place on the 1,000 List, so he intervened personally. [. . .]

There was great disappointment and indignation among the Long-Term Residents. The result is that many of them now live in terror of being sent to Auschwitz. [. . .] Again and again new lists turn up which were privileged at one time and are now being scrapped. Men and women stop one another on the

151

camp roads and ask: 'Where are you going, Theresienstadt or central Germany or Auschwitz?' The place is buzzing with questions. Everywhere you hear: 'Theresienstadt, Theresienstadt, Theresienstadt, Auschwitz, Auschwitz, Auschwitz.'

The whole mental life of the people here still centres round deportation and now those who have so far been able to disregard it as far as their own lives were concerned, baptized Jews, applicants for Palestine, Long-Term Residents, are finding it is their turn to worry about deportation. Also all the old men and women gathered together in hut 84 and mostly of German blood, who once lived in luxury and mixed with one another as if they formed a small, safe colony here, a complete whole, shut off from the outside world. Their living hut had become a kind of boarding-house for legal counsels, privy councillors, doctors, men of letters, an old folk's home that was at the same time a parliament where politics were carried on according to time-honoured custom, a club where people played games enthusiastically—skat or bridge—and erect old men, old soldiers with bristling moustaches like tigers appeared like ancient waxwork figures. [. . .]

Now this boarding-house is partly empty—several families were sent away with the last transport; the rest of them are going about with worried faces in spite of the privilege of going to Theresienstadt or central Germany. So what was perhaps the most striking institution at Westerbork is now disappearing.

Saturday September 11th: The weather is beginning to get cold and raw. Men are appearing in winter coats and women in coats with fur. Last night the flies left me in peace for the first time; today one or two are still roving about in the hut.

In the past few days camp residents dreading their departure for Germany have been fleeing like rats abandoning a sinking ship. A nurse, a female member of staff at the Applications Office, two members of the Hashera. The guards are evidently indifferent to these escapes. They have had quite enough of peering out day and night at all hours from their towers and patrolling along the barbed wire. They, like the Jews, want to go home.

Sunday September 12th: Yesterday celebrated the birthday of a friend of mine—a woman journalist who lives in my hut, in the women's room (but only sleeps there), and keeps house in the one-room dwelling of a Long-Term Resident and also has her meals there. Six people who know one another slightly, just as people get to know one another on board ship, assembled together round the festive board in a camp fairly shrieking with wretchedness. The host provided roses in bloom and the guests all brought presents, flowers, fruit. The dinner consisted of: hors d'oeuvre of egg with salmon, then sausages with green peas, and vanilla pudding as the sweet. The sausages were a gift of the gods—the tin said only "green peas". When it was opened, six sausages were found hidden inside. The guests were delighted with the sausages; they absolutely devoured them.

At the end of the dinner, as if it had all been planned, although it was, in fact, pure chance, the post brought six parcels on a wheelbarrow for the lucky lady, all from Amsterdam. It was like emptying out a horn of plenty—bread, cheese, butter, jam, truffles, notepaper, etc., etc. We shared in the excitement with our friend, a little enviously. Coffee afterwards, made from the real thing, which had come in one of the parcels just at the right moment. The coffee was sipped and praised to the skies. Pure coffee is hardly found here at all.

In the middle of the coffee one of the guests, also a Long-Term Resident, got up: 'Ladies and gentlemen, how would it be if I went and fetched a bottle of apricot brandy?' The host, perfectly calm: 'Yes, that would be a good idea.' I was speechless with amazement. Five minutes later a towering bottle of golden yellow liquid stood glinting there in the lamplight. Small cut-glass liqueur glasses too. Quaffed with a cigarette. A first-class drink. The glasses were emptied down at a single gulp as if everyone was in the habit of doing so. Stories about wild drinking parties in the camp. The friend whose birthday it was told me later that the drink was brought in by camp buyers.

Moved this morning to hut 83. We had to move en masse as hut 85 has been allocated to the "white Jews", Christians who have helped Jews and are to be coming here one of these days from the prison camp at Ommen. Hut 85 has been fenced off with barbed wire already. Great exodus with wheelbarrows. Everyone had to take his mattress with him. All the men and women had to wheel their own things—once again, for the umpteenth time, it looked just as if an ant colony had been disturbed. Including the mattress, my belongings now make up three barrow loads. I feel almost like a plutocrat. We left behind a great deal of rubbish—empty jampots, odd or worn out slippers and shoes, stale bread, tins, boxes, paper, with, glowing in the midst of it all, a few forgotten begonias or geraniums. But we have pulled the nails out of the beams and walls because these articles are very scarce, using one or two pairs of pincers which went from hand to hand, and we knocked them in again in hut 83 with the help of one or two hammers which also passed from hand to hand.

Hut 83 is exactly like hut 85 and we have all got back our old bed numbers, so we settled in at once. Lovely to feel so much at home straight away. I am occupying bed No. 439. From the point of view of amenities we have gone up in the world. The washroom of 83 has lacquered iron clothes-hooks, so we can hang up our pyjamas and towels properly. Certainly the gift of some rich man. But of the twenty-four windows in the opening frames there are seventeen broken, so there are plenty of draughts.

Monday September 13th: [. . .]

People are still haggling over the 1,000 List. Camp inmates who had been put on the list have been removed from it again, in order to make room for others who had been forgotten and had an unquestionable right to be on it. Of the former staff of the Jewish Council thirty per cent have been put on the list. Those who have been selected for this honour and privilege say pompously: 'I am entitled to it. I worked hard.' Or: 'I have done a lot.' They go about with an air of self-assurance or self-sufficiency. It is a remarkable fact that until now Theresienstadt has been reserved for German Jews who had served Germany well or for an occasional Dutch Jew who rejoiced in the favour of Mussert. All at once the portals of Theresienstadt have been opened to Dutch Jews who happen to be fathers or mothers of ex-members of the Jewish Council who came to Westerbork voluntarily, or are fathers or mothers of doctors, and so on. People just cannot understand this clemency, this new and delicate pattern of differentiation. Tomorrow things may be different again.

Was disgusted on a visit to the S-hut yesterday. In the washroom men and young girls were dancing foxtrots and so on to the sound of someone drumming on an upturned bucket. Men and girls perspiring from their exertion in the heat inside a hut with thirty or so people packed into it. An undignified exhibition. The S-hut has recently become a sordid hole—many men and women without any moral restraint.

Among the hut residents are a Catholic priest who helped Jews and a young Catholic man who wrote a letter about the racial question which was intercepted by the censors. In it he spoke out in favour of the Jews. [. . .]

The hut leaders are absolute rotters—they feel they are the chosen leaders in the room and not companions in misfortune, so they go haughtily through the huts with hardly a word of greeting and will hardly answer any question asked them. They confine themselves to going round the room in the morning and asking: 'Anybody ill? Anybody ill?' And to the evening roll-call when they read out the names of the residents. They also tick off people who have committed offences and paw any woman they can lay their hands on. They act as supervisors for the women's room too and they can and do get in there when men are denied admittance, after half past nine in the evening.

There is active contact between men and women. Every morning when I wake up the man lying behind me is being visited by his young wife, so I have to be the unwilling witness of an intimate tête-à-tête, which on Sundays becomes a long tête-à-tête. That is how people live here. You have to be careful not to let yourself be contaminated by the public sex life that goes on in all the nooks and corners. Human beings here have sunk to the level of animals. [. . .]

Last night a sixty-five-year-old woman in my hut committed suicide. Her application for Theresienstadt had been turned down, so she was to be going on the transport. Her daughter had said she was willing to accompany her voluntarily. She wanted to save her daughter from making that sacrifice.

Tuesday September 14th (five o'clock in the morning): Sentence was pronounced on me today without my knowing anything about it in advance. The Commandant himself compiled the lists, thus preventing my protector from keeping me here any longer. I have received my sentence very calmly, convinced that I shall see my relatives and friends again. Sincere thanks to my friends, including those at Westerbork, for the kind attentions they have bestowed upon me to keep me fit and well. I shall leave with happy memories of them. I hope you will all

155

be strong. Till we meet again. PHILIP MECHANICUS.

Tuesday September 14th (evening): The sentence has not been carried out—as yet. Thanks to the kindness of my friends, I had my things neatly packed: two blankets wrapped in a sheet and tied securely with string, a rucksack with clothes, a satchel with tinned goods, a bag of fresh provisions, a box of apples and pears, a water-bottle full of tea. Ready for a long journey. I had written my final greetings to my relatives and friends— on a card to show change of address with, under "new address", a heavy dash—"I don't know". This I had arranged to do. I said good-bye to all my friends and acquaintances in the hut and shook hands with twenty or thirty of them. A room-mate who had been temporarily given the job of barrowman wheeled my luggage to the train on a handcart, all except the bread bag which I had slung over my shoulder. A handshake every few feet of the way to the train. There I transferred everything to a wheelbarrow and took the unusual step of standing on the platform outside the train in order to intercept one at least of the powers that be from the former Jewish Council or from the Applications Office as they went on their rounds and through them put my case before Schlesinger. Schlesinger had assured me that I would not be deported. But this time the Commandant had compiled the list himself without respect of persons. There was a shortage of human material and anyone who did not have a valid stamp and had not been put down for the 1,000 List had to go along. That was the wish of the Grand Inquisitor.

Well-known people who had practically taken root here had been placed on the list. First came ex-members of the Jewish Council. 'We worked all night for you and now we are going too.' 'I have a good mind to cut and run. I don't want to go on this travelling pig-sty.' 'I wouldn't do that without making preparations. Just wait here. The legal way is the best. Things are sure to come right. Look—wagon 48.'

After ten minutes Dr. Ottenstein from the Applications Office came along, a dried-up looking, bespectacled figure in a straw-yellow jacket, frightfully smart. 'Just wait here. I'm coming back.' Ten minutes later he was back. Schlesinger in a black jerkin, leather riding-breeches and jackboots was coming behind him. A meaningful look. He rammed a letter into my hand with instructions to follow an orderly to the office of the Registration Department. On the note, in addition to my surname and first name, were the words: "Reason: by order of the *Obersturmführer*" with the stamp of the Camp Commandant's Office and, running across it, the signature of Schlesinger in a little snaking line. I spoke to friends and acquaintances at the entrance to the wagon which was already bursting with people and followed the orderly who wheeled the barrow piled high with my luggage past the guard posts of the OD.

In the offices of the Jewish Council I found I was the only mature adult among a group of about forty young men and women. My name was noted down on a long list, together with those of the others who were waiting there. 'You're surely not twenty-one yet?' And I saw the mocking smile of a boy of nineteen or twenty. 'No, not yet.' 'I can see that.' And the boy glanced at my greying hair. The young men and women turned out to be members of the Hashera. They were fetched out of the train by order of the *Obersturmführer* who had been mellowed by a telegram saying that 500 certificates had been made available for Palestine for members of the Aliyah. Actually they could only be members of the Aliyah up to their eighteenth year, but the age was forced up to twenty-one. As a result, thirty-seven young people have been spared the journey to the east, for the time being at least. The Commandant set the young people free because other camp residents volunteered for the journey in order to accompany relatives who had been called up for Poland. So long as the proper number was supplied. That was all that mattered.

Waited up to half past ten, until the train left. Then I grabbed a stray wheelbarrow standing outside the Registration Department, loaded my things on to it and wheeled it back myself. On the way back the same scene as when I was leaving —every few steps of the way a hand held out to congratulate me; from every window recess more hands to congratulate me. People thought that I had been terribly lucky—I had risen from the dead. They thought I was a lucky fellow. I let all these songs of praise simply slide over me, but I had a nasty taste in my mouth. I alone was back and so many good friends, so many good people, had been sent away. To hell? I had to pinch my arm before I could believe that I was still here and had not been blotted out from Westerbork. I tried to counter the nasty taste in my mouth by arguing that many of those

157

who have now been sent away had been here over a year, but I have only been here ten months.

Life is a lottery—here a lottery without any prizes, and why should I draw my blank earlier than I have to! Dreadful for those who are told they have drawn a blank and cannot throw it back in the urn! And what will happen in the future? Next week or the week after that the same performance again; in the dead of night a dazzling light and the expressionless voice of the Inquisitor: 'Mechanicus, Philip?' [. . .] Why do I stay here, why don't I run away? Running away is risky too. Everywhere round the camp are the peering eyes of the Inquisitor's henchmen who, when they lay hands on their victim, bring him back and hustle him into the S-hut as a doubly marked man to face—what destiny? I got to know the brutes at the Amersfoort concentration camp. That is enough and more than enough for one human life. And yet I am haunted by the thought: 'How can I get out?' At night I busy myself with plans for escape worked out to the last detail. Not that I am frightened of Poland or wherever else it may be, not that I dread death which will come one day in any case. But I refuse to be a slave, I refuse to be pestered and tormented, I refuse to end up in the clutches of my enemies. That is my right and I am fighting for it. [. . .]

There are just over 6,000 residents at the camp now. One is clearly aware that the camp is getting empty—few people wandering about on the roads.

Wednesday September 15th: Met Schlesinger this morning as I was sitting writing in the waiting room outside his office—an iron handshake. 'It was a mistake,' was the only explanation he offered in his stentorian voice. 'Can I see you today?' 'I have to go over the way now (office of the *Obersturmführer*), but if you are still here at four o'clock I can hear what you have to say then.' About five o'clock Schlesinger was still not back. There will be other days.

Thursday September 16th: Went to see the revue once again yesterday evening. Packed out. The ensemble have really got into the spirit of it and the revue is going like clockwork. The response of the audience is mixed. There is great admiration for the work of the cast and people laugh at the jokes and enjoy the words and music of the songs about the camp and the comments of the entertainer, Ehrlich. But the majority of the audience are not at all willing to let themselves go—they seem inhibited. The invitation of Camilla Spira to join in and sing the catchy choruses altogether gets a response only from some of the young people. The older generation keep quiet and cannot relax after all the suffering they have gone through and are still going through daily. Also in the matter of applause the older generation are restrained, but the younger generation are open-hearted and burst out from time to time into rhythmical handclapping. Many adults who go to the revue excuse themselves by explaining that they would rather not have gone, but that later on they will be glad to chat about everything that went on at Westerbork. Of course there is a lot of self-deception in this—they do not want to miss the revue, their evening out. At Westerbork they have nothing.

Many German and Dutch Jews refuse to go to the revue, the former because they find there is a painful contrast between the "fun" and the tragedy of the transports, the latter because they cannot enjoy themselves while their relatives, their wives, their husbands or their children, are suffering an unknown fate, joyless, dreary, deprived of everything. But the young people fall over themselves to get tickets for it. They cost only ten cents each. People have never seen a good show so cheaply before, and they will perhaps never see anything as good and as cheap again.

Over this whole revue an atmosphere of painful melancholy and suffering hangs like a haze. Silently protesting, they give way to the vital demands of life. And the performers who laugh and flirt on the stage feel their acting blood stir within them, but offstage they too have to bear their sorrows. Man wants to mourn with those who have been struck down by fate, but he feels compelled to live with the living. Is the *Obersturmführer* such a good psychologist that he knows this law of life and has put it into effect here? Or is he merely a brutal egoist who lets the Jews amuse themselves for his own amusement and gives them something at the same time? You cannot see the workings of his heart.

My desire to escape from the camp is just as strong as ever.
[. . .]
Went this morning to see Dr. Ottenstein of the Applications Office. He advised me to hand in an application on the basis of my dissolved mixed marriage with a child. He said I had a

good chance of being sent to Theresienstadt. It would appear that Schlesinger cannot keep me any longer and wants to be sure that at all events I shall not be sent on to Poland. When I asked, he told me that he could not see me today and referred me to Dr. Ottenstein. Fräulein Slottke who makes decisions in matters of this kind will not be returning here till October 15th. At all events I have been given a month's grace. A lot can happen in that time and I can consider what I ought to do.

Friday September 17th: Yesterday another member of the Hashera, a girl, ran away. Today the Commandant ordered that for the moment nobody is to work outside the camp any more.

In the night 316 Jews arrived from Vught, including all those still working at Moerdijk. Not a single one of them had a winter coat—they had been taken away from them. Several of them had literally no underclothing, no shirt, no trousers, no socks. 120 S-detainees from the concentration camp. The people were starving. Bread had to be collected for them.

There has been a change in my social life. A few days ago I was taken on as a table companion by the leader of the hut where only young unmarried men live. Some of them are employed in the carpenters' workshop and the smithy, etc. A good and ample lunch was served, prepared by a woman's hand. Potatoes ad libitum, cabbage ad libitum, a home-made sauce with pieces of fat bacon. An outsider joined in and ate his fill. My neighbour who sat with his girl-friend at the same table had a large bottle of vermouth standing beside his plate from which he served his table companion. The hut leader is a German from the Rhineland, a business-man who was in Palestine during the last war and has been flung from camp to camp in Holland. He has lived here for four years and knows the camp life inside out. A kind-hearted fellow, not educated, but with natural intelligence, natural refinement and a good brain—a thoroughly decent man. [. . .]

The relationship between the hut leader and the residents is absolutely different from that in the large transit huts. In the latter the leaders and the residents usually pass one another with cold indifference, but in the former there is a note of camaraderie and familiarity. [. . .]

Saturday September 18th: 350 Jews were brought in from Amsterdam during the night, including 124 who had been in hiding.

160

They have been put in the S-hut. There are also fifty patients who have been brought in from the Jewish *Invalide*. On the same train, at two o'clock in the morning, fifty Jews, members of the *Expositur* staff with their families, were taken back to Amsterdam as a token of recognition for their services. It is shameful to receive recognition from the hands of those who rob Jews because you have served those robbers so well. But it is better to go back to Amsterdam rather than travel to Poland. At seven o'clock this morning a number of Jews departed by bus on their way to catch the train to Barneveld. I was present when they left and felt that I just needed to step on board and I could have gone off with them. The supervision by the guards shows great indifference.

I have finally handed in to the Applications Office my papers relating to my dissolved mixed marriage with an "Aryan" child. I was given the assurance that these papers were adequate for me to be sent to Theresienstadt. At all events this means once again that my stay at Westerbork can be extended. A number of divorced partners from mixed marriages departed with the latest transport. The pattern of reasoning is as follows: Jewish fathers and mothers of "Aryan" children are at present given Theresienstadt as a mark of favour, whereas if Jewish men are found with "Aryan" women they go to a concentration camp where they are sometimes unlucky enough to be killed.

Sunday September 19th: Yesterday was another general moving day. Entire huts were given the order to go elsewhere with all their goods and chattels. [. . .] A friend of mine has succeeded in taking possession of a partitioned-off compartment for himself and his wife. 'I've slept with my wife for the first time for seven months. I can hardly believe my good fortune.'

An invasion of my hut too. A few old men and a few young fellows from Vught. [. . .] One of my neighbours has brought a wardrobe fit for a world tour; it hides three bedsteads. Three or four suits and a few coats hang neatly on coat-hangers from the bar of the topmost bed, just as if they were in a wardrobe. When I climb into my bed and get down from it one of the suits or coats always falls to the floor. [. . .]

This morning, a Sunday, came the introductions. The boys from Vught and Moerdijk told us of their experiences. They were treated like animals at the camp. At Moerdijk they

161

worked hard. 'We have been through the mill. We're not scared of Poland any more. Nothing new can happen to us there.' The old men listened in bewilderment. 'They killed a son of mine at Amersfoort. I never heard anything from him. Yes. All my other sons have been sent to Poland with their wives and children. I and my wife are the only members of the family who are still left.' [. . .]

It is hard to keep any feelings of sympathy. So many men are dying daily at the front in a state of wretchedness that cannot be measured or understood by the ordinary human heart. Why should we feel sympathy towards Jews who go to Poland, towards two old folk helplessly facing their destiny? What does it matter—two people more or less, ten, a hundred, a thousand, or ten thousand Jews? Man has become powerless in the face of the all-prevailing wretchedness. The misfortunes of one individual in normal times affect him more than the combined distress of millions in time of war and revolution. He has to throw off all soft-heartedness with regard to himself in order to hold out and he cannot indulge in any soft-heartedness towards other people without damaging his morale. Life and death play no part any more. Anyone who is cut down by the storm is simply cut down. The man who defies the storm and stays alive is lucky if he manages to hang on to life.

A new revue is being rehearsed. The man behind me, one of the stars, lies in bed in the mornings learning the words of his songs. [. . .]

Monday September 20th: Discipline in the camp has been relaxed in the last few weeks. [. . .] People can move about freely in the camp, unrestrained and unmolested. The OD attend mainly to the S-hut where they strictly supervise the movements of the detainees and the visiting for which there are special hours and regulations. They sometimes take harsh action against visitors. [. . .]

There was a row—about a box on a bed. The box had been there for a fortnight and nobody had bothered about it or taken any notice of it. Suddenly it irritated a resident who had slept badly. Many people sleep badly here. The resident began to grumble about the box. Why did the thing have to stand just there? It was in everybody's way. Whose was the box anyway? 'The box belongs to me and it has always stood there.'

162

'That's not true at all.' 'It's a fact.' 'Oh no, it isn't.' 'You're always making a row.' 'You're the one who's always making a row.'

That was the row. A tremendous din, and the whole hut was disturbed just because of a stupid box.

Tuesday September 21st: [. . .]

Once again a transport of 1,000 people, including sick old men from the Jewish *Invalide* and about 300 men who had come only last night from Vught, practically without any clothes. The Welfare Department provided clothing for the sick men and the people from Vught and also gave them proper equipment. Although it is beginning to grow chilly and the nights are cold, the emigrants may only take one blanket with them and not more than fifteen kg of luggage altogether. [. . .] The S-detainees were sent along with the transport in spite of the fact that a case of infantile paralysis had just occurred in the S-hut.

Yesterday morning, shortly before the transport left, the dead bodies of ten Aryans were brought in. They had been shot in Assen for breaking into distribution offices in Drente. Members of the Free Netherlands force. Five S-men from hut 67 were given the task of conveying the bodies from the hearse to the crematorium where they were burned. When they had done their work, they were taken straight to the train, white-faced after their frightening and nauseating experience, and their rucksacks were brought to them from the hut. [. . .]

The school has been closed because a case of infantile paralysis has occurred there.

Wednesday September 22nd: Mevrouw P., who had been given leave to buy books in Amsterdam for Aryan prisoners who are to be accommodated in the camp, did not return yesterday evening at the appointed hour to hut 83. Commotion in the hut. She had been on the point of being deported a fortnight before, but was fetched out of the train in the very nick of time. The deputy woman leader of the hut has been summoned by the guards for interrogation.

The first fur coats have been seen in the camp. Winter is on the way.

Yesterday the wife of a friend of mine was informed that there was a bag in a corner of the Post Office that was addressed to her. She went to have a look and recognized a bag of clothes which she ought to have received two months ago. For two months the bag had been standing there unclaimed. Nobody had attempted to send it to the correct address and nobody had laid a finger on it. Magnificent winter clothes came out of the bag. A phenomenon at Westerbork where people scrounge like ravens. Everyone is amazed at this case of "honesty".

The stoves have been got ready.

Thursday September 23rd: Two fresh cases of infantile paralysis among the schoolchildren. There is some word of stopping the transports to the east because of the infantile paralysis. Dr. Spanier has recommended to the *Obersturmführer* that the transports should be suspended for six weeks. Next Tuesday there would be no transport going in any case. People are sceptical about this rumour because in the night that has just passed another transport with 220 Jews arrived from Amsterdam and during the coming night another transport will be arriving from Vught.

During the night a large number of aircraft flew over Westerbork in an easterly direction from half past nine till one o'clock. The camp residents were wild with joy. 'Do you hear the music?' everyone asked. [. . .]

Eight months ago a baby was brought in here without its parents. A nurse undertook to care for the child, Moutje. The nurse had to go on the last transport. She did not want to leave the child behind and managed to arrange for it to go "voluntarily" with her. Shortly before the transport left, when the child was already on the train, news came from Amsterdam that the mother of the child had got a 120,000 stamp which the Aryan foster-parents in Amsterdam had obtained for just that sum. As a result, the child is free and can return to Amsterdam. [. . .]

Friday September 24th: [. . .]

On Wednesday evening two girls escaped. They belonged to the squad who travelled every day to the laundry in Meppel where the patients' washing was done. The Commandant has withdrawn permission for the squad to go to Meppel. Last night one of the men who unloaded the bodies of the ten Aryans in the crematorium escaped.

A scandal in hut 21 where young unmarried men live. After the evening roll-call two boys of twenty guided a couple of girls inside and made passionate love to them in full view of minors. The hut leader reproved the boys and reminded them of their position of responsibility with regard to their younger companions. He transferred them to another room by way of punishment. [. . .]

Sunday September 26th: Boxing match last night. Packed out. All the authorities present, together with all the heads of the departments. Also the *Obersturmführer* and Aus der Fünten, who had come over from Amsterdam. This morning the hut was full of the match.

The plague of fleas is raging in all the huts. On waking up, we no longer ask one another: 'Did you sleep well?' But: 'Did you have a bad time with the fleas last night?' At night, before going to bed, we sit down and carefully inspect the blankets for fleas. Old gentlemen who have nothing else to do during the day beat their blankets outside in the morning with beaters— as hard as they can, to scare away the fleas. At night you can find tormented souls in the washroom looking for fleas in their pyjamas which they have hung over a line. Really superior men who have probably never had anything to do with fleas before coolly bare their legs in public to hunt for a flea. Westerbork is one great flea-circus. [. . .]

Monday September 27th: Have been exactly one year away from home today. I tell myself that the time has flown, but I know for a fact that this is not so. If I look back, so much has happened to me in the past year that the time cannot possibly have flown. I know that every period of that year, my term in prison, my spell in the concentration camp at Amersfoort, my stay in the different hospital huts, as I remember them all, lasted a long time, sometimes an eternity. And yet the time has gone past like a film—a horrible, but enthralling film. That is what it is like now that it is all behind me. I did not see the film as a member of the audience from a comfortable seat, but as an actor who had to clench his teeth as he played his part. When you have to do this every day of the year it is tiring and is a great strain on the nerves. In my mind none of the events appears in perspective any more; they all stand side by side in a row, outside space and time—all the events of my life, including

165

those before September 27th 1942. I am only astonished that I am still here and have not yet been washed away to the east in one of those great waves of humanity. Pure chance. [. . .]

Those whose fate I shared in prison and at Amersfoort and who arrived here at the same time as I did were sent on to Poland, with one single exception, after only two days' rest and with their wounds bandaged—decently clothed, it is true, and provided with the necessities, as they were in those days—but they have been away for nearly a year. How are things going with these men, I wonder? Men who bore up well in the concentration camp and went bravely on their journey. Of all these exiles I have never heard anything more—nor has anyone else, as far as I know. Except in one instance. In March of this year mevrouw Landau received a letter from her husband, the well-known Dutch chess-player, who wrote to say that he was well, but he asked for food. [. . .] One year of isolation, of physical torture and mental torment is over. What will the second year bring?

Tuesday September 28th: A case of clothes lice in hut 60. Examination of all the occupants at the Quarantine Station. [. . .]

In front of the window where I am sitting writing a number of small children are playing on sewage pipes. They are discussing, as a perfectly ordinary topic of conversation, how many fleas each of them caught last night.

The Westerbork Café opened yesterday in the old Registration Hall. Packed out, almost all young people. A string orchestra.

Wednesday September 29th: At a quarter past four in the morning the alarm sounded for the members of the OD and NB. Great activity among the men, all trying to guess what the signal meant, but it was generally supposed that there had been another raid in Amsterdam and that a consignment of detainees was due to arrive. This supposition turned out to be correct. A hundred and seventy OD and NB men were selected to leave by lorry, presumably for Amsterdam to bring in Jews. All the men were heads of families, so the German authorities had a guarantee against escape. [. . .]

The Commandant had certainly thought it all out perfectly. He arranged for the alarm to be sounded in the middle of the night and the whole camp to be put into a state of turmoil and

166

upheaval, whereas the police already knew yesterday afternoon that something was afoot. The authorities in The Hague (or Amsterdam) had thought it all out perfectly too—a raid on the very eve of *Rosh Hoshanah*, the Jewish New Year festival, just like last year and just as at the time of other Jewish festivals. And in the doorways of the huts there were such kind notices saying that Jews could send greetings to their relatives outside the camp. Teasing and tormenting are a part of the cultural task that these gentlemen have set themselves.

The first consignment of detainees came in about half past one—in ordinary third-class carriages, with all their goods and chattels as usual. This time it was a high-class consignment: Asscher, Sluzker, Eitje and Van der Laan were there. Professor Cohen was still missing. Also Meyer de Vries, a partner in a mixed marriage. You could recognize them from afar off.

Many expressions of pleasure among the spectators at the discomfiture of these others: 'They're here too at last!' Many expressions of doubt at the justice of it all: 'They'll be going back home, no doubt! They'll have made sure of getting a good stamp.' Many expressions of vengeance: 'I'd like to get my hands on them!' Many expressions of contempt: 'They ought to have put a bullet through their heads!' Many attempts to excuse them: 'They're just weak men who did what they could and wanted to save their own skins too.'

In the disorderly queue were absolutely ordinary little men in the power of their persecutors. Nothing magical radiating from them, no glorious figures or faces. Just a few among many—miserable wretches among other miserable wretches. People clamour for their heads because they "betrayed" their cause, because they did not hand back their mandate at the first sign of treachery on the part of the Germans, but who knows what these miserable men, once bourgeois in good positions, will have to go through. They have had their first reward—they have been pushed back into the masses they once rose above. They too will probably have to go through the fire of slavery and accept the opportunity they will be given to purify themselves. They will, moreover, have to go through another fire—kindled by the contempt of their companions in misfortune. That is probably enough to atone for any guilt they may have.

At three o'clock, while the new arrivals were being registered

167

and Lippmann & Rosenthal were plundering them, a *huppah*, or church wedding, was taking place in hut 35. The groom was wearing a trim lounge-suit with a white aster in his buttonhole and the bride had a white veil. Both serious people and distinguished. A few hundred guests. Hymns and an address in keeping with the times and the marriage contract solemnly read aloud and signed. For the time being, this marriage is merely an act of witness because these young people cannot live here as man and wife—that is not possible. [. . .]

Thursday September 30th: Professor Cohen has arrived. He has been put in hut 62, a completely ordinary hut. Asscher has been put in hut 61, also a completely ordinary hut. Sluzker in 64. They are among the ordinary people, on rough mattresses, with their miserable bits of luggage around them, plagued by fleas. Yesterday altogether three transports came in, two from Amsterdam and one from Barneveld, with a total of 2,800 people. Almost the last of the Mohicans. The German authorities had intended that Amsterdam should be clear of Jews by July 15th and had announced this. It is now October 1st and Amsterdam is still not completely clear of Jews. It would appear to be not all that easy to achieve this. [. . .]

From Barneveld came the pick of the basket—700 men, women and children who have been accommodated all together in hut 85, the hut that was intended for the "white Jews". Behind barbed wire. There are men and women there with names that ring a bell—scholars, artists, heads of firms. But also a great number, and these represent the majority, of whom the world has never heard. [. . .] The 700 people, all mixed up together, were like a swarm of bees in a hive. After Barneveld they felt disappointed, upset and insulted; they thought they were having a raw deal. How well off they had been in their exile there—plenty of comforts, proper sleeping accommodation, their own furniture, their own books, their own musical instruments, a lovely dining-hall where everyone had a permanent seat at a well-appointed table, a wood in which to wander. Here a filthy stable of a place, bad enough to turn your stomach, and a grubby washroom.

To make matters worse, they had only been given an hour and a half to pack their things at Barneveld and in their hurry and confusion had forgotten to bring the most ordinary necessities of life with them. The luggage did, in fact, come on later. They had had to leave abundant supplies of food and drinks behind, to which, so it is said, OD and NB men treated themselves, like hyenas on a battlefield when the fighting is over. They ate their fill of creamy cheese, salmon, liver patty and sardines and they drank their fill of wines and spirits. They exchanged the old and crumpled suits under their overalls for the sometimes brand-new suits that the Barnevelders had had to leave behind in their haste, sometimes two suits, one on top of the other. They stuffed cases full of butter, coffee, tea and delicatessen and brought them by train to Westerbork for their own use. [. . .]

Friday October 1st: [. . .] The roads are full of gentlemen with high foreheads, well-fitting suits, well knotted ties, rasping voices and courtly greetings and their well dressed wives. A rather exotic interlude—Westerbork-le-Bain.

Professor Cohen, Asscher and Sluzker move like stars of the first magnitude among the crowd, with Barneveld behaving as if it were the new elegant class of Westerbork. Professor Cohen with his naive childlike face, good-natured eyes and black clerical jacket moves quickly and a little unsteadily through the crowd, all on his own, without any diffidence or the need to be noticed. He is evidently aware of the spiteful remarks that follow him about, but he does not choose any back ways when he is going about his business and, when necessary, he sits quietly and placidly in the midst of the crowd, waiting for his turn. Asscher is the picture of health and looks as if he has just returned from a long stay in the mountains. He strolls along, his head held high in a proud, self-sufficient manner, as if he has been here for years. He chats jovially and sociably with anyone who wants to have a chat. He has not the faintest idea of the contempt people feel for him, of the desire for vengeance that is building up against him. Or is he just pretending? He does not yet realize that here he is just one of many—transport material. In the canteen this morning he expected to be given precedence when lemonade was being served, but an OD man showed him his place in the queue. 'I am Asscher.' 'Then you must stand in line.' Needling.

Saturday October 2nd: This morning a tragi-comical accident occurred. The *Obersturmführer* was cycling along the Boulevard des Misères with Schlesinger—almost like two brothers. The

Ostu was on a brand-new bicycle with a double frame and gleaming, glittering rims in which the sunlight sparkled. Schlesinger was on a perfectly ordinary old bike painted a dull black. Carried away by the conversation, one of them made an awkward turn and suddenly the pair of them were lying flat on the ground with the Commandant underneath, as was right and proper. Helpful onlookers pulled the bicycles and the two great protagonists apart, but Schlesinger could not get up—he had broken his leg. You often find it is the wrong man who breaks his leg. Some people think it would have been fair if both of them had broken their legs. Now Schlesinger is lying in his house on a bed of pain and is receiving fruit and titbits from his admirers, male and female. [. . .]

The Barnevelders continue to attract attention. They have been put into jobs like everyone else here—the women peeling potatoes or on "inside work", daily cleaning of the huts, and the men in the different departments of the camp. The women are taking the change in their status in a pretty sporting way; they look at their black fingernails and their fingertips all engrained with dirt with an air of self-ridicule. And the men no less so. Eminent scholars in overalls wheel barrowloads of barrels and help to pull and push the mail cart with a philosophical smile. Light slave labour which they accept with resignation. [. . .]

The Commandant has ordered that Sluzker, Professor Cohen, Asscher and company should be treated exactly in the same way as everybody else at the camp.

Sunday October 3rd: It is definite that there will be a transport going again on Tuesday—those who possess Special Identity Cards, mainly members of the Jewish Council who have been made secure from arrest by the police in Amsterdam, invalids, S-detainees, applicants for the Calmeyer List who have been turned down. The Barnevelders have been promised semi-officially that they will not be sent away for the time being, as also have the bona fide holders of 120,000 stamps. [. . .]

People are at present taking the transport order with a pinch of salt. There is some doubt as to whether the transports can still get through to Poland now that the Germans have been thrown back in Russia and the Russians are already nearing the frontier of what was formerly Poland. It is said that the Germans have been busy for a few weeks withdrawing the

Jews in the east from behind the front to the large camp at Auschwitz and that the latest transports have not been able to go any further than Magdeburg.

Monday October 4th: This morning the news went through the camp like an electric shock—the transport train was not there! It normally comes punctually on the dot of eleven o'clock, but this morning the mangy beast did not come shambling in. There were all kinds of guesses as to the reason. In the course of the day it became known that the *Wehrmacht* had refused the request of the SS for a transport train—they could not spare a train. They desperately needed all train accommodation for themselves. Nothing like that has ever happened before. The transport list was all ready and waiting and the men in green were there. They had come from Amsterdam to accompany the slave transport. The barrels had all been filled with water. But there was definitely no train. In the past the trains may have come a day late, or a few days late, but nothing like this has ever happened before. What peace for agitated hearts, what a sigh of relief went up!

Tuesday October 5th: All quiet this morning—no transport train. The barrels of water were emptied out and the men in green departed yesterday. It is said that now there will be no transport going for a fortnight. A lot of things can happen in a fortnight. The Russians are continuing to press on. In the north, according to the latest reports, they are already on former Polish territory in a few places. In Italy the British or Americans have landed at Leghorn behind the Germans. The bombing of German cities is increasing at a great rate and is hitting home. The articles by Dr. Goebbels in *"Das Reich"* become more specious and insistent as time goes on. Sam de Wolff, the socialist and economist, who was brought to the camp last Wednesday (for the second time) states categorically that the war will be over around November 30th—the Germans cannot face another winter. All the signs thus point in a favourable direction. [. . .]

This morning I got a new blue stamp because of my half-Aryan daughter with the intimation that I would be going on the very next transport leaving for Theresienstadt. That will no doubt take some time. I am one of the fortunate people who have got rid of their S without paying a cent and have stayed

171

at Westerbork for a long time without any stamp at all—it will be eleven months next Thursday. Finally, I am one of the fortunate few who have acquired a blue stamp, again without paying out a single cent. Hundreds of thousands of guilders have been paid out to get rid of the hated S and obtain stamps which are often cancelled later on. The monetary stamps turn out in practice to be the worst, and the ones that are not paid for the best.

People ask me a dozen times every day: 'What do you really do?' I really do nothing, that is to say, I have not been enrolled in any individual branch of the labour organization. [. . .] As a journalist I go round the camp and sit in all the nooks and corners. I speak to people and keep my diary up to date. In the midst of my other activities I play chess, on my old pocket chessboard which is now nearly twenty-five years old and on which I used to play so many games with my newspaper colleagues during the night. At the moment I am busy with two contests.

It is not so simple to answer the question: 'What do you really do?' I usually pass it off with a joke: 'Everything and a bit more.' [. . .] People look at me in amazement, but do not question me further. I certainly cannot say to everyone: 'I'm writing a diary.' [. . .] It is forbidden to write diaries here, except in the case of simple souls who begin as follows: 'When I came to Westerbork on such and such a date . . .' So far the *Obersturmführer* appears to have heard nothing about my clandestine occupation. Only a small number of initiates know about it, but not all of them keep their mouths shut. [. . .]

Thursday October 7th: The Barnevelders received their luggage today, some of it ransacked. Lippmann & Rosenthal had stolen linen, tobacco, toilet soap and articles of value from the cases. Some cases reached their owners completely empty. What the Barnevelders left behind at Barneveld has been brought here in lorries. The Commandant and his staff are picking out what they fancy and are reserving the rest for purposes as yet unknown.

Saturday October 9th: Yesterday was the Great Day of Atonement, marked by prayers in all the huts. While the devout men and women fasted and were busy saying or singing prayers in a corner of my hut, the others were carrying on with their normal

172

lives, amid the clatter of pans and the clinking of spoons and forks. Today the devout prayed all day long.

The agents of Lippmann & Rosenthal left today, carrying in their waistcoat pockets many fountain-pens which they had appropriated for their own use; they also had gleaming brief-cases (ditto) and in their suitcases articles which they had filched from the Jews. They released the letters still in their possession, all more or less unopened. Tens of thousands of letters were poured out over the huts like an avalanche. Some people got ten letters at once, the oldest of which dated back to the beginning of August. The agents did not know where they were going—they might equally well be sent to Amsterdam or to the eastern front. It is good that the post is free from control once more.

In the night a transport of 300 Jews arrived from Amsterdam, mainly S-detainees. Yesterday night twenty Jews arrived from Arnhem—the members of the Jewish Council. The night before last the members of the Jewish Council from Groningen. The S-hut is crammed full, more than 500 Jews. People and baggage lie higgledy-piggledy like a great skein that cannot be disentangled. People trip over one another and you have to shout above the continual droning of voices and the shuffling of feet to make yourself understood. The men do digging and a great proportion of the women work in industry, under supervision of OD men.

The Barnevelders are still packed close together. Since they got back part of their baggage they too are in a hopelessly topsy-turvy state with all their belongings. [. . .] All the huts give the impression of a second-hand shop, but the Barnevelders' hut is like a bazaar, with colourful garments, beautiful wickerwork and cloths hanging on the walls and from the beams. For the most part the Barnevelders are happy to be here because they no longer find themselves in a false position, also they have been freed from the constricting feeling of being just one group of people gathered together. Today they got their blue stamps. For the moment they are happy with them, but they definitely realize that they have not been brought to Westerbork just so that they can stay on there—especially if the war goes on for a long time. The document they got from Frederiks states that they are exempted from employment in Holland or abroad, but it does not say that they are exempted from being sent abroad. What indeed is a promise from

173

Frederiks worth, accompanied by the tacit guarantee of the National Socialists? How many promises have been broken by them and how many lists smashed by them here!

In the past few days there has been something new. They have once more handed out green stamps to a number of people employed in industry, in particular to workers in the metal industry. This is an extra for people who have been put on the 1,000 List and have been given the mark "ST" on their Camp Cards. The "ST" means "*Stammliste*", or Basic List. Holders of this type of Camp Card can at once get into the small comfortable huts which others have had to vacate. They also enjoy special privileges. This week each of them was given a packet of soap powder as a gift. The Commandant knows how to reward hard work.

Sunday October 10th: According to a statement made by the detectives, thefts in the huts have recently been increasing rapidly in number and scale. In the past few days crates and cases containing provisions and clothing have been completely emptied in some of the huts. This has coincided with the decline in the number of incoming parcels. Many Jews now receive nothing from outside as they have no relatives left in the city. They are feeling the pinch.

Tuesday October 12th: There is a feeling of tension in the camp as a result of the IPA rumour that the Germans and Russians are busy negotiating a separate peace behind the scenes. No reports from outside the camp to confirm this rumour. Naturally all kinds of conjectures—and fear in case things do turn out like that. The rumour sounds highly improbable, or it must be that Germany is trying to secure a separate peace— Russia has all the cards in her hand at the moment.

Wednesday October 13th: In the last few days fresh cases of infantile paralysis have broken out in hut 82B of the hospital. And in the orphanage. There are also many cases of diphtheria and jaundice, which have been occurring in the camp for some time. Strict quarantine has been announced for the affected part of the hospital and the orphanage—a cordon of barbed wire separates it from the general public and visiting is not allowed. Nevertheless—doctors and nurses go freely in and out and mix with the public. [. . .] In view of the infantile

174

paralysis, Dr. Spanier has recommended to the German authorities that there should be no transport next Tuesday. The *Obersturmführer* has passed on this recommendation to The Hague.

Thursday October 14th: Sick visit to Schlesinger. Yesterday evening at half past eight. Room full of people. Schlesinger in his night-shirt. When you go in, a mighty wave of the arm, as if he were a dictator bestowing favours, a firm handshake and the dramatic words: 'Well, my friend!' With a vigorous tug he turns back his blanket, revealing a plaster dressing extending up to the hip. He looks at me proudly—the plaster has been written on from the top almost to the bottom with a copying pencil, straight across and at a slant. There are dedications, short poems, signatures of friends and admirers. His eyes say: 'Well, what do you think of that? Isn't that wonderful?' I gaze at him paternally. Every new visitor has to be shown his plaster dressing, as if it were the covering of a mummy, something of historical value. [. . .]

Friday October 15th: The thought of the hostile atmosphere between the different groups keeps on nagging at me. Again and again fresh cases of animosity come to light. Went to Schlesinger to suggest that a proclamation should be drawn up. It would be published when peace came and would appeal to the hearts and consciences of the camp inmates to preserve harmony and rise above their own petty feelings. It would be signed by a number of prominent Dutch and German Jews. Schlesinger was delighted and at once gave his approval to the draft I put before him. He undertook to have the proclamation printed secretly. Trottel, who had accompanied me, also gave his approval to the plan. I said I would nominate two other Dutch Jews to take part in the scheme. Schlesinger would, in turn, nominate three German Jews.

The German authorities have turned down Dr. Spanier's recommendation. So a transport of 1,000 Jews will be going next Tuesday. Uneasiness in the camp. I have found that Dr. Willy Polak and Professor Meijers will be willing to co-operate with the German Jews in the interests of keeping the peace.

Saturday October 16th: Visit to Schlesinger together with Trottel

175

to inform him that my mission had been successful. I had previously established contact between Trottel and Professor Meijers. Frau Schlesinger is not entirely satisfied with Professor Meijers—she does not trust him and is afraid that he is playing a double game; he does not look people straight in the eye. I naturally sprang to Professor Meijers's defence. 'Who are the men on your side?' Schlesinger replied: 'It isn't so easy to find them. Each one of our people, in fact, has other commitments.' Frau Schlesinger agreed. Once again we went through a list of high-ups: Wachtel, Spanier, Neuburger and the rest. Nobody was found suitable. Schlesinger was to hold the appointments over. [. . .]

Sunday October 17th: Attended the première of the new revue yesterday evening. Absolutely packed out. Old numbers that had been refurbished, well acted. A great part of the programme consisted of dancing by revue girls with bare legs. The *Obersturmführer* present with Aus der Fünten. Went home with a feeling of disgust. [. . .]

Watched a sports contest on the parade ground this afternoon. Running, relay races, tug-of-war for seniors and juniors. A thick wall of spectators, including all the big-wigs of Westerbork. People spoke ironically of a "trans-sport contest". [. . .]

Monday October 18th: Camilla Spira, the star of the revue, has departed for Amsterdam, Aryanised. A great loss for the revue.

A Jew doing outside work at Hooghalen has escaped. The Commandant has officially announced that his mother and sister have been transferred to the S-hut (67) and will be put on the S-transport.

Following a report by an OD man, a Jew who was found behind hut 73 near the barbed wire—which is forbidden, although this is not generally known—has been put in prison. He will go on the S-transport.

Tuesday October 19th: The transport has left, 1,000 persons, S-detainees, a group who came in from Vught during the night without winter clothes, people without stamps. [. . .] This time, owing to the danger of infection from infantile paralysis, diphtheria and jaundice, the train was hermetically closed off with lead seals. [. . .] The last member of the

Plutocrat Club (apart from myself) went on that transport—a dentist from The Hague who was an S-man. The Hague took away his S, but at the same time removed his Puttkammer stamp and ordered him to be deported. He was a popular man in the camp where he went on practising as a dentist. His friends tried in vain to get him off the transport. [. . .]

Thursday October 21st: Yesterday we suddenly moved house. [. . .] This hut has once again become part of the hospital owing to the high incidence of infectious diseases. [. . .] The inmates have been spread out over all the other huts. I chose hut 71, the former "exemption" hut, to which I had been brought on November 7th of last year when I arrived from the concentration camp at Amersfoort. My reception started off on a discordant note. The room leader was in a grumpy mood. When selecting a bed, I innocently asked if there was a baggage bed available too. Answer: 'If you're not pleased with the bed, you'll just have to go elsewhere.' As if mine host the room leader was a hotel owner with too many guests. The peremptory tone of the Germans which the Dutch Jews complain so much about. A little later in the evening a spontaneous demonstration on the part of the inmates of hut 71 against the room leader who had snapped at one of them for no reason at all—a deputation to the hut leader to lodge a complaint. Explosion from the hut leader (also a German): Anyone who wasn't satisfied with the room leader appointed by the authorities could just lump it. Exeunt the demonstrators grumbling. [. . .]

A restless night. In the middle of the night a plaintive child's voice: 'Daddy, where's the pottie?' Daddy: 'In the corner.' Child's voice: 'I can't find it.' Angry man's voice: 'Can't you get all that done before you go to bed?' From various beds: 'Sh!' At half past five an alarm clock went off with a penetrating noise: 'Ru-tu-tu-tu-tu-tut.' At six o'clock another alarm clock standing on a stoneware plate. It sounded just like a bird beating its wings against a lattice. At the same time the *Shul* service began in the kitchen between the two wings of the hut, with the tenor voice of the precentor rising high above the singing of the congregation. *Simchath-Torah.*

The hut leaders and room leaders have looked after their own comforts. They have cubicles screened off with pieces of material and sleep there with their wives. That was forbidden

177

in hut 83, where the motto was: What is sauce for the goose is sauce for the gander, or, in the Dutch idiom, all monks wear the same cowl. In hut 71 the hut and room leaders do not want to be monks. Understandable. [. . .]

On the recommendation of Dr. Spanier, the *Obersturmführer* has ordered strict quarantine for the camp. [. . .] Official trips and leave have been suspended, also the discharge of residents from the camp. The outside squads have been done away with. An exception has been made in the case of OD squads needed "for special purposes in Amsterdam". That is, for collecting transport material. All incoming goods have to be handed over at the entrance beside the barrier. The railway staff on incoming goods and transport trains may not leave the train inside the camp. All gatherings, for talks, tuition, etc., have been discontinued and the performances of the revue have been suspended. People are forbidden to eat unpeeled fruit and are advised to drink as little tap water as possible. Every camp resident is obliged "to wash stripped to the waist" night and morning. The huts have to be cleaned more thoroughly and beds, blankets and baggage aired more often.

The quarantine is of course a farce. As long as the living huts are too full and are filling up more and more all the time, the measures that have been adopted are quite pointless. The huts are swarming with people and yet a simple course of instruction or a lecture is not allowed to take place! [. . .]

In the camp people feel that the quarantine is not being taken seriously and believe that Dr. Spanier is in league with the *Obersturmführer*. That would, of course, be completely contrary to any proper idea of quarantine, but it is not as crazy as it seems. They might well want to alarm the German authorities in The Hague and Berlin and so get the transports stopped—Dr. Spanier because he wants to put an end to this beastly traffic once and for all and the *Ostu* because he wants to hold on to his position as Commandant at Westerbork and avoid being drafted out east himself. The incidence of disease is, in any case, serious enough to justify the quarantine.

Saturday October 23rd: Great rejoicing. The Russians have broken through the German front between Kremenchug and Dnepropetrovsk. There is an IPA rumour that Turkey has made her territory available to the British and American forces as a supply area. The radio does not confirm this. [. . .]

178

The holders of 1,000 stamps have each been given an allowance of forty cigarettes. Not so long ago they were given soap powder. The other camp inmates had the pleasure of watching them. Divide and rule! The eatables taken out of the baggage of the Barnevelders [. . .] have been disposed of by lot among the camp residents employed on the sorting of scrap metal. This branch of activity is important for the German *Wehrmacht*. Mountains of scrap metal, for the most part from confiscated radios, bells and cables, lie heaped up in the camp. Also piles of wrapping paper with a lining of silver paper intended for the tropics, which is being collected for the processing of aluminium. The linen of the Barnevelders has been washed and mangled and deposited in the store. Their furniture, after the Commandant and his friends of both genders had taken their pick, has been installed in the small huts where the holders of 1,000 stamps have been or are to be quartered. What a grand idea to live amongst furniture stolen from one's fellow-Jews! An antique cabinet belonging to a friend of mine has found a place in the Commandant's villa. This same friend has been elevated to the post of honorary sculptor to the Commandant in place of the sculptor who escaped recently. [. . .]

Sunday October 24th: Every morning the small children who have not been going to school for a long time because of the infectious diseases go for a walk under the supervision of women teachers. They play all kinds of games and sing all sorts of songs out in the open field. One of their little songs goes as follows:

> "We're having a lovely walk between the huts
> And go with teacher nicely in a line,
> Past the great, tall chimney
> And the little houses,
> Then along the railway and so back home."

[. . .]

Monday October 25th: Was put down for sorting legumes yesterday. That means sorting peas and beans. Convict labour. The Commandant is keen that everyone in the camp should work. [. . .]

I reported to hut 78 promptly at eight o'clock this morning, in accordance with the instructions on my duty slip. A sea of men and women at long tables busy sorting dried broad beans. Greetings from friends and acquaintances on all sides. It was as if I had never done anything else in my life other than check through broad beans, instead of books and newspapers. On the ceiling was genuine home-produced tobacco in bundles that had been put on sticks to ferment. An imitation of finest Java tobacco. Miserable bunches without a hint of tobacco aroma. Had a chat about the war. People agreed that Germany was feeling groggy and was waiting for the coup de grâce. Was tapped on the shoulder. I turned round and found myself face to face with a woman of my own age, with a wrinkled brow, owlish glasses and a few gold teeth. 'You don't recognize me.' 'No, who are you?' 'I used to be juffrouw So-and-so.' A shock seemed to go through my heart. I had sat with her at school and been a little bit in love with her and I had not seen her in all those years. Now she was a mother with grown-up children. 'Oh dear, how quickly life passes! But here you see everyone you used to know.' I scouted round a bit more and got in everybody's way. A friendly request from the work leader to go away. 'I haven't got a place for you, but come back again this afternoon.' I went away. As I came out, I noticed that there were others who were not working. That eased my conscience. [. . .]

Tuesday October 26th: Returned yesterday afternoon to sort beans, but was given the day off when I asked for it, as I still had so many other things to do.

Today they brought into the hospital a Jew who had been shot in the leg by the *Obersturmführer* in person. Fortunately it was only small shot. The Jew had ventured too close to the barbed wire and, when summoned to move away from it, he took too long to do so. [. . .]

The Commandant has issued an order forbidding frying or roasting for private purposes in the Central Kitchen. This offence was being committed on a large scale. He has also issued an order forbidding the consumption of alcohol.

The number of cases of infantile paralysis is increasing.

Wednesday October 27th: [. . .]

In the end I was not taken on for legume sorting after all. Trottel intervened on my behalf with the "Minister of Labour", Samson. He made it clear to Samson that it was scandalous to inflict a soul-destroying job like bean-sorting on a man who daily exercised his natural function as a writer and was working for reconciliation between Dutch and German Jews under the direct protection of Schlesinger. Samson recorded my name on a memo list and put me down for a better and less time-consuming type of work. [. . .]

Thursday October 28th: [. . .]

A number of the S-men have been wearing for some time the indigo and scarlet convict outfits intended for the prisoners who were to be coming from Ommen. The S-men stand out with these outfits and their close-cropped heads, but they actually look very distinguished and a woman with some flair for colour and style could not devise any smarter colour combination for a very chic dress. The S-men certainly do not go about with bowed heads under their stigma, but go merrily singing and whistling through the camp on their way to work and come back from it singing merrily once more. These bright colours bring a bit of sparkle to the grey camp huts. Until now only the latrines brought a vivid touch to the camp with their red brick. They have been given a special name: *les châteaux rouges.* Since the coming of the Barnevelders who brought in a French note. Whenever someone has to go on a certain errand, large or small, he now says: 'I must just go to *le château rouge.*' The stink is just as terrible as ever.

Saturday October 30th: My desire to write has been curbed recently. The daily struggle against the disgust of communal life, against noise and triviality and vulgarity uses up a lot of energy. In writing I found a diversion which often helped me to forget the disgust. And in chess too. Recently my energy has left me in the lurch and I have felt no urge to make my notes. Have I looked out at the camp and become indifferent, like so many others who have been here a long time, to what is going on here among human beings? It is a fact that life here has a dulling effect and you must fight this all the time if you want to make anything of your life. [. . .] I am one of the few in the camp who officially do nothing, but I am not ashamed of this. Most of the work is carried out, when all is said and done, for the benefit of the German *Wehrmacht.* And I do not feel called upon to help in this. It is more important, I feel, to record the daily happenings for those who in time to come will want to get an idea of what went on here. So I have a duty to go on with my writing.

Sunday October 31st: A bright day—soft sunlight over a wide autumn landscape. Nature gives a sense of peace. Everyone enjoys his free day. In the afternoon I lay lazing in a wheelbarrow in the open field, as far as it is possible to laze in a wheelbarrow. There is only a little green in the open patches between the camp and the barbed wire—it is nearly all covered up with sand. Part of the field is used as a place for sorting rubbish which lies scattered about in large heaps, either in sheds or in the open air and gives off a musty smell. Horrible. [. . .]

A fresh case of infantile paralysis today in hut 85, the hut of the Barnevelders, a girl of seventeen. Great consternation in the hut.

In the afternoon listened to a sermon in hut 73, the hut for the baptized, by Gottschalk, the male nurse, who was acting as parson. A caustic sermon in which, without putting it into so many words, he lashed out at the persecution of the Jews by the National Socialists. He preached on the theme: "An angel flew through the heavens." The congregation sang "A safe stronghold our God is still", the verses of which took on a note of passionate feeling. [. . .]

Monday November 1st: Case of infantile paralysis with fatal consequences in hut 64, a man in his fifties. [. . .]

Van Dam, the Dutch *Untersturmführer* appointed a short time ago, is taking very rigorous action. He has made a few camp residents who could not establish their identity properly bend their knees or roll in the mud in public. [. . .]

Last night an *Unterscharführer* came storming into hut 71 very noisily after the camp had settled down to sleep. One of the residents whose sleep had been disturbed shouted out: 'Shut up!' Whereupon the intruder bellowed: 'If I hear another sound, you'll march twenty times round the hut with me behind you. Report tomorrow!' When the resident reported this morning, the *Unterscharführer* appeared not to remember a thing about the incident. He had been blind drunk. Not the only time.

Tuesday November 2nd: No transport today. A fresh case of

182

infantile paralysis, in hut 85, a girl of twenty-two. There are 500 people living tightly packed together there. An order has been issued, definitely forbidding all visits to the hospital, also to huts 61, 62, 64, 69 and 85. But the inmates of these huts can go on moving about freely. [. . .] Every day Jews still leave for Amsterdam on official trips. [. . .]

Wednesday November 3rd: Had an interview this morning with heer Eitje of the Jewish Council, with heren Eckman and Hanauer, couriers of the Jewish Council, present as intermediaries. Heer Eitje told me he had noticed that there was a very hostile atmosphere between German and Dutch Jews in the camp and asked me what chance there was of bringing about co-operation now and in the future so as to put an end to this hostility. I put him in the picture about what was being done in that respect and told him that the leading members of the Jewish Council were on the whole viewed with mistrust and contempt and I said that it was best if men without other commitments handled the task of reconciliation. Heer Eitje thought that it was reasonable for the different factions to speak out against one another to clear the air and that the differences had already been underlined here in the camp. People should work together. I said that I for my part had no objection if this could be done and that I would be glad to discuss the subject with Schlesinger and my confidential partners, but that certain persons who already had other commitments ought to stay in the background. Heer Eitje asked if he too was classed with these men who had other commitments. I could not, of course, answer that and I said that it was a delicate matter and everyone should know what position he ought to take up.

Thursday November 4th: Have heard on authority that the nineteen cases of infantile paralysis which have occurred so far are bona fide cases. Also that the head of the medical service and the *Obersturmführer* are working together to have the transports stopped because of the outbreak of infectious diseases. [. . .]

Friday November 5th: Icy cold this morning. The ground was covered with black ice. Men in winter coats, women with hoods on or scarves round their heads. Bitterly cold in the huts. Two base-burning stoves in the hut, one of which is a miserable little thing which burns badly and gives off little heat from the peat which is the only fuel available. The top surface is sixty centimetres square. Close to this little stove is my bed. Every evening there is the usual crowd round the little stove— men and women with mess-tins, pots, kettles and jugs to boil up or heat up left-overs. Every evening the same squabbling about who is to come first. Men and women with tins or baskets full of slices of bread and butter for toasting. Everyone toasts bread here. [. . .] In the small gaps left on the stove between the mess-tins and the kettles the slices of bread and butter lie basking and browning in the heat, or get all charred if the fire blazes up too fast. The stove is the meeting place and battleground of the gourmands. [. . .]

Sunday November 7th: Anniversary of my coming to Westerbork —one year ago—to the same hut as I am living in now. Celebrated it by a small party with a woman-friend at a corner of a table in my hut. [. . .] Not to commemorate the fact that I have been here that length of time, but because I have gained a year from Poland. A nicely set table. The tablecloth was a piece of dress cotton with a floral pattern. Menu (in the order stated): fried potatoes, consommé, hors d'oeuvre—egg with mustard sauce, ryebread with cheese, biscuit and cheese, roll and sausage, pear compote, apple, coffee (ersatz), cigarette. A small tonic in this awful place. Great interest shown by passers-by. [. . .]

Monday November 8th: [. . .]
Have got a new stove which has come from the Maginot Line—a low affair with a top surface about a metre square on which a great number of mess-tins and pots and kettles and jugs can stand at the same time. A great rush from the whole hut, also from the wing where the women live. [. . .]
Invasion by Turkish, Spanish, Rumanian, Italian and South American Jews from Amsterdam. All at once the hut has acquired a cosmopolitan character—the Turks and the Spaniards are like sparrows chattering away loudly and quickly in their respective languages, with plenty of rolled r's. They converse with the Dutch Jews either in Spanish, which they have held on to, or in French spoken with a strange accent. The noise has increased. If it is true that man is a product of circumstance, I would not be surprised if I came away from

here with four ears.

A small colony of Turks, parents and children, have settled close to my bed. They live all day long round the stove and, as they are so numerous, they monopolize it for their own use and take an active interest in the cooking operations of others. They are terribly kind and anxious to help. The children chatter in a mixture of Turkish and Dutch—lively, agile children, as bright as a button. Things have become terrible in the passage by my bed and in front of my bed. Whenever I come back I have to push my way through a bunch of people and ask them to make room for me. That is how people live here—hemmed in, barricaded.

Talking of my bed, there is still one other personal point. I am sleeping three tiers up and each time I have the same problem—how do I get up? There is no ladder or chair available. You have to clamber along the edges of the bedstead, sharp edges that dig into your hands. With dirty and sometimes muddy shoes you scrape along the mattresses and sheets and blankets of the people below. That is how people live here. You develop into a sort of ape-man. I sometimes think my arms are getting longer. [. . .]

The bedstead is of light metal and it always trembles and quivers like a ship vibrated by the screw. When the man below me coughs, my bed quivers like an aspen leaf in the wind, and when he turns over it seems to be dancing on the waves. When my neighbour on the right turns over, my bed quivers, and when my neighbour on the left turns over, it quivers. It is quivering all the time, so long as people are not completely at rest. But in the middle of the night there is always some bed creaking or groaning. The bed is the symbol of the camp—we are on a journey, a voyage on a creaking ship on a heaving ocean.

Tuesday November 9th: Visit to Schlesinger. Half of the plaster on his leg, the upper layer, has been removed. That half, sprinkled with short poems, dedications and signatures, is standing resplendent against the wall like a trophy. Schlesinger is proud of it. Reported on the interview with heer Eitje. The latter had himself been to see Schlesinger in the meantime. Schlesinger shares my view that there need be no objection to co-operation on tactical grounds and he invited me to co-operate with him. He evidently does not want to rebuff the members of

185

the Jewish Council. He might need them and is covering himself on more than one side. I feel this is like a comedy in which all the parties are making fools of one another [. .]

Wednesday November 10th: Evening visit to Korman of the Hut Inspection Bureau—a large gathering of Germans at the sick bed, including the head porter of the hospital, the Cerberus of Dr. Spanier, who was also present. Dr. Spanier was indignant about the undesirable contacts between nursing staff not working in the hospital huts which were under quarantine and the patients who were nursed there. Members of the staff perform various tasks and duties for the patients through the barbed wire. Dr. Spanier has given the order that all those who are caught in the act are to be deprived of their food cards for the hospital staff mess. Arising out of photographs in the German national periodical "Signal", there was a discussion as to whether the German charge that the Russians had shot Polish officers at Katyn was based on sound evidence or was merely intended as propaganda against the Bolshevists. Opinions were divided. After Dr. Spanier left, an animated discussion about the industrial future of the Soviet Union in relation to Germany.

Two cases of infantile paralysis, one in hut 64 and one in hut 62.

Untersturmführer Van Dam today made the punishment squad from the S-hut lie in the mud and then get up again because one of their number had not taken off his cap promptly enough. Great indignation in the camp.

Thursday November 11th: Case of infantile paralysis in hut 5. In hut 85 there are eighty people ill.

Friday November 12th: Untersturmführer Van Dam, driving to Hooghalen at night at 100 kilometres per hour in the *Obersturmführer's* blue car, ran into a tree. The car was reduced to a twisted mass of iron and tyres. Van Dam was admitted to the doctors' room in hut 1 with concussion and flesh wounds in the face. Gloating among the Jews because of his behaviour towards the S-men. The *Obersturmführer* was furious. [. . .]

Case of infantile paralysis in hospital hut 81B. Quarantine ordered.

In the past few days, owing to incessant rain, the camp has

become a great pool of mud through which one must literally wade. Anyone who has clogs goes about in clogs; anyone who has not, tries to get some at the store. [. . .] Life is becoming more trying, wetter and muddier.

Saturday November 13th: Suddenly the rumour has popped up that there is going to be another transport on Tuesday. Unfortunately it seems quite definite. The quarantine is just a farce, the only point of it being to hinder or obstruct contact between Jews and Aryans. A piece of wry National Socialist humour from *Oberstabsarzt* Mayer: 'Is it any wonder that the Jews fall ill when they live so close together?'

Sunday November 14th: The Palestine List has smashed. What people were afraid of months ago has finally come to pass. From Berlin a list has come with 395 names on it (from the First Veterans List). They are Jews whom Berlin finds suitable to be exchanged for German prisoners-of-war. These Jews, who have proper certificates, remain exempt for the time being. The rest, several hundred of them with their families, [. . .] have been released for deportation. The artistes from the revue and the members of the orchestra have also been made available for deportation. Great dismay.

For about a week the Camp Cards of all camp residents have been examined hut by hut by the Registration Department to see the type of stamp on them. Every resident considered suitable gets a special stamp classification. There are four main categories: the Blue Z (Z means deferment), the Green Z, the Basic List, and the so-called Fourth List. The Blue Z is for baptized Jews, foreign Jews or Jews of dual nationality, the Jews from the Calmeyer List (of Aryan origin; Portuguese), the Puttkammer Jews who have purchased the so-called 120,000 stamp with diamonds or have acquired this stamp through the German or Dutch authorities, the Jews from the Frederiks List (the so-called Barnevelders), under 800 of them, and partners from mixed marriages who have been divorced and have half-Aryan children. The Green Z is a so-called "work stamp" for persons without stamps who are employed in "vital" work sections (metal industry, shoemaking, clothing manufacture). The Basic List includes those who appear on the 1,000 List and because of services rendered to the camp are to be sent to Theresienstadt. On their Camp Cards the letters "ST" (for

"Stamlijst") are marked in red. Will they ever get there? The Fourth List consists of Jews whom the Germans acknowledge to be of economic value to Germany (about 450); they are Dutch or German Jews who had good trading contacts with foreign countries. They have special exemption from the Camp Commandant's Office. [. . .]

Monday November 15th: Inoculated against typhoid—the first injection, high up on my left arm.

Conversation with a woman in a bent position behind the bars of the prison through a broken window pane. 'How did you get in there?' 'I'm an Aryan, a doctor's wife. My husband is half-Aryan and he's at the Vught concentration camp. My son was in the Labour Service and spoke out rather strongly about it in a letter to my husband. They brought me here with my family out of spite. There was an argument when we arrived and the *Untersturmführer* said: "Your husband must certainly look like a Jew." To which I replied: "You look more like a Jew than he does." I got a smack from the *Untersturmführer*. And so I said: "You're a hero—you'll have to go to the eastern front." That is why I'm sitting here in this dreary hole. But they won't get me down.'

In the evening in the light of the cell you can see men moving about behind the bars in a bent position like baboons behind the bars of their cage at the zoo. Friends smuggle in bread and titbits and cigarettes through the broken panes, just as they would poke titbits through the bars to baboons.

Farewells between men and women, husbands and wives, sisters and brothers in the mud behind the S-hut. The men and women are going tomorrow on the S-transport to Poland. They are not allowed to receive any visitors on the eve of their journey and they are no longer allowed, with the connivance of the OD men on guard, wrapped in their long blue capes, to chat in front with their relatives and friends at the barrier or behind the barbed wire. So the final farewell is at the back, opposite the latrine, between two rows of barbed wire, with a no man's land three metres wide in between. On one side the indigo and scarlet prisoners, on the other the civilians with their feet firmly sucked into the mud, in the background a damp haze in the falling dusk.

Shouts criss-crossing from one barbed wire fence to the other. 'I'm definitely going tomorrow. I'm very upset about it.' 'Don't be so spineless now. You've always been brave, I know. Keep your chin up, lass.' 'Oh, would you just call out Daniel Belinfante for me. From the Post Office.' 'And get me Emil Cohn!' 'Belinfante and Cohn. I'll see if I can find them.' 'Have you heard anything from father?' 'Do you need anything?' 'Have you enough bread—and butter?' 'Are there any cigarettes still to be had? I haven't got any.' 'I can't hear you—it's the noise.' [. . .] 'Good-bye now, keep your chin up, we'll soon be seeing each other again. Good-bye, good-bye!' 'I'm stiff with cold.' 'How is mother getting on in the hospital? Give her my best wishes and tell her that I'll bear up. I'm not scared at all.' 'What is that you say? I can't understand you with all the noise.' [. . .] 'Is the train here yet?' 'No, but it will be coming tonight.' [. . .] 'Write a letter to your wife! I'll see to it that it gets through.' 'Damn it all, what a racket there is here!' 'Would you call out Klaartje de Beer for me!' [. . .] 'Ugh! How filthy it is! And cold!' 'Well, bye-bye and keep smiling. Don't be scared!' 'I can't hear a thing.' 'Now, Dan, be strong! You're a fine strapping fellow. Good-bye, we'll be meeting again soon. Good-bye!' [. . .]

Tuesday November 16th: Transport of over 1,000 persons. [. . .] There were many young men, hospital staff and patients. The quarantine proved to be no obstacle. On Monday morning it was lifted for the purpose. Parents who were dreading deportation and had children in hospital demanded to have them because they did not want to leave the children behind on their own. [. . .] There are still about 8,500 left. For how long? Just to make sure, Schlesinger has transferred me from the list for Theresienstadt to the one for partners from mixed marriages who, in principle, are not considered for deportation and so are not subject to scrutiny. [. . .]

At present the stove is being monopolized by the Turkish colony who settle round it from early in the morning till late at night. "Settle" is the right word for it. They are not to be pushed aside. The women do their bits of cooking on it or sit with their arms folded on chairs or benches they have managed to scrounge. The men stand among them with a cigarette between their lips and talk and talk and talk. At certain times these domesticated gipsies are surrounded by a circle of people wanting to cook meals, and round these people there is sometimes yet another circle, all with their pots and pans. Just think what disasters can occur when such a crowd gathers together. [. . .]

The Turkish colony remain unmoved by it all and there in the innermost circle go on living a life of contentment and domesticity—like cats in a basket. That is what happens evening after evening, always according to the same pattern.

I remember with nostalgia the ineffectual little stove with its niggardly contours, where life was not so sociable, but at the same time there was not the same rush of people.

Wednesday November 17th: Had a temperature yesterday evening from the typhoid inoculation. Went to bed early, about half past eight. 'Well now,' I thought, 'I'll just read a bit. So nice to be between the sheets!' It is not as nice as all that, however, because I lie under an air-shaft through which the wind comes rushing merrily when it feels like it. But I am keeping this bed as it stands close under a good electric globe which radiates a sea of light. What will a man not do for a good light in a hut which is mostly plunged in darkness! So I thought: 'I'll read for a bit.' I had got hold of a crazy book by Jules Romains, borrowed from a friend: "Les Copains", a grand piece of nonsense—a band of poets who freely indulge their spite against a few provincial towns which they have taken an aversion to on the map. The language and the style are delightful.

The hut was crammed full. Below me the twittering Turks talking incessantly. I thought to myself: 'I'll read through all that.' A little bit every hour. But I was making headway and managed to keep my mind on it.

In the corner behind the Administration table a woman suddenly began to laugh. "Laugh" is not the right word—she was screaming with laughter—long drawn out screams of laughter. A young fellow was making love to her in his own way, a little crudely, and she too was responding in her own way, a little boisterously, but so that everybody around was aware of it. People were polite and well-disposed and did not say anything. [. . .] So the screaming woman just went on rhythmically expressing her feelings for her lover. [. . .] Behind me on my left a row of children began to shriek and romp about like savages from the backwoods, raucous and inarticulate. I tried to read on without saying anything. What could one do about it? What can one do about anything?

The Turks have a right to converse. A young woman visited by her sweetheart has a right to scream with laughter as an outlet for her titillated emotions. She cannot do otherwise. And children will be children and must get rid of their surplus energy somehow or other—even though it is a bit late in the evening. If only I had not got a temperature. They could not know that I wanted to read a nice book just then, a book which was difficult into the bargain. This is not a clubroom after all. No, you could not exactly call it a clubroom. [. . .]

Celebration yesterday evening in the Moor Camp for the SS and the guards. Compensation for not being able to go home on leave owing to the quarantine. That, at any rate, was what the Commandant stated in his address. No toast to Hitler. Although his portrait was up there on the wall. The guards made no secret of their feelings. One guard to another (pointing to the portrait): 'There he hangs.' One to the other (pointing to fir branches on the tables): 'The flowers are there all ready.' The guards took the lead all evening with their favourite cowboy song. [. . .] They were busy playing cards. At ten o'clock the Commandant left, because he was bored, so they say.

Thursday November 18th: Announcement about mail. From now on we are no longer allowed to write letters to relatives or friends in Holland except on special forms on which the recipient must also write the reply (once every fortnight). Also, we are no longer permitted to send cards to confirm the receipt of parcels. [. . .] In future it will be possible to send correspondence to relatives in the labour camps by every transport train. How many transport trains will still be going?

The wife of a friend of mine came back into the hut from her work this afternoon with bare legs. Frozen. [. . .] A case containing clothes had been stolen from under her bed. From the Welfare Department she could not even get a pair of stockings to cover her legs. [. . .] Yesterday a woman cut up rough in the Welfare store because she could not get stockings either. 'It's all right if it's for the Germans!' Touché. It is a fact that the German Jews, the Long-Term Residents, through their good relations with the German heads of the Welfare Department, have been given preference as far as clothing and footwear are concerned. Now that winter has set in, many of the Long-Term Residents are going about dressed up to the

191

nines—good suits, lovely heavy overcoats, heavy water-tight shoes and boots—coming for the most part from the Welfare Department. [. . .]

But many people must be annoyed that the Dutch men and women who arrived with hardly any clothes on their bodies should in most cases have been sent on wearing only rags. You cannot help thinking about these men and women all the time. How do they manage in the icy cold of Poland without any proper equipment? Many letter cards have come in from Theresienstadt and Lublin from Jews who write to say that they are getting on well. These cards date from the month of July and have not been written according to a standard model. They are varied and often detailed, but strictly personal. There is nothing about their environment or their work activities.

Friday November 19th: Palestine, Palestine, Palestine. In the past few days we have heard nothing but 'Palestine' everywhere in the camp. Fräulein Slottke is preparing a transport for Celle, near Hanover, consisting of Jews who are on the Watik List, the list of the so-called "Veterans" who are to be exchanged for Germans. As a matter of fact, there are four waiting lists at the moment, drawn up at different times. Originally the transport was to have consisted of only 500 Jews, with the result that only the first two Watik Lists were recognized as being valid and the other two lists were declared to be null and void. Fräulein Slottke arranged for each person to have a note, saying that exemption for the purpose of the Palestine exchange had been cancelled, so they were to prepare themselves for going to Poland shortly. Great disappointment among the Palestine candidates who went around with sorrowful faces.

Suddenly an order came from Berlin—the transport had to number 1,000 persons. Fräulein Slottke whirled round like a leaf on a tree. She arranged for all the Palestine candidates to come and see her and any who could at all satisfy the registration or certificate requirements and any who could give adequate proof that they were of British nationality as well as Dutch were informed that they could go. [. . .] People are viewing the prospective exchange with great misgivings and think that Berlin, as has happened so often in the past, will not keep her word and has some cunning scheme in mind. Nevertheless there are many who are not worried about going to Celle and believe that there really will be an exchange. Nobody knows what form the exchange will take. There is only guessing. Palestine, Palestine, Palestine. That is the only word you hear, just like Auschwitz, Auschwitz, Auschwitz earlier on. Cynics who believe that people who have been allocated for exchange or have opted voluntarily for it will end up in Auschwitz nevertheless speak scornfully of the *"Austauschwitz"*— the "exchange joke". It sounds so very like Auschwitz.

Saturday November 20th: Great celebration held by a family of twenty persons, men, women and children, to mark the *bar mitzvah* of one of the boys. At the back of the room a banquet for the occasion at which all were assembled round rabbi Philip de Vries, from Haarlem. Choice pastries. A speech. Jewish songs. Impressive ceremonial. This whole family, all convinced Zionists, are going on Tuesday with the transport to Celle. They are delighted to be able to stay together and have an opportunity of going soon to Palestine, the Promised Land.

Jews who have come from Vught confirm that the other day a transport with a thousand men and women was sent straight on to the east. Men coming from the concentration camp were put on the train in their striped prison outfits without any further clothing to protect them. Only ten blankets were available for every sixty persons. In weather like this—it is bitterly cold already! Jews coming from Amsterdam told me that they had been kept for twenty-four hours in the *Hollandse Schouwburg* without food. [. . .]

Owing to the escape of two persons from the S-hut just before the last transport, the Commandant has arranged for the S-men to be deprived of their jackets, trousers and overcoats. They now wear their indigo and scarlet overalls over their vests and underpants in the cold and the rain. [. . .]

Sunday November 21st: There is a boom on the Palestine market. Many who had been sceptical to begin with about the call-up for the Palestine exchange almost seem to be wanting to go along on the transport next Tuesday to Celle, near Hanover. Fräulein Slottke has still not succeeded in making up a full list. Evidently as a result of this she has today sent for the holders of double options: Barneveld—Palestine, Protestant—Palestine, to give them the opportunity of choosing, in the hope, naturally, that they will choose Palestine. She has not applied any pressure, nor has she given any hint as to the relative value of the options. Those she summoned, except for one person who is a determined Zionist, have not chosen Palestine, because they think that Barneveld or Protestant will provide a better safeguard for the time being. Nevertheless the Barnevelders and the Protestants still do not know exactly where they stand. As far as the former are concerned, there is a rumour, supported by semi-official statements, that they will be considered as a Dutch Theresienstadt and will remain in Holland. As for the latter, they are clinging fast to the agreement between the Synod and the German authorities and the declaration made by those authorities that Protestants would not be sent away to the east.

The Barnevelders have been pretty much at loggerheads with one another as a result of the visit to Fräulein Slottke. The true Zionists among them have been criticized because, when they were given the chance to emigrate to Palestine, they did not take it, but clung desperately to their Barneveld exemption in order to remain in Holland. Those who had exemption because of a Palestine option, but were not Zionists —there are several of these, just as there are among baptized Jews who do not bother with religion—have been criticized because they had no right to an exemption based on Palestine. Sharp recriminations on both sides. [. . .]

Monday November 22nd: The 1,000 for the train to Celle have at last been scraped together by hook or by crook. Fräulein Slottke once more summoned the Barnevelders who had Palestine exchange papers and confronted them with the choice: Barneveld or Palestine. Only three Barnevelders opted for Palestine. [. . .] Those who were included so that the full train quota could be made up had the following note: "Because of an official decision you are being transferred to another camp on the transport leaving tomorrow."

In the camp people are saying it is a swindle. But those who have good Palestine papers are walking on air. The train arrived this morning, a train with good, clean third-class carriages, with seats and proper carriage doors and windows that can be pulled open. Such a thing has not been seen at the camp for months—real passenger coaches, for Jews, as if they are going on a pleasure trip. There can be no further doubt.

The Germans are acting in good faith as far as the Palestine exchange is concerned. 'There you are,' say the Zionists, 'a third-class train. We can take our baggage with us and we can take two hundred and fifty guilders. We're not going to Auschwitz, we're going to Celle. Perhaps we'll even be given Red Cross parcels there.' The Palestine folk are living in a state of intoxication and are almost falling on one another's necks for joy. Haven't bags of apples been loaded on the train, and cake and cigars and cigarettes? There are definitely apples—I saw them being loaded myself. Cigars and cigarettes? Well, you must leave some scope for the imagination. 'You see! We're going—at last!'

Others who have not been put down for Celle, but have to stay on here awaiting an uncertain future are envious and wide-eyed with amazement. They would like to go too—in such a beautiful third-class train! One should go just for the fun of it. The sceptics shake their heads at the sight of so much shallowness and frivolity. You can never trust the Germans, can you? It's like this today, but tomorrow. . . . Go easy!

The check on postal packages and registered parcels sent by letter post has been intensified. From now on, they will be opened before they are sent on to the huts and will be searched by officials of the Camp Commandant's Office for money and luxury goods. There goes our tobacco, there go our cigarettes! The only luxury that we have ever enjoyed! [. . .]

Tuesday November 23rd: Great consternation during the night. At half past twelve men from the OD, "by order of the Commandant", so they declared, collected from all the huts the passports of foreigners and Jews with dual nationality. Strange that it should happen just when the train is standing ready to carry away Jews with dual nationality! At half past five it was announced that the transport was not leaving and everyone was asked to go to work as usual. [. . .]

People were simply speechless with amazement. Just fancy that! Such a thing had never happened before. Those marked down for Palestine were bitterly disappointed. People wondered what the reason could be. The continual cases of infantile paralysis? The heavy bombing of Berlin? One could only hazard a guess. In the course of the morning, the foreigners got their passports back, but many who could claim dual nationality did not, for example, British and American women,

195

married to Dutchmen or Germans.

A sensation. A new exchange list is coming, for South America. [. . .] It is understood that they intend to exchange 10,000 Jews in Europe for 10,000 Germans in Brazil; these would include 1,000 Dutch Jews. People who have been put on the list must pay down a hundred guilders. They are to leave for South America via Portugal.

The story of Fräulein Slottke's efforts in connection with the Celle transport had a funny ending. She instructed a Jewish orderly to take away a petticoat and have it ironed. Things like that *can* happen. Even in the most critical situations a woman remains a woman. The orderly just left the petticoat lying somewhere on the way and later could not remember where. Fräulein Slottke urgently needed the petticoat and had an announcement made in all the huts that she had lost the garment in question and asked for it to be returned to her speedily Riotous merriment in the camp. An Aryan petticoat had actually gone astray among the Jews! It turned up in hut 65. In the spinsters' house, of all places, the residence for single women. Quite amazing in a camp where things hardly ever turn up again. Fräulein Slottke was overjoyed and merciful—a true woman! She did not send the orderly to the S-hut. What a bit of luck for the orderly! Many a Jew has been put on the S-transport for more trivial offences than that. People are still talking about Fräulein Slottke's petticoat, not always too respectfully. It will certainly occupy an important place in history.

Late this evening the train departed empty for its place of origin. The camp residents feel triumphant (with the exception perhaps of the Palestine people). A train has gone away without any Jews on it! How can that be possible?

Wednesday November 24th: A howling gale from the south-west with lashing rain. The camp is flooded. Mud, nothing but mud. [. . .] Filth everywhere. The few tiled roadways have sunk below the sea of mud which has accumulated all round. Anyone who has no rubber boots or clogs or overshoes is utterly wretched and suffers twice over from the filth of the camp.

The forty-eighth case of infantile paralysis has occurred. Nearly all the cases have turned out to be slight.

Weinreb has departed for The Hague with his wife and children. Asscher and Professor Cohen are getting a small house which they are moving into. A small privilege due to men of note who have done so much for the Jews. Small hearts have small desires.

Young girls and women have been put to work on the road roller which they pull along by their combined efforts. People cry shame on Samson, the so-called "Minister of Labour", who gave the order for this. Samson has had his bust fashioned by the sculptor Wertheim. It shows him smiling with self-satisfaction, the head of a little man with nothing in it. Fried, one of the departmental heads, has also applied to be done. An opportunity like this of having yourself immortalized by a clever sculptor free of charge only comes once in a lifetime. The sculptor apparently has nothing better to do with his time here. [. . .]

Friday November 26th : Many hundreds of British or American, or British and American 'planes have flown over the camp a few thousand metres up, some in an easterly direction and the others in a westerly direction. The whole camp was in a turmoil and absolutely delighted. Everyone who was fit rushed out to the edge of the camp. Berlin had just been bombed for the third time in a week, by night. People had listened at night to the heavy roar of the aircraft. They had flown over in waves. We lay in our beds as if we were listening to a beautiful concert. 'Oh, it's like music! Do you hear that? Music in my ears!' So we had music in the midst of the moor of Drente and a strong and vital contact with the life outside. No British or American aircrew will drop their load of bombs here. They know that this group of huts is occupied by Jews, the prisoners of the Germans, people stripped of their possessions. And now for the first time hundreds and hundreds of 'planes were flying over the camp in succession by day, in an almost clear sky. A formation went over not long ago, but it was mostly hidden by the grey clouds. Like shoals of fierce pike in the translucent water of a brook they rushed through that other element—air. Narrow, slender white bodies, the engine with a vapour trail, formations of thirty or nearly forty, positioned behind the leader. What a sight, what a miracle of form and speed! What a deep roaring through the ether! Music, music! Macabre music, a death march, but music nevertheless! Music for feverish, overheated minds, a soothing melody for tortured and tormented hearts. One 'plane crashed. The occupants reached

197

the ground by parachute.

An order has been issued, saying that all camp residents must hand in passports, identity cards and other papers revealing their nationality to the authorities. [. . .]

Up to this point everyone in the camp has been allowed to keep all the documents he brought with him. Anyone who shows reluctance and does not hand in the documents asked for is threatened with preventive detention, which means the concentration camp. Nobody knows what lies behind this, but it is thought that the purpose of this measure is simply to rob the Jews of their identity papers and make do with the Camp Card on which only name and date of birth appear and not nationality. Do they intend to make the Jews here stateless, in anticipation of their despatch to the east? The Jews are naturally not keen to relinquish their passports and other proofs of identity and so hand themselves over body and soul to their oppressors.

There is an order that children under twelve years of age must be in bed by eight o'clock in the evening. So far they have stayed up till ten o'clock and often made a deafening racket as they played about.

Bought two cauliflowers and some tomatoes from the greengrocer who visits the camp every week to deliver a large consignment of vegetables to the Central Kitchen. Long-Term Residents in particular take advantage of this opportunity to provide themselves with illicit vegetables and fruit from the greengrocer. They sometimes besiege his lorry in droves. [. . .]

Saturday November 27th: Ten airmen came down yesterday by parachute on the Drente moor near Westerbork, all Americans. They were brought into Westerbork Camp. One turned out to be seriously injured and had to have an arm amputated. The arm was broken in three places. The crew of the 'plane had decided to land to save the life of their wounded comrade. A second volunteered to donate blood for him. All the Americans had copper discs on their chests indicating the blood group to which they belonged. They were dressed in electrically heated overalls. The uninjured young Americans were taken elsewhere to be interned. The other two were admitted to one of the rooms at the Camp Commandant's Office. The camp is taking a lively interest in the wounded man and has woven all kinds of romantic phantasies around him. While men are

198

falling at the front like flies and towns are being flattened by bombing, the only person who exists in the eyes of the camp at the present time is the wounded young American, the hero of the day. [. . .]

A transport of fourteen persons has arrived from the concentration camp at Amersfoort, wearing only pyjamas and without stockings, severely undernourished. They had been five to six months at Amersfoort. From what they said, there are still a number of Jews who cannot be moved for the present. Five died during their time there. A total of about sixty persons has arrived from the prison at Scheveningen and from The Hague.

The marriage room has been done away with. Two days ago a young couple who had just got married wanted to apply for it, but their request was refused. The huts or a place behind the huts in the darkness is good enough for a Jewish honeymoon. Indeed it is an outdated institution since German officers and soldiers began having "war brides" who know nothing of the state of matrimony and who therefore have no honeymoon. There are always the Long-Term Residents who live in little houses and will oblige newly married couples. But this goes together with coarseness and crudity.

It has been officially announced that a thousand Jews can apply for the Weinreb List for transport to Portugal or Morocco. Being put on the provisional list does not mean exemption. The final list will not be drawn up till later. The deposit fee is one hundred guilders per person. [. . .]

This morning no stove was lighted as a punishment because yesterday and the day before nobody volunteered to fetch peat.

Sunday November 28th: All day long a grey leaden sky with exasperating rain streaming from it. The camp is one mass of mud, black, black, black all over. [. . .]

A quarrel going on round my stove between the Turkish colony and the Dutch Jews. The Turks monopolize the stove. [. . .] They are popularly called the Dardanelles—through which nobody can pass because they are hermetically sealed.

I spent a great part of the day and evening in excellent company in the waiting room outside Schlesinger's office—rest and warmth from the central heating. We had it all to ourselves. Looking out at the streaming rain and the mud and the grey-black huts, but thankful to be away from the oppressive atmosphere, the noise of the human monkey-house, out of the squabbling, the stench, the feeling of being packed together, the crowd, the jostling, the congestion, and to be able to carry on conversations that were not sawn up into a thousand pieces, with only the memory that I was trying to say something lingering on in my mind.

In the evening I went thankfully and contentedly to bed, rested by the restful atmosphere I had been in. Underneath me people were going on about the curse of a free Sunday when your only refuge is the stinking, steaming, growling and grumbling hut. A man grows selfish here. I jealously kept my mouth shut about my hiding-place, fearing that people would go there next Sunday and then my self-created privilege would be no more. Man is like that. He needs to withdraw from the filth and nastiness, from the chattering and the ravings of the masses.

Tuesday November 30th: Everyone in the camp has a cold. Everyone is coughing, wheezing, sneezing, young and old, large and small, and everyone is swallowing tablets and powders. The wet and the damp, the draught rushing through all the doors that are forever being opened or slammed and stealing through 'crevices, the chill given off by the wooden walls—all this is making people ill. There are sore throats, influenza and colds galore in all the huts. Everyone is shivering and snivelling. The people look grey and pallid in their wretchedness. They ask one another: 'When will all this misery end?' They complain: 'We can't stand it any longer!' The small children are going about with swollen, running noses and pale lustreless eyes. Women wear themselves out, dividing up their time between their jobs in the metal or textile industry or some other work section and their meagre housekeeping and attending to their ailing husbands and children. In the hospital huts patients come and go. In the living huts slightly sick folk lie in rows. Along the roads OD men come and go, carrying stretchers with patients. It certainly seems like a hospital camp where the fit are only there to visit their sick relatives.

Weinreb is the favourite. Applications for his list come streaming in. The majority want to go to Portugal, or at a pinch to Morocco or Brazil. [. . .] Prudent folk ask themselves: 'What part is Weinreb playing in all this? What is his list worth?' [. . .] What a running and a trotting about, with everyone asking everyone else and no one knowing. Not even Weinreb. He says: 'It is a good type of exemption as long as the list lasts. But you must be careful not to lose any other good exemption you have, so that you can use it if and when my own list fails to come off.' So he himself is apparently not convinced that the scheme may not be based on phantasy after all. [. . .] He is a terribly unassuming fellow, the gauche scholarly type, naive. [. . .]

Wednesday December 1st: The *Obersturmführer* is indignant. Careless people have spread about a story that the SS steal from the parcels they search. Yesterday evening an announcement was made in the huts that he felt insulted to the depths of his being and that, unless the rumours ceased, he would have the scandalmongers unearthed and punished—sent on the S-transport. [. . .]

An order from the *Obersturmführer* obliging camp inmates to bathe, i.e., to make regular use of the shower facilities. The *Ostu* can give what orders he likes. Anyone who does not want to bathe will simply not do so. [. . .]

A heavy blow has fallen upon us. The Commandant has laid down that, as from December 15th, men and women who are on their own can only receive a parcel of foodstuffs of not more than two kg once every six weeks, families with not more than two children one parcel every four weeks, and families with more than two children a parcel every fortnight, but only from Jewish relatives or from relatives who are partners in mixed marriages. Berlin has ordered this restriction on foodstuffs. In a German newspaper it was pointed out that the Jews at Westerbork lived far better than the German population. [. . .] Many have sent letters secretly out of the camp, urging their relatives and friends to send as many parcels of two kg. as possible before December 15th. Camp residents are secretly buying as much butter as their financial resources will permit. [. . .] Tobacco is getting scarce. [. . .] People who have tobacco are looked upon as rich men, as "plutocrats". The hut leaders still go on smoking hard. They have their own secret sources of supply. Yesterday I myself received a parcel with cigarettes and a letter enclosed. It had evidently eluded the censor.

Had an interview with Mr. Proosdij who had come from The

201

Hague in connection with the Aryanization of a number of Jews. A friendly interview. He advised me to apply to Mr. Kotting in Amsterdam for Aryanization. At once wrote a secret letter to investigate the possibilities. Several Jews have already left the camp, as Aryans. I took a look at myself with this in mind. My nose is not all that curved, I have thin lips and my name can easily pass for that of an Aryan. Why should I not have a try and see if I can leave this squalid place and go about once more as a free man. Relatively speaking. There is no disgrace about passing oneself off as an Aryan, although it is not pleasant to accept a gift from the hands of the oppressor. The main thing is to get out of his clutches.

Have got a new job—sorting foil. [. . .] My "special mission" has got rather bogged down, as, in actual fact, nobody knows exactly what can or should be done when the war ends. It does look now as if I shall have to do foil-picking after all, i.e., take silver paper off condensers from stolen Philips wireless sets. Six hours per day.

I started with two days "off duty" owing to a "painful reaction" to the typhoid inoculation in my arm. A piece of good luck—splendid walking weather. It had frozen hard in the night and the young fir trees and the barbed wire were covered with hoar frost, so that the barbs looked like knobs. A fine empty winter landscape. The barbed wire seemed like a system of rough cords stretched round the camp. A softer system than the rusty iron wire from which the barbs stick up like spikes. The sugar-coated fir trees sparkled in the sun.

It is healthier to stride along the barbed wire and go in and out among the fir trees than to go and pick foil in a hut—for the German *Wehrmacht*, nota bene. I do not feel enthusiastic about it—I am no part of the German *Reich*. But on Monday there will be no help for it because of my call-up note.

Letter despatched to Amsterdam by courier regarding Aryanization.

Yesterday evening a transport from Amsterdam—54 healthy people, nearly all of whom had been in hiding, and fourteen mentally sick people from Den Dolder, nine men and five women. To begin with, the insane were locked up in the same prison cells at the *Weteringschans* as the healthy prisoners. Only after a protest from a member of the prison staff were they placed in separate cells. They have been admitted to hospital here and put among the ordinary patients. A scene of misery and wretchedness.

Thursday December 2nd: Aus der Fünten shooting hares and partridges. OD men as beaters.

Fräulein Slottke [. . .] has arrived. She has summoned the holders of Palestine exchange stamps who have a second stamp as well, in order to make them choose one of their two stamps. The great majority have chosen Palestine. A call to the applicants for the Weinreb List to enrol on Friday and Saturday next. Otherwise they will find the door closed.

Friday December 3rd: [. . .]

Spoke to Schlesinger about the Weinreb List. In his opinion there is nothing to be lost by appearing on it. The only thing one should do here is try to spin things out and the Weinreb List gives one a fine opportunity of doing so. I have decided to put myself down for it. [. . .]

Two men complained to each other this morning beside the stove about how wretched they felt for want of bread. When I called out to say that I could probably let them have some bread, they pounced on my bed like pirates boarding a ship. They asked to come another time.

Sunday December 5th: In all the huts in the camp the festival of Santa Claus has been celebrated in a lively fashion. This morning I found a parcel with a big M on it at the head of my bed. It contained marzipan sprinkled with chocolate, together with a poem and an affectionate letter from the best woman-friend I have. A moving token of affection. [. . .]

Every child got a small present. Mere trifles, often home-made articles. But it really was Santa Claus, Santa Claus as of old. In my hut an apple was stolen from a shoe that a little chap had put out ready for Santa Claus, and from another child a little scarf with animal figures embroidered on it.

Tuesday December 7th: Have been thirteen months in the camp today.

Yesterday picked foil for the first time in hut 57—silver paper pressed hydraulically on to paper impregnated with paraffin wax. A soft job, or rather a greasy one, as your hands become covered in grease from the paraffin wax. Eighty men on one side and more than a hundred women on the other.

Camp Cards handed in as a guarantee against scrimshanking. Six hours' work, from one till seven. Typical convict labour. Much talk in the midst of it all—about the war, Zionism, Russia, Judaism. About six o'clock a general state of fatigue from the work; people grouping round the stove which was at its last gasp. The supervisors turned a blind eye. Evening prayer by the devout Jews in a corner of the hut.

Was today appointed as a foil-picking supervisor. I let the responsibility for the appointment fall squarely on the work leader. I said that I felt I was not competent for the post, I was not cut out to be a slave-driver. The boss set my mind at rest. It was only a temporary post. He had something better for me in mind, in keeping with my abilities. I felt highly flattered. Just wait and see! My first day as supervisor was spent in discussions at the different tables about Russia. I have the reputation of being an authority on Russia. Nearly all the Jews had read my articles about Russia in the "*Algemeen Handelsblad*". If it had not been for these discussions I would have been bored to death. [. . .]

Wednesday December 8th: Great preparations for Christmas in hut 73. Christmas wreaths are being hung up and a choir is rehearsing Christmas carols. The period of frost is over once more. Westerbork is again a sea of mud. [. . .]

The wife of a friend of mine has discovered quite by chance that her sister's two small children are living in the orphanage. The children had been in hiding. The parents still are. The children had been in the orphanage for four weeks. Apparently on instructions from their parents they refused to give their names. When they were spoken to by their aunt, and she asked them to say what their names were, they gave their first names; they had forgotten their surname. It just so happened that they had not been sent on to the east.

Debate about Palestine in Korman's house. It has been arranged that I shall give a talk on the subject next Wednesday.

Thursday December 9th: A search of the small huts occupied by the Long-Term Residents who were caught smuggling goods into the camp. Amongst the belongings of one of them a large sum in American dollars was found. One of the hut leaders who was sympathetic about his arrest sighed: 'What a pity!

He was one of the people I could get little extras from.' Large slices of meat and full jugs of milk used to appear regularly on his table. That is over and done with for the time being.

A transport of sixty persons from Scheveningen in goods wagons, mostly people who had been in hiding. Transport of twenty people from Rotterdam, the last members of the Jewish Council.

A final decision on the part of the German authorities that Westerbork should continue to be a labour camp. As time goes on, more and more Jews are being transferred to the metal section, mainly for sorting foil and taking out batteries. Work in shifts—one shift from seven till one, the other from one till seven in the evening.

Friday December 10th: [. . .] The newspaper accounts of the bombing are being read avidly. They pass from hand to hand. Great satisfaction among the Jews—the Germans are now experiencing what they inflicted on others. The words of Hitler are repeated scornfully: 'We will wipe out the English cities!' [. . .] There is a general fear that the war will go on for a long time, too long for the Jews. People nearly always look at the events of the war in relation to the fate of the Jews. The transports have been provisionally suspended till the middle of January. [. . .]

Around six o'clock a general disinclination for work is evident among the foil-sorters. Men and women leave the tables and gather round the stoves or stay talking at the tables. This afternoon there was community singing—Jewish songs, songs from the Westerbork revue. High spirits. Leaders and supervisors powerless and unable to deal with this. In their hearts they care just as little about the work as the "workers", who include professors, lawyers and other intellectuals. I myself have been writing my diary and have read a bit of "*Les Copains*" by Jules Romains, which I am trying to finish. Order from the Commandant forbidding the holding of prayer meetings during working hours.

Saturday December 11th: Trottel called me to one side: 'I've saved four more Dutchmen. They're holders of the 120,000 stamp.' He showed me a letter from Mr. Mendels, requesting that these four men, ex-lawyers who had obtained an exemption from the German authorities through the kind offices of the dean of advocates, should be kept at Westerbork as long as possible. [. . .] Trottel got Schlesinger interested in the ex-lawyers. With a wink: 'You see, I have an interest too in keeping them here for the future.' Sly old dog. He is stateless and does not know what will become of him at the end of the war. Do any of us know that? But everyone is playing his own little game here—each clings fast to the other, out of fear, with the idea of being dependent, with hope for the future. Strong people who were once lions have become docile and timorous sheep here. [. . .]

General complaint that the parcels are coming back looted from the censor. Bread, butter, cigarettes are missing. I myself have no cause for complaint. I received six parcels this week, all of them opened, but not rifled. [. . .]

The shortage of bread is getting greater. A doctor yesterday asked friends of mine for crusts of bread for his wife who is working as a nurse at the hospital and can hardly keep going.

In clogs today for the first time—a bother to walk in, but beautifully dry, warm feet. It brings back the concentration camp at Amersfoort.

Sunday December 12th: Bitterly cold. I am still lying under an open air-shaft with the wind blowing through it, an east wind. Right through my blankets; I have three. First I was told: 'The hole will be closed up in a few days.' Afterwards: 'There's no covering material available.' Yesterday: 'The building consultant has definitely refused to have it done.' Result— permanent ventilation. When I am dressing, I am nearly blown away, and when I am undressing too. [. . .]

A mother asked her eight-year-old son: 'Hans, what would you like best of all when we're back home again and Daddy is back?' (Daddy is in hiding.) Hans: 'Mummy, I'd like to sleep for a whole day and then for another day and not see any people for a long time.' That is how many adults feel here.

A nine-year-old girl [. . .] went on a visit to a young professor's wife in a small house, a sort of little gingerbread house, of which you find a row here and there, colourless, faded looking and silent. You have to twist and wriggle to get inside. In the large huts people pour in and stream out in the maelstrom. The girl looked round bashfully: 'Do you know what's so wonderful about this place? The quiet. In the huts there's always such a noise. And you've got chairs here. Oh, and you've got real china cups too. It's lovely.' The lady of the house told us the story and said: 'Those poor mites get worn down in the large huts among the grown-ups and don't know what quiet is. They have no place of their own and just run wild.' [. . .]

A commotion yesterday evening—at the roll-call two young men were missing by name: the food server in the kitchen and a member of the Flying Column. A rotten business! The room leader was beside himself and went about cursing. An icy silence among the residents. We'll see how it all turns out.

At half past twelve heavy footsteps and the lights were turned on, hurting the sleepy eyes of the inmates wakened from their sleep. The woman room leader cried out hysterically: 'Wake up, all of you!' The hut leader thundered: 'Wake up, all of you! I have a very unpleasant announcement to make. Van Dam says that he suspects there are two men who know something more about the affair. If they report to his private quarters by ten o'clock tomorrow morning, they will be let off without punishment. Otherwise they will go on the S-transport. And twenty-five men from this room and ten members of the Flying Column as well.' Consternation. The lights stayed on. The men went to sleep again.

This morning pandemonium. Everyone chattering and talking and shouting out his views on the incident. A roaring noise filled the hut and hung like a dense fog over and between the beds. [. . .] After ten o'clock two OD men appeared and a resident who was a friend of one of the men who had escaped was arrested and transferred to the prison in hut 51. [. . .] The whole camp is in confusion. All the huts know about the incident—the news has spread like wildfire. It is Sunday and everyone is at home.

Around noon an order from Van Dam, the acting Commandant: 'All men present must line up on the parade ground.' Punishment drill: lying down and standing up under the command of Zimmern of the OD—pretty tame stuff. I missed the punishment exercises. I had had a premonition of it and left the hut in time, like several others. I shut myself up in Schlesinger's waiting room—peaceful and silent. [. . .] After two hours the men came back in excellent spirits from the drill field—it was all humbug. [. . .]

In several huts there are still swarms of flies about and it is the middle of December. A doctor gave me the following advice: 'Kill them! Every winter fly is equal to two million summer flies.' I have definitely killed fifteen today. [. . .]

Four marriage announcements put up—girls of nineteen and twenty and the men getting on for thirty, also a lad of nineteen and a girl of eighteen. Westerbork marriages, for the sake of Celle—exemption marriages.

This evening had a meal in Schlesinger's waiting room, bread and butter in my hand—peaceful and silent. The silence is audible—it hums like music in my ears, like the rustling murmur of a gentle gas flame. The noise in the hut sounds to me like the thundering of a train in a tunnel. Silence outside—not a footstep, not a breath of wind, not a sigh, not a rustle. I am in the middle of the moor, the bare, empty moor. [. . .]

Monday December 13th: Yesterday evening there was a repetition of the punishment drill. About ten o'clock Zimmern came to announce it with four OD men, Long-Term Residents in long dark blue capes and imitation police caps. The men had to line up outside. Marching by the side of hut 71 on the freezing ground under an overcast sky with the light of the moon shining through, under the command of Zimmern and supervised by Van Dam, surrounded by his OD men, like walkers-on with no lines to say. Zimmern with his little finger on the seam of his trousers and his head bare had already announced: 'One hundred and seventy-one men from hut 71 line up!' Van Dam ordered that men over sixty and those who were on night duty were to come to the front and they were sent home. An act of mercy—towards Jews! 'In step, quick march!' 'Left turn!' In response to these two commands a merry march by fantastically attired men in the gloaming, without variety, without bullying, without abuse, without any lying down or standing up. How was it possible? On the dot of half past ten back home with a threat uttered by Van Dam in his childish little voice: 'As long as nobody comes forward with information about the men who have escaped, this will take place every evening.' Nobody was impressed by this feeble threat. On the contrary, they found, for the moment at least, that it was an excellent thing to go for a walk like this before turning in. People felt that Van Dam had gone rather too far with his threat to send twenty-five men from the hut to the S-hut without having the necessary authority to do so, and that now he wanted to save his face by ordering punishment drill. But only for half an hour and such tame stuff! It was ridiculous, verging on imbecility.

In the meantime, yesterday afternoon, a member of the hut Administration reported to Van Dam that one of the two fugitives had come to ask him for a loan of a hundred guilders, but the man did not know what this was for. A stupid thing to do. If you say anything, you have to answer for it. Result—the administrator went into quod, taking the place of the escaped man's friend. That is what our overlords are like. They promise that no punishment will be meted out, but, when they have to redeem their promise, they break faith. We shall see later whether the arrested man is to be punished, but to imprison him after he made his statement was, in any case, a beastly thing to do.

Tuesday December 14th: Yesterday evening punishment drill again for half an hour. During the roll-call another appeal from the acting Commandant: 'Has anyone got anything to say about the two men who cleared out—*die zwei Leute, die getürmt sind?*' An icy silence in the three lines of men out in the open air. You could have heard a pin drop. The acting Commandant stood there with his OD men, embarrassed by the silence. Almost scared. 'Then we shall go on till someone does come forward. Otherwise the whole hut will be deported!' A voice like a flickering candle, faint and anaemic. The voice of the virile and warlike German people. The old men had to step out and go back home. 'In step, quick march!' 'Left turn!' 'Straight ahead!' Amid sniggers drowned by the noise of marching feet and masked by the darkness, we did our square-bashing. Nursery gymnastics. [. . .] The party of men began to bob up and down and jostle one another. I played at tag with the man in front of me. [. . .] The acting Commandant let his pocket torch play over the faces of his Jews. He stopped in front of a young fellow. 'How old are you?' 'Seventeen.' 'Go on, off to bed, and look sharp!' What a heart of gold! Touching sentimentality. The boy stammered in confusion: 'Good night, sir,' and ran off home like a hare. [. . .] 'Hands up! Knees bend! Anyone who doesn't do it will be shot straight away.' 'Knees bend! Up! Down! Up!' We went round nearly ten times. The men with their half-bent arms above their heads or with their hands pulled back on to their shoulders and their hind-quarters sticking out looked in the half-light like rabbits or kangaroos preparing to jump. A fantastic sight, all those rabbits and kangaroos in a row on the moor. [. . .]

Two Dutch Jews have been dismissed from their posts as officials at the hut Post Office. Two Germans have been appointed in their place. The Dutchmen have been put down for foil-picking. They were excellent Post Office officials, hardworking, helpful, honest. [. . .]

Was given a mild ticking-off at my job. The controller, a young German with hard steel-blue eyes and a jockey cap on his fair curly hair, asked: 'How is the work going here?' 'Very well.' 'Are the people willing?' 'Very willing.' 'Last week production was very low. I am the controller and the blame falls on my head.' 'I see.' 'You must make sure that people work here. Production must be kept up to standard. You are responsible for that. If things do not go right, you will lose your job.' I looked mockingly into his cold eyes and said: 'I see.' The controller disappeared with an air as if to say: 'I have told him straight.' [. . .]

A birthday visit to hut 84 where the elderly live. Took with me as a birthday present a little branch of catkins picked by me from a tree in the camp. Others had taken as gifts a pair of shoe laces, a little jar of Nivea, a nailbrush, a packet of toilet paper, pieces of chocolate or sweets. Was treated to a slice of apple tart.

Wednesday December 15th: Yesterday evening the last punishment drill took place. The high-ups did not themselves put in an appearance and left it to Pisk, the man sketched in charcoal and like a creation of Walt Disney, the supreme head of the OD, and a few of his assistants. Gemmeker the *Obersturmführer* is back. He apparently cannot be bothered with all the fuss made by Van Dam. It is a generally known fact that he does not like Van Dam. Pisk acted as if he held our fate in his hands: 'If you march well, it is very likely that this will be the last time.' We saw through his pomposity at once. What power! A kind of snort went through our ranks. On no evening had we ever marched so rebelliously before. Like naughty, high-spirited boys we went bobbing up and down and jostling one another, in time certainly, but bobbing about nevertheless. [. . .]

Waylaid by a hut leader who was busy collecting cigarettes for the man who is locked up in prison and is suspected of knowing about the escape. Sympathetic souls dipped into their

210

pockets, but the *communis opinio* was that he deserved to be imprisoned. 'He shouldn't have been so stupid as to open his mouth.' All at once a row flared up. [. . .] Absolute silence among the bystanders who evidently had no opinion on this delicate subject. The row quietened down—the hut leader no longer had the courage to go on begging cigarettes for his friend. He gave them back to the donors. Like conquerors who had just beaten off a large-scale attack we clambered up into our beds.

All the occupants of hut 71 were examined for clothes lice at the Quarantine Station. Like ducks one behind the other. Outside in the passage we stripped to the waist. Inside the room examination of the hair on our heads with a magnifying glass, also our shirts and pubic hair. The findings were negative; everything in order. [. . .]

Start of the chess contest. Thirty taking part. Gave a lecture on Palestine in Korman's house.

Thursday December 16th: For three days I have been arriving half an hour late for the foil-picking. I just cannot manage to crawl out of my bed at a quarter past six—overtired. I have not had any ticking-off. The room boss is a decent man who allows for the fact that I am "in a senior position": a supervisor. The silver paper annoys me. It lies in long streamers along the tables, crawling like snakes and glinting in the artificial light till my eyes sting and I have to blink them.

A woman has been appointed as deputy leader—from a prosperous background. She wears a magnificent woollen jerkin with matching slacks, clogs and a coloured scarf. She certainly does wear the trousers. A hard face. She commands operations like the captain of a ship and acts as if the work section were her very own. The men frown and the women screw up their noses. She does not find me a good supervisor. I am too half-hearted and have no enthusiasm for my work. [. . .]

Towards the end of the working period: 'Supervisor, why have you not collected the knives?' 'You must ask the room leader and he'll sort the matter out with you.' Madam swept off to see the room leader. A moment later she shouted across the room: 'Supervisor, collect the knives!' 'Very well, madam.' I raised my hat. 'But I hope you will adopt a different tone in future. It won't do. I'm not your slave.' Madam looked at me in extreme amazement. Her lips opened, but she said not a word. What was going on in that hard brain?

The men and women sang again today. [. . .] One of them, an ordinary working-class woman, gave an imitation of Heintje Davids in a series of comic songs about Westerbork and Vught. [. . .] A full-scale cabaret. In the meantime the women had fashioned a complete dinner-set out of silver paper and, while the room boss was absent for a moment, they deposited it on his table. The work is utterly dreary and the women are full of life. They say: 'Anyone who has worked here for a day can safely be admitted to any prison or penal institution.' At all the tables there is a lively discussion about politics.

In hut 73 (where the baptized people are) women sleep under umbrellas to protect them from the condensation water dripping down from the roof.

Had news from Amsterdam that Mr. Proosdij is to be dealing with my case. Had an interview with him here today. He does not find my case a very easy one, but he will see that it is attended to promptly. [. . .]

Friday December 17th: A number of women who had been working for a few days at the Moor Camp, Long-Term Residents, have been given a punishment—cleaning out WC's in the camp. They made the beds of the SS men with gloves on. That could not be allowed; that was not right and proper for Jewesses. [. . .]

The Long-Term Residents generally carry on a barter trade in goods they have scrounged. Anyone who wants a nice coat goes to a tailor from the Club, who works for a few hours a day in the tailoring section, but works for a great part of the day in his own little house on his own account with material, the origin of which should not be too closely investigated. If the tailor wants to indulge in a pair of jackboots, he goes to the shoemaker who works on the same basis. So they can pay each other without opening their purses. They can pay with foodstuffs coming from the black market which carry a profit. There is a lively traffic in money between the Long-Term Residents, much of it based on the black market. This traffic got a knock the other day with the arrest of a couple of black marketeers who regularly supplied meat and dairy products, poultry and tobacco from outside. This certainly does not mean that these activities have stopped. Many a woman has a business of her own, e.g., an illicit ironing business, where for exorbitant prices she does the personal laundry of persons of the highest rank in the camp who can afford an extortionate price, the wives of the camp dignitaries. They represent the high society of the camp. They know all the mysterious ins and outs. Just as the men turn out in smart coats, good suits and sturdy gleaming jackboots, the women appear in well-fitting coats of good quality.

A number of these "parasitic" wives were sent to the Moor Camp to replace the previous team. They were furious. For some of them this meant that a part of their livelihood had gone. A tremendous upheaval in the lives of the Long-Term Residents. And now some of these women have to clean WC's in the camp as a punishment. The status of the Long-Term Residents has been lowered and undermined. [. . .]

Another regulation is aimed at "work-shy" women. [. . .] Women stay away from work on the slightest and most trivial pretext and get a note from the doctor exempting them from their duties. Understandable. A large proportion of them have never worked in the true sense of the word and the work does not suit them or seems pointless. Also many do not have the strength needed for the work and they are bowed down with worry about their family and their neglected children. They are short of sleep at night and are in a state of agitation. Others shirk work because they are naturally lazy; the mirror is the centre of their interest and they pretend to be ill. Well-fed women with some understanding of social relationships can struggle through better and more courageously than the others. The above order is evidently intended to scare them, but it also shows how the system is becoming stricter. Westerbork is at present being treated as a labour camp and there has recently been a tightening of the reins.

Saturday December 18th: Yesterday evening a Yule party for the SS in the old building of the Registration Department. About a hundred men, all prominent SS officers from the Central Office in Amsterdam and The Hague, with their wives, together with the guards from the camp, made up the guests. The hall was decorated from floor to ceiling with fir branches and on the platform the swastika flag was set up side by side with the SS standard. At half past ten the party was over—officially. Van Dam and his closest friends went on celebrating until far into the night and drank more than was good for them, to put it mildly. They also fought among themselves and so the medical service had to step in. [. . .]

Since the order about handing in papers, many camp residents have surrendered their passports. A good number of them have concealed their passports or have sent them secretly out of the camp. The order would appear to apply only to passports and similar documents specifically indicating nationality.

Monday December 20th: Shoals of British and American 'planes over Westerbork. Again and again fresh formations appeared out of empty space like fishes ranged round their leader. Fighters flew round the bombers like paper streamers. An uplifting sight, not because of the aim they had to accomplish, but from an aesthetic point of view. Aesthetics in the service of technology. Not birds which create an aesthetic effect by the movement of their wings or fishes which do the same by moving their fins and tail, but rigid machines which are propelled from inside by an invisible force. The aesthetic aspect is to be found in the composition of the formation, in the swinging movement, in the combination of 'plane and vapour trail, in the speed of flight. General elation and many people beside themselves with joy.

Tuesday December 21st: A speech by the controller in hut 57, the one where the foil is sorted. It boiled down to the following: the Bureau for Non-Ferrous Metals in The Hague which superintends the metal section at Westerbork is not satisfied with the yield from the foil-sorting operation. 'If production does not improve in the immediate future, there is a chance that the daily working period will be extended to eight hours. You will have nobody but yourselves to blame and you cannot say that you have not been warned in good time. You are not hustled and you work under the supervision of team bosses whom you know. See that you appreciate this!'

Rather perplexed faces. How are we to take it? Can we treat it all as a bit of a lark as we have done up to now, although we did a lot of work even then, or must we respond to the call and take the threat seriously? A problem, as there are men and women who argue: 'The less I do for the Germans, the better I am pleased.' They do not wish to help their enemies or injure their allies. That is the theoretical side. Practical considerations come into it quite a bit too. The camp has officially become a labour camp which, they say, can provide permanent work for four to five thousand camp residents in the metal industry, thereby safeguarding them from deportation to Poland. That is also something worth while considering. If these workers are able to achieve and maintain a level of production that will impress the German authorities, then the camp will remain in existence. If they are not capable of doing so, the camp will be closed down and they will go to Poland. People familiar with the work section assert that the whole business does not amount to much, but the Bureau for Non-Ferrous Metals is blowing it up into something big and making the Germans think it is a worthwhile scheme, in order to play into the hands of the Jews. From the little bit of colouring yielded by the aluminium which is extracted from the silver paper you could not even spray a 'plane propeller. It sounds fantastic. Naturally the whole thing is exaggerated. The Bureau for Non-Ferrous Metals is not a philanthropical institution and it can naturally come to an arrangement much more cheaply here than on the open market. The Jews, being slaves, cost very little—less than forty cents per day. The open market is very much more expensive. In all probability the secret lies in the fact that a nice little profit can be made out of the slave labour. Be this as it may, the Jews have no choice but to take a fairly serious view of their employment and see to it that they produce enough for the work section to be a paying proposition, which will mean that they will not be sent to Poland.

The *Obersturmführer* is feeling once more that people have been treading on his toes. An over-sensitive man. He has had the following order posted up in all the huts:

"Concerning Rumours in the Camp:
Arising out of the Yule Party organized by the Camp Command, many irresponsible rumours regarding my guests and myself have been spread around the Camp. On several occasions I have made known my views about rumours of this nature, both orally and in writing, and I have threatened the adoption of punitive measures. As these punitive measures have in no way achieved their purpose and rumours concerning myself are still being circulated almost daily, I now hold all

215

Camp residents responsible for these rumours arising or remaining unchecked. The punitive measures to be adopted are as follows:

1. I forbid all festivities connected with the coming Jewish and Christian festivals (*Hanukkah* and Christmas). Violation of this rule will be punished in the severest possible manner.
2. On the festival days falling within the period from December 22nd to January 3rd work will be carried on as on a normal working day and I would point out in particular that Saturdays are also considered as normal working days and work will therefore go on until the evening. Should Camp residents evade the work ordered by me by means of doctors' lines or in any other way, a special punishment will be imposed.

Should rumours continue to circulate in the Camp even after the present punishment order has been announced, or should the measures adopted prove to be inadequate, I shall institute punishments which will ensure that no further rumours will arise.

The Camp Commandant, Gemmeker. SS-*Obersturmführer*."

Those impudent Jews, sending irresponsible rumours out into the world that bring the conduct of the Commandant and his guests into disrepute! The punishment affects the children most, both the children of devout Jews and those of baptized Jews, who had been preparing hard for their different festivals and had been looking forward to them. From the punishment it can also be concluded that the regime has become sterner. Last year the Commandant honoured with his presence the celebrations for *Hanukkah* held in one of the huts and he showed signs of being moved by the ceremony. An enigmatic character with iron hands covered in velvet. [. . .]

Saturday December 25th: Yesterday evening OD men checked in hut 73, the hut of the baptized Jews, to see whether the inmates were complying with the order that Christmas must not be celebrated. Not a single sprig of greenery, not a single candle was allowed. The *Obersturmführer* has also privately forbidden the baptized Jews to hold their usual Sunday service. We have looked for a reason for the Commandant's irritability. His resentment at the unkind rumours concerning what went on at the Yule Party seems to be excessive. We think that the underlying reason is that he is annoyed at the unfavourable course the war is taking and the concentrated bombing of German cities. The Commandant has just been to Düsseldorf on leave and would have seen the devastation with his own eyes. He probably realized that Germany was losing the war. He is supposed to have said something of the sort the other day.

Arrest and imprisonment of a young girl, Lotte W., because she had an understanding with a guard. This is not allowed. The guard was sent to the concentration camp at Vught.

Arrest and imprisonment of Juda van den Berg, Sluzker's chauffeur, for black market activities. He was found in possession of 650 packets of cigarettes and two parcels of foodstuffs. He was one of the important links between the highly placed Jews in the camp and the outside world. He got thousands of letters secretly out of the camp.

Yesterday evening a check made after the evening roll-call by Van Dam and Van Eck in all the huts. They tore into No. 71 like the wind. '*Achtung!*' Everyone who was still up rushed into the spaces between the beds or on to the actual beds. I was smoking my pipe and slipped it away like lightning into my trouser pocket. Van Dam unexpectedly went into the screened-off cubicle of the woman who is deputy hut leader. It was pitch dark inside. I moved along the narrow little passage by my bed to the other side in order not to be confronted with the aroma of tobacco emanating from me. Van Eck had just passed along that side. He turned round and bellowed: 'Cap off!' I had forgotten to take off my hat. I snatched my hat from my head and stood stiffly. [. . .]

In hut 85, where the Barnevelders live, there was a similar performance, but the tone was less friendly. Van Eck stopped in front of a greying elderly gentleman, Praag, a former general. 'Cap off!' 'Do you know that I was a general in the Dutch army?' 'General, my foot! You're just a common Jew.' Van Eck, who was once a meat porter at the abattoir, knocked the hat from the general's head. The general muttered between his teeth: 'Damn!' 'I'll give you "damn"! You'll go into the S-hut for three weeks.' The general is now in hut 67 and does convict labour, slave labour under the supervision of OD men.

Monday December 27th: Christmas passed cheerlessly amid punishment chores. One consolation was that the weather was mild.

A minor conflict in the foil-picking section. I was instructing a woman and allowed the grease from the condenser to melt on the edge of the stove to make it a bit easier to handle. A protest from the stoker. Me: 'You're interfering in things that don't concern you!' The stoker called in the German supervisor, my colleague. 'That thing must go!' A movement of the hand in the direction of the condenser. 'That thing is not going. You have no authority in the matter.' An altercation, slightly heated. He bellowed and I shouted. Me: 'You Boches must always be forbidding something, otherwise you're not happy.' Him: 'Boche did you say?' His eyes started from their sockets, ominously. 'You are not a good comrade. We are all Jews here.' I did not mean to hurt him and later went after him and took hold of his arm to attract his attention and settle the affair. But he wrenched himself free and went angrily away. Later the work leader, a Dutchman, said at the roll-call: 'You have had words. Try to settle the matter, or I'll have to report it. Otherwise he will do so and I'll be made to look a fool.' Me: 'I've tried, but he doesn't want to. Why don't you try and convince him that it wasn't meant as seriously as all that?' 'Very well.'

The controller (the German lad with eyes as hard as steel and curls under his jockey cap) appeared at the roll-call: 'You said "rotten Boche". That is an insult. It won't do. We're all Jews here.' 'I'm putting things right.' 'Yes, but I can't accept that sort of thing here in this section. I must report it.' Me: 'That's your affair, but real men accept apologies from one another and shake hands on it if a word has been said in anger. That is the custom here in Holland.' Him: 'If Nussbaum is willing, I think that will be all right, but you will have to apologize publicly.' 'Very well.' The controller turned away in Nussbaum's direction. Enter Nussbaum with outstretched hand. Me: 'Nussbaum, I did not mean to insult you by what I said, but, if you feel insulted, I want to tell you I am sorry.' Nussbaum, with feeling: 'That is splendid.' The conflict was buried in the din from two hundred and fifty voices. Only people sitting nearby were aware of it at all.

I had made up my mind not to have a fight. But the dictatorial tone of the Germans gets on the nerves of the Dutch, and that includes mine. Dutch people who sit at the same table as Germans can be heard to swear: 'Those damned Germans! I can't bear the sight of them any more and I can't bear to hear their language.' The same story everywhere. 'We don't like them. After the war they must get out. They have the faults of the Prussians and the faults of the Jews all rolled into one.' Love of one's fellowmen is put to a hard test here.

Tuesday December 28th: Juda van den Berg has been released from prison and has returned to Amsterdam with Sluzker and Blüth. He enjoys the exalted protection of Aus der Fünten.

Thursday December 30th: Transport of eighty persons from Amsterdam, almost entirely made up of people who had been in hiding. The S-hut is packed once more, about 650 men and women. [. . .] In the morning they go through the camp to their work in long lines of fifty wearing their fancy dress outfits which look as if they have been borrowed from Breughel, under supervision of OD men, muffled up in their blue capes, one in front and one behind and a few along the side. They do not walk now as they used to in the summer and autumn. They crawl along the road in dismal silence. The men have been deprived of their suits and the women of their dresses and they are feeling cold. A considerable number of the S-detainees are little old women who jog along looking grey and decrepit, often leaning on the arm of a younger woman. Life in the hut is frightful. They are packed tightly together like herrings in a barrel. Quite often they have to stand for an hour to get their hot food and hunk of bread and they are forced to stand eating it with their spoons till their mess-tins are empty. [. . .]

Friday December 31st: An S-man condemned to stand by the barbed wire for eight hours on end on three different days under supervision of an OD man. He had given Zimmern, the head of the punishment squad, a slap in the face. Zimmern is known to be a dreadful fellow, a brute who shouts and flings out taunts and abuses exactly like an SS man. He is universally hated; people would like to kill him on the spot.

We are forbidden to celebrate the Old Year. The hut leaders have advised people to go to bed promptly at ten o'clock as they fear a raid by the SS gentlemen, as happened on Christmas Eve. Old Year visit to various huts to wish friends and acquaintances Peace and Freedom.

Saturday January 1st 1944: Everyone is working today, still as a punishment for circulating rumours harmful to the Commandant and his guests at the Yule Party. In the meantime it has been definitely established that people attending the party did indeed come to blows and Dr. Spanier treated one of them personally for a dislocated collarbone. Also the day after the Yule Party the camp was searched for a brand-new trilby hat belonging to one of the guests which had been lost on the way home. There was no wind blowing at the time.

Sunday January 2nd: Dismissed by letter from my post as supervisor in the foil-sorting section:

"Department 12.
Mechanicus, Philip. 17.4.89. Hut 71.
Your duties as Supervisor in the Foil-Sorting Group have been terminated. You will, however, continue to be attached to the Foil-Sorting Group and will there carry out the same work as all the other persons employed in that Group.
Dept. 12—Administration. Salinger. Westerbork Camp. 2.1.44. S/Sp."

I would very much like to meet the great Salinger who permits himself the luxury of signing without initials. I had never heard of him, either outside or inside the camp. [. . .] I had a long wait. The gentleman in question was in conference. A little fellow with an undistinguished shape of head and dark, sombre, beady eyes. He could not give me the reason for my dismissal. It had been ordered by Herr Beyer, the work leader, who had just left on an official trip to Amsterdam and it could not be held over. [. . .]

I have my own thoughts on the subject. Foul play on the part of Cats, the man with the inhuman eyes—resentment because I had classed his colleague Nussbaum with the Boches. Cats is hated for all kinds of reasons. Last week he gave one of the foil-sorters three hours overtime for being cheeky to one of the work leaders. One does not readily forgive a "companion in misfortune" for doing such a thing. [. . .]

Monday January 3rd: As an ordinary foil-sorter I took my seat at table 1 and was received with a quasi-emotional inaugural address from one of the gentlemen who has set himself up as chairman of the table. Speeches all round, such as are normally made at the meetings of professional bodies. 'Mr.

220

Chairman, I have a proposal to make,' and so on. Nothing done, not a single piece of foil picked off. Good company provided by others who have taken idleness as their motto. Even touching a knife to rip open a condenser is in flat contradiction to our principle: 'Be idle, but do it well and systematically—it is for a good cause!'

During the afternoon I and three other foil-pickers fetched tea for the hut from the Central Kitchen—two large mess-kettles on two wheelbarrows. Two men wheel the barrows and the other two keep a tight grip on the mess-kettles to prevent them from toppling off. Visit in the meantime to the canteen to buy tinned dabs and gulp down a paper cup of clear soup (ersatz) for ten cents. Our five minutes there and back had been stretched into an hour and a quarter. Swinging the lead, as people say. Anything to kill time. When we took back the mess-kettles we scrounged some carrots from the Central Kitchen to augment our diet. The lunch helpings are getting very meagre. In the evening a handful of copper deposited in the latrine—the fruits of a day's labour by four pickers.

Wednesday January 5th: [. . .]

Met a good friend today who has been here for a fortnight in a hut which we were both visiting. A remarkable case—a Portuguese called A. Ricardo, formerly financial editor of the *"Nieuwe Rotterdamsche Courant"*, later editor-in-chief of the *"Financier en Kapitalist"*, and later still editor of *"Handelsberichten"*. He had pointed out that he was descended from the Portuguese aristocracy and had family connections with a famous Anglo-Portuguese economist, and was, moreover, a member of the Remonstrant Church. For that reason he had been given a dispensation from the *Reichskommissar* nearly two years ago, making him out to be an Aryan. His wife had been brought here with him and placed in the S-hut. He said he did not know why, but she herself declared that, although she was entirely Jewish, she had made a false statement, alleging that she did not know the origins of two of her four Jewish grandparents. She goes every day to the Potato Kitchen with the punishment squad.

Thursday January 6th: Positive rumours about a transport next Tuesday, taking members of the Palestine exchange list to the camp at Celle near Hanover. The early enthusiasm of many people has waned. Long faces—the end of the war is in sight and people, when all is said and done, do not have any faith in this business.

Yesterday evening a very lively bridge drive in my hut. Great animation. A woman, a well-known artiste, L.H., has escaped from hut 85 where the Barnevelders live. At seven o'clock this morning she was at the foil-picking, but shortly afterwards she disappeared. She herself had intimated that she was going to disappear in a letter to her brother. In it she said that she could not stand the life at Westerbork any longer and had therefore decided to end her life. But her body has not yet been found. It is known that she had fits of melancholy, but also that she could not get on with her husband and was pondering on ways of getting out of the camp and rushing off to find the new lover she was hankering after.

The acting Commandant, *Untersturmführer* Van Dam, has punished hut 85 in the absence of the Commandant who is away in The Hague. He sent twenty residents, ten men and ten women, to the S-hut. [. . .] He had the husband of the "suicide case", who was lying ill, removed from his bed and transferred to the S-hut. In the course of the day he was taken to the hospital. Van Dam personally arrested Herr Rosenbaum, the executive head of Department 12, because he had omitted to report the absence of the "suicide case" from her work at the proper time. When he reached the S-hut with his prisoner, he met De Jong, the sergeant of the guard. The latter asked Rosenbaum: 'Why have you come here?' Rosenbaum: '*Untersturmführer* Van Dam has arrested me.' De Jong: 'You'll go straight back to your office.' Van Dam was silent. Exit Rosenbaum. In place of Rosenbaum Van Dam arranged for heer Gokkes, room boss in the foil-sorting section, to be arrested and transferred to No. 67. In hut 85 there is great despondency and indignation centred on the woman responsible for the calamity.

Order from the *Obersturmführer* regarding "association with S-detainees":

"I would once again draw your attention to the fact that it is strictly forbidden for any Camp resident to speak in an unofficial capacity on the road or at places of work to S-detainees. Any violation of this rule will be severely punished by me.

The Camp Commandant (Gemmeker)."

In the work huts ordinary camp inmates and S-men and S-women sit so close together and the personal relationships are often so intimate that not speaking to one another would demand superhuman willpower. So they do speak.

Thursday January 6th: [. . .]
Arrest in hut 71 by the Camp Police of mevrouw Z.-S., a spy working for the *Sicherheitsdienst* (Security Service). The Police had intercepted a letter written by her to the SD in which she had criticized certain actions of the *Obersturmführer*.

Friday January 7th: Was sitting working yesterday evening in Schlesinger's waiting room in Department 2 when a young man put his head warily round the entrance door: 'Is Herr Silke (head of Department 2) in his office?' 'Not as far as I know.' 'Have you been here long?' 'Yes, three-quarters of an hour or so. But I'm here on a purely private matter.' 'Look here, I'm coming here with a girl. Would you be good enough to turn your back?' 'Certainly, if that's what you want.' The young man pulled a cigarette case out of his pocket and opened it: 'Here you are.' 'Thank you very much, but I don't need any. You don't have to recompense me.' 'Take one all the same. I've got plenty.' I did not want to be rude. The young man disappeared and came back after a time. I disappeared. He unlocked the office of the head of Department 2 and slipped inside with the girl. The head of the department had done the same thing a week ago and the week before that too—he had had a rendezvous in his office in the twilight with the girl of his fancy.

Of two thousand kg broad beans given out to be sorted, one hundred and fifty kg have disappeared. Evidently spirited away. This happens wherever foodstuffs are given out for preparation or distribution. In these last few weeks men and women could be seen everywhere beside the stoves, busy roasting broad beans on the ashes. The shortage of bread is becoming more marked every day. In the middle of the day men and women with mess-tins swarm round the Central Kitchen like wasps round a pot of honey, to get a spoonful of gruel on the sly from friends in the kitchen. Cigarettes play an important part here. [. . .]

My foil-sorting table has been given the title of the "élite table". From the start of their working day the men adopt a sleeping posture, with their heads reclining on their elbows which are resting on the table. This continues the whole time until shortly after five. Then I appear on my return from the tea-fetching operation with the "*Nieuwe Rotterdamsche Courant*". When I say: 'Gentlemen, here is the newspaper,' they start up, crane their necks and open their eyes wide like captive tigers which have caught the scent of their lump of meat. They are very keen on the paper. It enables them to verify the rumours going about the camp and to find out the war situation and read of the effect of the bombing on Berlin. From the "*Korte Berichten*" (News in Brief), printed in brevier type, they can dig up important war news that is not mentioned on the radio and is carefully tucked away by the newspaper. The paper afterwards goes the length of the nearest tables, passing from hand to hand. So much for our foil-picking!

Rain—the camp is a great pool of mud once more.

Saturday January 8th: Yesterday evening Dutch subjects of foreign extraction and those who are on the first two waiting lists for the Palestine exchange have received a written notice, telling them to hold themselves in readiness for "transfer to another camp".

Arrival of a number of gipsy caravans which have been set up, partly inside and partly outside the camp. Purpose unknown—the guard say they are for evacuees from Bremen.

The hut teacher asked the boys: 'What comes from Gouda?' 'Candles.' 'What comes from Schiedam?' 'Holland gin.' 'What comes from Beverwijk?' 'Strawberries.' 'What comes from Barneveld?' 'Jews.' [. . .]

Bridge drive over. Speeches all round.

Sunday January 9th: Chess competition over. Yesterday evening an improvised musical evening in one of the rooms at Schlesinger's office—piano and violin. Pieces by Corelli and Mozart.

Monday January 10th: It is now definite that the transport is leaving tomorrow for Celle. In all the huts people are busy packing. At the last moment Fräulein Slottke put down 130 camp residents who had obtained an exemption from the Camp Commandant's Office owing to their international contacts. They would be going to Celle for exchange too. A disappointment. Many people who had a double option were asked to choose—one or the other? Anyone who was being considered for Palestine, but was thought to be essential to Westerbork, could remain here, provided that he renounced his Palestine exchange rights. Many have taken this risk in the hope that the war will soon be over and they will find some other loophole to save them from the hardships of Poland, which people are gradually ceasing to believe in. Among the Barnevelders, a few people have finally opted for Palestine, and from the hut for the baptized a married couple as well.

Tuesday January 11th: Forty illicit letters confiscated from a driver. A number of doctors and male and female nurses arrested and transferred to the S-hut and the driver put in prison.

At one o'clock today the departure of the exchange transport began immediately after the arrival of the passenger train. For the first time we had a transport leaving in the middle of the day, and the men and women were not drummed out of their beds in the dismal light of the early morning. Fräulein Slottke had said to one of the applicants who was wavering: 'This is a unique transport. But it's up to you.' We shall see later on if it really is a unique transport in the full sense of the word. In the limited sense of the term it certainly was unique— an exodus with all the odiousness of deportation dispelled by the passenger train. The applicants could also take all their goods and chattels with them. The residents who were not going on the transport had to be in their huts at one o'clock to avoid confusion round the train. From nearly all the huts the emigrants departed in a procession with a final farewell, with a wave or a clasp of the hand at the open windows, where those who were left behind crowded together to watch the departure. Except for those who, hardened by their long stay at Westerbork, just went on playing chess or cards.

There was a flicker of hope about this transport as the emigrants had a chance of reaching the camp where their friends were very soon. The only regret was that they were pushed out in their poverty and nakedness and had to accept a favour from the hands of their enemies. They could not go their own way as free men and women. With this transport the pick of the basket has gone from Westerbork, with the exception of the Barnevelders. Even old Trottel, who as a man with international services to his credit had a special stamp from the Camp Commandant's Office, had to go on that transport against his will and so saw his hopes of remaining on Dutch soil fade away. He was deeply moved. The Commandant consoled him by saying that he should look upon his departure for Celle as a great mark of favour.

Wednesday January 12th: The discovery of the illicit despatch of letters has led to an order being passed which virtually seals Westerbork off hermetically from the outside world. [. . .]

So no more parcels, no more letters, no more newspapers, no war news we are able to verify. The authorities have taken the opportunity of introducing a measure that they probably had in mind for a long time. The only thing we could still buy in the canteen yesterday evening was vinegar. To make things even sourer. [. . .]

Two young men have escaped from the S-hut. The whole camp is in a turmoil, dreading further collective punishments, for the S-hut and the other camp residents.

It has turned out that, under pressure, a patient in hut 81 gave the names of a few individuals who had sent illicit letters. This morning Van Dam made all the women from the S-hut and those from the Sewing Room line up on the parade ground because of hints contained in the confiscated letters. Of the women from the S-hut all those called Beppie and from the Sewing Room all those called Clär had to step forward, and the Beppie and the Clär who were supposed to have written the illicit letters were called upon to reveal themselves. Deathly silence. In the OD barracks they later had to produce a line of handwriting for comparison with the letters. And the stokers mentioned in the letters in some connection or other had to line up also. Two of them were sent to the S-hut and the others were condemned to do marching as a punishment. The camp is chuckling at the silliness of Van Dam, although they are sorry for the people who are suffering from his arbitrary show of authority. [. . .]

Transport from Amsterdam and from Arnhem. A total of 120 persons, mainly S-detainees. From Arnhem a number of children from one to nine years old. The S-hut is crammed full, about 800 people. Here and there they are sleeping with three people to every two beds, and five to every three beds. The place is crawling with fleas. This morning an S-man in the foil

226

section let me see his arm. All the flea-bites made it look like a map of Central Europe.

One of the two men who recently escaped from hut 71 was on the transport from Amsterdam; he was put in prison.

Thursday January 13th: The two men who got away the day before yesterday from the S-hut were picked up at Appelscha.

The word "Theresienstadt" is resounding through the camp. The Commandant is preparing a transport for Theresienstadt. A whole host of decisions are being taken with regard to pending applications. I too am being considered for the transport. When I questioned him on the subject, Schlesinger replied: 'I am sorry, but I can't do anything for you. The Hague and Fräulein Slottke are arranging all these transports. The only thing you can do is fall ill. But don't let Dr. Spanier know beforehand.' Through Dr. de L. I asked Dr. Spanier if I could be admitted to the hospital to evade the transport. Dr. Spanier refused. Since my discharge from hospital in August I have not been in poor health and the strictness of the German authorities about whether a person is "fit for transport" or not would make any pretence in my case impossible. It would be too patently obvious. Through the Applications Office I applied to Mr. Kotting for a statement that he was dealing with my Aryanization and a request to keep me here for the time being.

Friday January 14th: Weinreb was at the camp to complete his list. He gave me the assurance that I too appeared on the list, but when I asked what I ought to do if confronted with the choice: Theresienstadt or Weinreb, he advised Theresienstadt. From this it can be inferred that Weinreb has little confidence in his list and does not dare to take the responsibility of advising anyone to choose his list if that person has a better guarantee of exemption. [. . .]

The existing 1000 List has smashed again—a great number of those who, according to the original intention, were to be remaining in the camp until the last and then be sent to Theresienstadt have been put down for the transport next Tuesday. The Berlin authorities want a transport of a thousand persons and the Commandant has to see that they get it. [. . .] This time there was agitation only among the Long-Term Residents who after four or five years have to give up their

227

little middle-class houses, their bits of furniture and their stove and take their place as newcomers in another camp where they will count for nothing. They have to leave Dutch soil where, as stateless persons, they thought they could find a suitable haven of refuge for the future. Now they will find themselves in a country which hates the German language even more than Holland does at present (Czechoslovakia) and where they do not have the slightest contact with the native population. [. . .] More than half of the remaining Long-Term Residents are to be going and these include many of the most prominent. [. . .] The camp is indeed breaking up now that its leaders are disappearing. It is true that a new 1,000 List is being compiled, but most of the people appearing on it work in the metal industry, which allows them to extend their stay in the camp for a short time at least.

Saturday January 15th: Got an authenticated extract made from my personal identity card and signed by the acting burgomaster of Westerbork. On inquiry I learned that the personal identity cards of people who are deported on the transports to the east are sent to the place of origin and are lodged there with the note: "Gone abroad". So it can be assumed that nothing is known of the whereabouts of Jews who have been deported and that they have left their hearth and home of their own accord. An extract is of importance for "going abroad".

Have been officially directed to hold myself in readiness for the next transport to Theresienstadt. [. . .]

At once approached the couriers of the former Jewish Council to hurry things up and have it explained to Mr. Kotting that I urgently required a proper certificate. This afternoon the courier who is in Amsterdam will be asked by telephone to do this. I do not want to go to Theresienstadt. A friend gave the following picture of it: 'Theresienstadt is the cat's whiskers, but the cat stinks.' My old idea of escaping has returned. The weather is ideal for this—pitch dark at night—but I reflect that if I escape the interests of many people might be prejudiced and also the risk involved in escaping is quite considerable. Recently people who had been in hiding have been pouring into the camp. I am an old S-man and, if arrested, would be in danger of getting a double S.

Sunday January 16th: Yesterday evening took my leave of most of my friends, mainly in hut 85. Also Dr. Spanier whom I thanked for all he had done for me. He gave me an introduction to his parents at Theresienstadt and at the same time presented me with a household medicine chest. Once more I had the impression that I was dealing with a man of some stature, a good man.

Yesterday evening again, as I was walking in the dark, I toyed with the idea of escaping, but consciously rejected it again. And at night in my slumbers I still indulged in thoughts of escape. The idea goes on absorbing me like a kind of hobby. I imagine myself going along the railway line in the darkness in the middle of the night and reaching Zwolle, from where I could catch a train to somewhere or other in the morning. The thought fascinates me.

Monday January 17th: Early this morning I went to the office of the couriers of the Jewish Council to find out if any news had come in from Amsterdam. It appeared that the courier had returned with a statement from Mr. Kotting to the effect that he had duly referred the matter of my ancestry to the office of the *Reichskommissar*, but that for the moment he was not in a position to hand over the petition and the full documentation, as they were in the possession of other authorities. What a blow!

Could I stay? I dashed to the Applications Office. Dr. Ottenstein read the document and said drily: 'It's all very fine, but it's not enough. If you're not on the Calmeyer List, it's no use. Do you know what? I'll ring up The Hague right away and I'll send you a message presently.' Like an arrow from the bow he disappeared into another room to go to the telephone. Within the hour I was called back. 'It's all in order, mijnheer Mechanicus,' said Dr. Ottenstein drily and held out his hand to me with an austere smile. The first time I have actually seen him smile. [. . .] Once again I have escaped the hazard of deportation and there are no more transports going to Theresienstadt for the time being.

Two OD men have fled, one in Amsterdam and one in Zwolle. Forty OD men have been allocated to go with the transport to Theresienstadt. The two who escaped apparently wished to decline the honour.

Tuesday January 18th: The train departed again this morning with clockwork precision, but this time the transport was, of course, quite different from the transports to Auschwitz, and also different from the exodus of exchange Jews the week before. [. . .] This time there was once again a train made up of third-class carriages with luggage vans for the sick and livestock trucks for the provisions. The travellers could book their seats in advance, especially the Long-Term Residents, who were informed in good time by their friends, just as if it were a Lissone or a Cooks trip, and they could deposit their luggage in the train on the previous evening. The invalids got bedsteads with specially made mattresses on them. For the first time since the transports to the east the huts were not closed up while the transport was leaving, so those staying behind could see their friends off beside the train and go as far as the cordon of OD men. They could watch it leave as if they were on a platform and were free to wave back when the departing travellers waved good-bye. A pleasure outing to Theresienstadt.

The word "Theresienstadt" has had a magnetic effect on people's minds, like Wengenrode or the Isle of Wight or Capri. Fantastic tales were going the rounds. It was said that life there was so good that the residents were not imprisoned behind barbed wire, but could move freely through the little old fortress town and live in small houses. The young people were keen to see a fortress town. It is situated in Czech territory after all, isn't it—on friendly soil? How credulous man is, how naïve and ready to imagine that the place where he does not happen to be is better than the place where he is, at present, relatively speaking, quite well off. [. . .]

So the train departed with men and women who took their leave of Holland and their friends with rather heavy hearts, but consoled themselves with the thought that they were going to a place remote from the scourge of war, the cruelty of the concentration camp and the callousness of the slave-driver who is master in Poland. A pleasure train and a little bit of sight-seeing—although it *was* going to take a fairly long time. On one side of the engine in large white letters, painted on in italics: "Victory first—then travel." On the other side: "Wheels turning for victory."

Hitler wants to exterminate the Jews. He has said so more than once. Yet he calls for the Jews in trains fit for human beings and takes them to a favoured spot in Europe: Theresienstadt. He exterminates them in separate classes, just as a firm of undertakers buries its dead clients according to different categories. [. . .] Hitler is playing the part of the undertaker and he takes off his hat to Jews who occupied privileged positions in their lifetime.

Wednesday January 19th: A large-scale moving operation—the Turkish colony have been shifted to hut 72, the hut for foreigners and people with dual nationality, from which last week 200 went on the transport to Celle. Hut 72 had a bad name in the camp—the tone was extremely rough and brawling was the order of the day. The inhabitants of hut 71 are delighted that the Turks have gone—much less noise. On the same day the residents in hut 66 were shifted, a few hundred people, to make room for the overflow from the S-hut where 900 people are now crammed together. One of my friends there had to wait this morning from ten past five till twenty to seven outside the WC before it came to his turn. [. . .] They are now sleeping with five people to three beds placed together. [. . .]

Eighty men, women and children have come to hut 71 from 66. There is quite a crowd in my hut. As a result, I have lost my baggage bed. I have deposited my cases with a friend in a partitioned-off space under one of the beds. My boxes, pans and shoes I have stacked up ingeniously and placed on the tie-beams, so my sideboard, my library, my bedside cabinet, my shoe-cleaning box and my writing materials and so on are all to be found up there. I am in terror lest the whole show should come tumbling down one day, and myself with it. [. . .]

Thursday January 20th: About 400 Long-Term Residents went on Tuesday on the transport to Theresienstadt. Many who had a choice between Theresienstadt and the Weinreb List opted for Weinreb. Unless it was absolutely necessary, they did not want to be parted from their little houses and their comforts and so they rejected the gift of Theresienstadt offered to them by the Commandant. The latter was furious and told them that they would in due course be removed from their houses and would have to shift to the large residential huts. So they were being given notice to quit. The Long-Term Residents who left got a parcel from the camp containing butter, sugar and jam; the others got nothing. People who knew about this said it was a disgrace—unheard of favouritism. The Long-Term Residents had already done very nicely for themselves, thanks to their contacts in the kitchen, but still went on about

231

the bad time they had had five years before. The houses which have been or are to be vacated will be made available to the new people on the 1000 List. [. . .]

Had an interview with Mr. Pr. and informed him about the Theresienstadt developments. 'I know,' replied Mr. Pr., 'but you surely don't believe that a petition has actually been handed in. Having any father other than your legal father is something that could not be accepted. We would have begun a genealogical investigation, but the man dealing with that has been in prison for a month and a half. The day may come when you do have to move to Theresienstadt. You must just act according to circumstances.' 'I have no intention of doing otherwise.' I wonder if Ottenstein is in the conspiracy too and only made a pretence of 'phoning to The Hague. He smiled in such an enigmatic way on the Monday in question. From this small incident one can see that there are many ways of saving a person from deportation. [. . .]

Friday January 21st: The indigo and scarlet colours of the S-detainees are turning up everywhere in the camp—in the outside work, the laying of sewage pipes, the Potato Kitchen, the metal industry. They are to be seen all over the place among Jews who are not undergoing punishment—at the Applications Office, in the Out-Patients' Department, at the dentist's. Today five S-detainees were relieved of their S.

This afternoon I visited hut 56 where foil is picked and at one of the tables the S-women—all Barnevelders undergoing punishment—were sitting playing a party game instead of picking foil. They were throwing dice fashioned out of silver paper and holding a quiz on zoology, Biblical knowledge, music, sport, painting and so on. [. . .] In my own work hut the zeal of the supervising officials has waned somewhat. They have been placed on the 1000 List, which was apparently the reason for all their keenness in the first place. My table is still an élite table—people still sleep at it and one of the sleepers is generally known as the "arch-sluggard". I confine myself to fetching tea and spend the rest of the time strolling about inside or outside the hut like a vagabond.

Saturday January 22nd: There has been a gale howling since this morning. Westerbork is once more a great sea of mud. In the night it was pitch dark—you could not see your hand in front of you. In my hut the crowd which had gathered mainly round my bed beside the stove under the bright light was quite unbearable. It was like a stock exchange. Men and women stood in the passages between the blocks of beds, talking away about the war and the coming transport to Auschwitz, often quite wildly. It is so hard for people to be silent and when they do open their mouths they speak a lot of rubbish. Fresh squabbling over the stove, fresh voices, fresh accents, but basically things are just the same as they were the other day when the Turks were still here, blocking up the stove. People have to keep their nerves well under control if they are not to explode with rage or sink into despair. In the daytime the women bewail their sufferings and at night the men heave the sighs they have suppressed during the day.

People cannot escape from one another. They are chained to one another hand and foot. The adults curse other people's children because they run wild and shout and shriek in the hut and bump into everyone and everything as they career about with youthful high spirits. The children rebel against the adults who try to curb their natural exuberance, although there is no other place where they can use up their surplus energy. They are mutual enemies. Owing to these cramped conditions of coexistence, the children are also drawn into things only intended for the eyes and ears of adults who have lost a great deal, if not all, of their reticence towards the children. Young children spy upon their elders in the washrooms, in the unpartitioned WC rooms. In the work huts men and women visit the same WC. All sense of modesty disappears. Women of some standing say to justify their behaviour: 'I would never have done that at one time.' One person enters into the private and intimate life of another without wanting to. The sharp edges of respectability are being gradually rubbed off and feelings of reticence hardly exist at all any more. What will become of the children, living as they do?

Next Tuesday a transport to Auschwitz, mainly S-detainees. The relatives of the S-people are down in the dumps and are rushing about everywhere, trying to get their relatives out of the S-hut at the last minute. But the chances are nil.

Sunday January 23rd: In the night part of the roof of hut 65 was blown off. The rain made the whole place soaking wet. A wall of hut 66 was pushed in. The wind is still howling. The scraggy little trees are being shaken to and fro: 'Och! Och! Och!'

I have heard that I am on the Weinreb List. [. . .] It is like a kind of roulette now. At last I too have more than one guarantee of exemption: Theresienstadt and Weinreb. I may shortly have to choose between the two. I also have the imaginary Calmeyer. A complicated situation. It is as if we are all sitting together at a gaming table and have put our money on different numbers and are waiting to see which number will come up. We hope it will not be our number. We are not playing of our own free will, but under duress, and we hope that the bank will break one day. [. . .] People are uncertain whether the Weinreb List will ever reach the exchange stage and are inclined to believe that the List will smash one fine day and those who are on it will be sent off to Auschwitz, bag and baggage. Unless the Russians are approaching or actually reach Auschwitz before then, in which case Auschwitz would no longer be a possibility. Weinreb still involves a leap in the dark.

The camp has its potato hunters. Every day you can see men and women delving into the heap of potato peelings that are deposited on a small piece of ground in front of the main entrance to the Central Kitchen near a large cask. They are searching to see if any stray potatoes have landed among the peelings. [. . .]

Hunger is growing in the camp and is making itself generally felt. At the same time women with generous stocks of things still bake quantities of rolled oat biscuits and other delicacies every day with butter and sugar. But this cannot go on for long as there is not a single parcel coming in from outside.

Yesterday my doctor prescribed an extra daily allowance of milk gruel. I had chronic stomach trouble, probably caused by having too much cabbage. [. . .]

There are persistent rumours of a raid in Amsterdam upon partners from mixed marriages. Jewish partners in mixed marriages living here and waiting to return to Amsterdam are growing uneasy and are afraid that they will all be left here. Nothing is known about this in official quarters. [. . .]

A dreadful hullabaloo going on round the stove—a regiment of mess-tins, poor facilities, materialism and lack of tolerance. [. . .] The Turks have gone, and the clan of "Aunt Rose", a grandmother with children and grandchildren, with the menfolk encamped in star formation round the stove, is now in command of the ground. She fries on all the stoves at

234

once, with the assistance of the female members of the family, and is in charge of large pans which go into position early in the morning. She swears black and blue that the stove will not be commandeered for longer than a quarter of an hour. Anyone who answers back is engulfed in a torrent of unpleasant language. With her heavy iron frying-pan she rules the stove, but she fries potatoes superbly and all the people around feel their mouths watering.

This afternoon half of my mess-tin of rolled oats was lost owing to the clumsiness of one of my fellow-cooks. I fried potatoes; waited from seven till nine, when the fire went out. Hastily stoked up a small wood fire.

Monday January 24th: The Barnevelders who had been shut up in the S-hut as a result of the escape of L.H. were discharged from there today and have returned to hut 85. One of them had been sent away on the latest transport to Theresienstadt. The husband of the woman who escaped had to remain in the S-hut.

A number of Jews left for Amsterdam to buy things for the shop which is being set up at Westerbork.

A. has been shifted to hut 1. A lovely hospital hut—square rooms with ten or eleven beds painted in pastel colours, central heating, small cupboards above the beds and a model operating theatre which can compete with the best in Holland —at Westerbork of all places!

Tuesday January 25th: [. . .]

In a tearing gale and pouring rain a transport of 1,000 persons left for Auschwitz. Once more in cattle trucks. The majority were supplied by the S-hut—590 people. The rest were young men of the Aliyah, old men from the hospital and thirty-one small nameless children who had been in the orphanage and whose parents were either in hiding or had already been sent on to Poland. Among these children was a ten-year-old boy with a temperature of 39.9°, i.e., a tenth of a degree too low for him to be included among the lucky people who were "unfit for transport". They were clearing away S-detainees and unproductive folk who were nothing but a burden on the camp budget. People still do not know what happens to the deported Jews in Poland. They curse the National Socialists and search for names to express their feelings which are a combination of contempt and loathing, horror and hatred, but nobody can find the right word. They stand there powerless, heaping up one word on top of another, but they have to give up looking for a suitable epithet and finally give just an exclamation of disgust.

'When will the war be over, when will the misery of these weekly transports come to an end?' lament the women. 'The war is going well! But there is a transport going every week,' the men say scornfully to those who are confident that the war will soon end in an Allied victory. The winter is far on now and they fear that if the decisive blow does not fall this winter the war will go on throughout the summer and not a single Jew will be left on Dutch soil. Hope alternating with fear. Where are we going? What will our fate be? What lies in store for us?

Wednesday January 26th: [. . .]
Patients from the diphtheria and scarlet fever hut were sent on yesterday's transport, also a man with tuberculosis who was considered "fit for transport". [. . .]

The telephone wires are humming once more: Celle! Celle! Celle! Wherever you go in the camp the residents are speaking of Celle. Next Tuesday another transport is expected to be going there and there is good reason to believe that it will consist of persons in possession of 120,000 stamps. Their turn is coming at last. There are three types: the contacts type, the accumulator type and the achievements type. The contacts stamps are given out to those who have good foreign trade connections which the Germans hope to take advantage of somehow or other if they win the war—if! The accumulator stamps go to those who have paid with "black" money or money belonging to others. The achievements stamps are handed to people who have been outstanding in some sphere or other and have, as a result, awakened the admiration of the Nazis or have appealed to their practical sense—as, for example, in the case of experts in the diamond industry—and so have managed to induce the authorities to save them from being deported to Poland. [. . .]

Thursday January 27th: [. . .] Many people who were once in a good position always go about with a bag of some sort, a briefcase or a shopping bag, in the hope of picking something up on the way—potatoes or carrots. Some have a small tub

236

for collecting odd lumps of coal. The whole camp population is out on the prowl to see what they can pick up. [. . .] During the morning I saw a woman on the kitchen staff fill up a bag on the side of the potato centrifuge with enough boiled potatoes to feed ten people. The same scene again and again in the kitchen—petty thieving going on on a large scale. The people are short of things, but they are over-greedy. [. . .]

Friday January 28th: Yesterday evening a transport of 180 people, including about eighty for the S-hut. Among the hundred others were some with Captain Sommer exemptions—120,000 stamps. The holders of these stamps had worked for the German metallurgical industry and had, it is said, earned a lot of money on the black market. These were more or less the last exempted persons left in Amsterdam.

Saturday January 29th: Great agitation and indignation among the holders of 120,000 stamps—Fräulein Slottke has called up the holders of accumulator stamps in groups and given them the choice: either make up the deficiency or the stamp will be declared null and void. So they will go, not to Celle, but to Auschwitz. They are mainly the wealthy Jews from the diamond industry who are on the so-called Ros List. [. . .] They were given a week in which to set their affairs in order. They naturally felt cheated and spoke of blackmail. Of course they called it blackmail. The first stage of the proceedings was also blackmail and was aimed at extorting black money from the Jews. The Nazis evidently mean to squeeze the last guilder out of the wealthy Jews—money or else Auschwitz! And the Jews are hurrying to fork out, if they still have anything left and can get through to the people helping them, because they do not want to go to Auschwitz. [. . .]

The 1,000 List has grown to thirteen hundred members. They have been officially notified that they can move into the little houses that have fallen vacant as a result of Long-Term Residents leaving for Theresienstadt. They are delighted—anyone with a wife can have his wife with him.

Sunday January 30th: The Commandant has put an end to the doubts besetting the holders of two options. Anyone who has a 120,000 stamp and is at the same time on the Weinreb List must give up his Weinreb option. Today the notes have finally been issued, telling the holders of contacts stamps to be ready

237

to travel on Tuesday next. Those who are on the remaining exchange lists for Palestine have been notified as well. Also many with dual nationality, including Dutch people who had purchased a Paraguayan, Honduran or other Latin American passport. They are evidently not looked upon as foreigners suitable for exchange, otherwise they would have been interned. What is going to happen to the Barnevelders, the baptized Jews and the Portuguese with four Portuguese grandparents remains a mystery. By order of the Commandant the lists on which they appear have been taken out of the cardindex. So for the present they are not being considered for deportation.

The Sommer case is interesting. The Jews who worked for the German *Wehrmacht* enriched themselves to such an extent with black market transactions that the Gestapo had them arrested and brought to the Amstelveenseweg. Thanks to the intercession of Captain Sommer, however, they were well treated. In Westerbork too they received preferential treatment and were accommodated in little houses. [. . .]

Monday January 31st: Tumult and tension in the camp—packing for Celle. The German authorities are once again providing a train suitable for decent people. Travel regulations have been put up in writing today in all the huts. [. . .] Just as if it were a pleasure trip—with everything well organized, just to make sure! Those kind National Socialists! Yesterday they were not able to reach the target of 1,000 travellers, the number needed to fill the train. This morning they were still 200 short. Fresh call-ups for it at one o'clock today. [. . .]

Tuesday February 1st: Yesterday afternoon a farm in the neighbourhood went up in flames. An NSB farm. The flames blazed up high and the farm was reduced to ashes. Satisfaction among the camp residents.

1,000 people on the transport to Celle. From my hut fifty-two people, from hut 64 over 120; the latter hut is swarming with holders of 120,000 stamps. The rest of the population had to remain in the huts until the train had left. At the last moment the Hungarians, numbering about twenty, were called up for the transport. They had to leave without their wives. That transport was coupled to the train for Celle and went, as far as could be ascertained, to Weimar. The women were to be following next Thursday. It is thought that politics entered into this—German displeasure at the defection of Hungary who recently decided to withdraw her troops from Russia.

Early this morning the Americans and the British went by bus on a transport to Assen and from there to The Hague for transfer to internment camps in Germany with a view to exchange. They departed rejoicing. The Jews going to Celle departed with sorrow in their hearts. Many of them were convinced that the war would only last a short time and they regretted having to leave Dutch territory for that short time. German families who had lived in Holland for years and had become familiar with Dutch customs and traditions and spoke Dutch fluently and correctly were doubly sorry. 'How can we get back to Holland?' many of them asked. 'Why do we have to return to the rotten country of the Boches?' [. . .]

A dreadful feeling to see these men, women and children you have been friendly with for such a long time and whose life you have shared here go off as poverty-stricken emigrants with a few cases or bundles of rags, certain that they will never see Holland again and will remain in the east, destitute and dispossessed. Many a fist was clenched today and many a curse and many an oath were directed at Germany. And feelings of vengeance were kindled once again when people saw the shameful humiliation of the departing Jews in spite of the fine clean passenger train they were travelling in. Whatever Celle is like, they feel suspicious. They know that the Germans are taking the Jews to Celle for a sordid barter deal and, if it miscarries, they will be flung on the dunghill like the hundred thousand other Jews, most of whom were carried off to Poland in cattle trucks.

Dutchmen and Germans unite in hating the Germans with a hatred so fierce and fiery that nothing is capable of extinguishing it. But at the same time the Dutch hate the German Jews with a hatred almost as fierce, because the German Jews are tarred with the same brush as their non-Jewish compatriots. 'A rotten people!' they say here, referring to both sections of the nation. They are either sweetly spoken with treachery oozing from them or else they are so rough that you feel like knocking them down. That is the general complaint. [. . .]

We were not emotional about the good-byes, nor have we ever been, at least as far as the Dutch are concerned. We have kept the sober restraint of our country and our language, but

239

we had a lump in our throats nevertheless, as we have had so often before at those farewell moments. They represent a great sea of misery, with all the feelings of pity and horror welling up from our hearts which on ordinary days are held down by the work of the camp and the discomforts of hut life. Every good-bye is like another splash in the sea of misery. It makes us rake up the sufferings and anxieties we have already gone through and try to imagine what the unknown future will be like. Thousands and thousands have gone away like this with the courage of despair in their hearts. In the eyes of those who have stayed behind they seem to have disappeared into a dark cavern which closed again behind them. Where are you, you thousands and tens of thousands who have been carried away from one place to another—what has been your fate? You are silent because they will not let you speak. We stand there breathless with agitation and disgust and indignation—the emotions awakened in us by each successive transport. The tragedy in Holland is drawing to a close. The National Socialists have played with us for a long time in the Westerbork mouse-trap. The majority of us have been chased into one mouse-trap after another with the same dismal game being repeated again and again. Will the final small remnant be kept safe from transfer to these other traps?

Wednesday February 2nd: [. . .] This morning the camp was suffering from a hangover perhaps worse than any it has ever had before. In the severely depleted family that has been left behind and is thinning out more and more all the time we are very keenly aware of the absence of so many people—so many acquaintances who were here for months on end. Where have all the familiar faces gone? How bare it has become, how thin the ranks are!

Yesterday a small transport of thirty people who had been in hiding came in from Rotterdam, also Argentinians. They included one who on arrival here found papers ready waiting which stated that he was an Aryan. He can therefore go back home unscathed. This evening a transport of 120 Portuguese from Amsterdam. [. . .] The Portuguese were left in the dark about their position for a long time. Even now they are still in the dark and are being allowed to believe that they will be sent back to Portugal which was once their native land, where they became mixed with the *marranos*. All imagination, of

240

course—since leaving Portugal three hundred years ago they have become thoroughbred Dutchmen and never thought of Portugal as their native land. But now that the need has arisen they have had their family trees traced and have had lengthy documents compiled, proving that they are still Portuguese to the core. [. . .]

It is now understood that they will leave on Saturday next on a special transport, together with the Hungarian women. Also the Ros men, in spite of the fact that they were unable to make up the deficit. [. . .]

Thursday February 3rd: Once again Jan Ros tried to make a coup. Yesterday evening he arranged for a doctor with a 120,000 stamp to be summoned and demanded the sum of 9,000 guilders as a supplement, otherwise his exemption would be withdrawn. He sat behind the table with a big fat cigar and heavy gold rings set with diamonds on his fingers. We can assume that these were bought with the commission on the proceeds from the 120,000 stamps. The doctor refused as it was impossible, but at the same time pointed out that nothing could happen to him as he was Portuguese. [. . .] Ros did not trouble the doctor further. On the same day he summoned a Jew who had paid 34,000 guilders, but had got no 120,000 stamp, and he now asked for 4,500 guilders as a supplement. The Jew put up a stiff fight and said that he had been given a contacts stamp later on without paying a cent for it. Ros realized that he had blundered and, to save his face, he patted the Jew on the cheek and said: 'I'll go on taking care of you.' Just what you would expect from a generous man like that!

Yesterday evening I had another chance of escaping on a train returning to Amsterdam. Dead easy. But I was wearing clogs and, what is more, I was completely unprepared. I just want to mention how easy it really is to get away from the camp. But one would have to think out what to do next. That is not so easy. The temptation is great—it is just as hard to resist it as to give way to it.

Yet another list has smashed—the Weinreb List. People had been afraid of this for some time since Weinreb himself had seemed so sceptical about the value of his list. A grotesque farce. [. . .] The sheet-anchor of a thousand people who had hoped to evade deportation to Auschwitz has been roughly swept away. The old saying has come true: 'A list is just there to be

241

smashed.' Was it a game being played by The Hague and did Weinreb have a part in it? Why? What for? The Hague plays with the Jews like a cat with a mouse. Why did Weinreb have to be a party to it? Is it any wonder that people do not put any faith in the transports to Celle or Theresienstadt? [. . .]

A potato peeling machine has arrived—the women have become redundant. Release from beastly slave labour.

Friday February 4th: Yesterday had a spot of bother with my immediate superior, Brauner, just a lad to look at, with a short black coat and a cap which quite submerges him, but a devil of a fellow. He watches and spies all day long with his sneaking eyes. He has got his knife into me because he saw me writing at the table instead of picking foil. 'Just you come along with me,' he said in a little voice that did not ring true, 'I have a nice light job for you.' [. . .] There were a few others going along with me behind the broad wall of the coat. It was resplendent in its newness and it was clear to be seen that it had not come from any honourable source. In procession to the rubbish dump. 'Just get cracking on these, gentlemen, if you please, and cut them open!' And he pointed to a fair-sized stack of mattresses from the different huts, all badly damaged by bed-wetters. I did not fancy that. It was drizzling. 'That is out of the question,' I said. 'I suffer from rheumatism.' 'Have you a doctor's certificate on you?' 'No, would you expect me to have a thing like that all ready and waiting?' 'Then you must stay here. This work is good for rheumatism.' 'You know nothing about it. Let me go and fetch a certificate.' 'I can't. But you can work in the shed there.' (He pointed to a shed where the rain was actually pouring in.) 'No thank you. It's no use. Let me go back to the foil today, then I'll come with a certificate tomorrow morning.' 'That's no good. Then I'll get into trouble from the others.' 'That has nothing to do with me. I'm dealing with you and not with the others.'

Brauner then left me standing there without another word and I stayed out in the heavy drizzle, watching the others tear open the stained mattresses and take out the straw or the seaweed or grass. Shall I go away or simply stay and watch? If I go away, he can accuse me of sabotage and I have no desire for a row over nothing at all. As I was considering this in my own mind, the supervisor, a heavily built man from Groningen, came up to me and said: 'Do you know what we'll do? We'll make you the fireman.' I took a look at a young man who was busy piling up the straw and making a little fire. The straw obviously had to be burned. That suited me perfectly. I am a real pyromaniac. 'All right!' I said. I grasped a rake with iron prongs and raked the straw together and fed it gradually to the fire, from which the wind carried away a dense cloud of smoke. So the problem was solved. Together with the other "firemen" I felt just like a typical Amsterdam urchin making a bonfire. How splendidly the straw burned!—although it was damp.

The fun went on till half past five, when it was growing dark. We then extinguished the fire with tubs of black-looking water, wet sacks and rolling barrels to prevent a real fire from breaking out. Oh dear, what if a spark leapt across and set the whole show ablaze? There would be no holding it. And yet a little devil whispered: 'What if the whole show did catch fire and this beastly rubbish heap went up in flames!' But there are too many human lives involved. My punishment afternoon had gone off well. When the job was nearly done, Brauner came up to me in his large coat: 'Are you still angry with me?' I made no answer to that childish question. Who could be angry with such a stupid child. [. . .]

Saturday February 5th: A "high-explosive bomb" came down on the camp today. With the exception of the baptized, the Barnevelders, the members of the 1,000 List and the partners from mixed marriages, all exemption stamps belonging to hospital patients have become invalid. A blow like this has never fallen on Westerbork Camp before. It means that a large proportion of the approximately 850 patients must prepare to go on the transport to Auschwitz next Tuesday. It is the work of Aus der Fünten who is staying here. He has a bad reputation —when he comes to stay at Westerbork something terrible always happens. People are searching for the reason behind it. Viewed objectively, the hospital is, as it were, the hydrocephalus of the Westerbork child. At the moment the camp numbers about 6,000 residents, and of these about 850 are bed-ridden in the hospital, and there is a correspondingly large number of nursing and administrative staff assigned to look after them. Undoubtedly Westerbork has a large number of bona fide invalids as a result of the high incidence of infectious diseases and inflammation of the throat, nose and ears, but at the same time the hospital huts provide a haven for many chronically sick people and would-be invalids. These are under the protection of the doctors who try to save them from being sent away for as long as they can. It is obviously the intention of Aus der Fünten to make a drastic clearance on a large scale and turn Westerbork into a camp with only a small hospital. But he is striking out with an iron fist and also hitting many people with stamps who live outside the hospital and are unfortunate enough to be related to the patients there. [. . .]

Sunday February 6th: [. . .] Those who considered themselves lucky to be living in the hospital and so managed to evade the most recent transport to Celle have now got the wind up because they will have to go to Auschwitz. The blows do not always fall in the same quarter, nor is safety always to be found in the same quarter. You have to be lucky here—for as long as it lasts. The mouse-trap has many doors which are left closed or are opened quite at random. [. . .]

The Calmeyers—those who claim to be of Aryan origin and the Portuguese in particular—have had a terrible knock too. Fräulein Slottke has cancelled the exemption of 140 who would have sworn by the beard of Mahomet that their famous 10,000 stamp represented an absolutely sure form of exemption and also thought they would, as a result, be going no further than central Germany, on a passenger train, even though it had to be third class. Now they, or at least a large proportion of them, are going like cattle to Auschwitz next Tuesday. They might as well throw their long and well-thumbed lists of family ancestors on the fire. They too realize that anyone who trusts in the word or the actions of a National Socialist is standing on quicksand and will sink down into it. Auschwitz, ladies and gentlemen, there is nothing else left for you. They, and others with them, feel the transport stealing closer like some filthy and monstrous reptile—their laugh of self-assurance is hushed, deep wrinkles appear like furrows carved on their foreheads— we too have been struck down by fate.

In the administrative section of the hospital the Germans have called in the list of patients whose exemptions have been withdrawn and who are considered "fit for transport" and have sent it back with a harsh note to the effect that only those who are dying can have their names deleted. That means hardly anyone. Deep despondency among the sick. Only those who are dying can be saved! So unfitness for deportation does

244

not exist any more. About 350 have to leave, making 675 with their relatives included, and with members of the hospital staff over 700. Forty children from the orphanage are going too—unproductive persons who impose an unnecessary burden on the camp budget, also the chronically sick who are merely mouths to feed. The law of the jungle—away with anyone who cannot stand the pace, anyone who is not productive! A clean sweep. [. . .]

In hut 71 a girl was arrested and transferred to hut 51 because she had publicly declared that she would "take to her heels" if she got the chance. That was an unwise thing to say— the enemy is on the look-out, even among the Jews. The guard stood beside her bed as she packed her things, watching her with a pitying expression and a look on his face as if to say: 'You stupid little thing, why weren't you more careful!'

Monday February 7th: Today marks the beginning of the sixteenth month of my stay at the camp. I have had more than enough of it, much more. Man should beware of pride and judge his fellowmen with gentleness and long-suffering, but I am well on the way to becoming a misanthropist. I thought it was wrong to confess it to others, or a sign that one was lacking in charity towards one's fellowmen, but when in an unguarded moment I spoke of these feelings of mine the other day in front of a very decent man he said eagerly: 'I'm turning into a misanthropist here too. And I've never been like that before.' He had apparently been waiting for a chance to speak out about it. Just like me. We are not the only ones who are becoming misanthropists here, or have already got like that.

People in the mass, especially if they are living under bad conditions, are the most hideous and repulsive thing imaginable. It is a loathsome degradation of human life, with the chaotic, immoral passions of twenty, a hundred or a thousand human beings all packed together in a small space. Downright selfishness comes to the surface and makes itself felt in things large and small and there is no consideration or courtesy. [. . .] Life begins early in the morning with the shouting of the room leaders and goes on the whole day like that with shouting from the very ordinary mouths of all the different little leaders who were never of any importance before, but are gathered together here and live life to the full with all their sneaking and abusive little ways. A man should not be haughty and judge his fellow-

245

men more harshly than he judges himself. But I hate the masses whom you can only reach through demagogy and things that are easily understood and who react just like children.

I have been demoted once more. After losing my position as a supervisor, I was appointed as a coffee and tea fetcher. On Friday hail was falling and the stones pricked my face like needles as I was taking back the empty mess-kettles. I took refuge for a short time in the Central Kitchen where the German on duty bellowed at me: 'You have no business here. Get out!' [. . .] I stood quietly where I was, together with my companion. Quite by chance my boss, the illustrious Brauner, with his expensive coat and pimp's cap, came striding into the kitchen. 'What are you doing here?' The kitchen johnny bellowed: 'Those characters have been standing here for an hour!' I said: 'Five minutes.' Brauner: 'I'll put you to work again at the rubbish dump.' I thought to myself: 'Go to hell, you rotten swine!' This morning came the dénouement. The female room boss came to tell me without any warning: 'Department XII says that you are not to fetch coffee any more.' I thought to myself: 'Go to hell!' I have lost my contact with the outside world and the fresh air and also a great deal of my freedom of movement. [. . .]

Such small incidents poison the relations between the Dutch and German Jews living here together. We get over these minor upsets and just laugh at them. But I am not going to do a hand's turn. I have books with me and there are still ways of getting out of things and hiding yourself away in the camp where you want to be or have to be. This morning I went to the canteen to hand in a fresh doctor's certificate for vegetables which had to be countersigned, and I went to the kitchen to scrounge a carrot or two, and to Schlesinger to plead for a friend who is on the transport list for tomorrow, and to my friend's hut to tell him that he is safe. I am satisfied and content and can laugh at little Brauner. [. . .]

Tuesday February 8th: Another amputation has been carried out and the mangy snake has crawled away again this morning with a full belly. 277 invalids with their relatives, and the rest made up by Weinreb people [. . .], Central Office stamps that were no longer valid, Calmeyers declared to be null and void, S-detainees, orphaned children. [. . .] Although word was given out that only those who were dying were unfit for trans-

246

port, several seriously ill people succeeded in getting off the list. They have been lucky. Others too have been lucky. A few Calmeyers from the smashed list have been reprieved from transport to Auschwitz and have got a Theresienstadt. Clemency on the part of the Commandant. A whim.

Another group, Long-Term Residents, had renounced the Theresienstadt privilege granted to them by the Commandant and had picked Weinreb. They numbered forty-eight families and nothing could save them from being sent away. Anyone who turns down a favour from the Commandant cannot expect any mercy. Except for the chief of the hospital kitchen who as a person has the worst reputation in the whole of the camp, but maintains good relations with the people who have so often benefited from his presence as head of the kitchen, when holding parties, etc. People had been glad that this man with his red moonfish face was at last going on the train to Auschwitz. At the last moment he was hauled out by a strong arm. A stout supporter of corruption and blackmail has been preserved. [. . .]

I have the same feeling again and again every week. Although I am not allocated for the ordinary transports, at least not so far, I am never sure in my own mind that a mistake will not be made which will carry me away into the maelstrom. I feel as if I am standing on a high diving-board over icy cold water, with my feet on the edge, and I am waiting for the order to jump, along with most of the other camp residents. I am tottering on the outermost edge of the quivering plank and see the others beside me and opposite me tottering too with anxious faces, many of them in dire distress. Only when the order is given will I know if I have to splash into the icy cold water or can turn round and go back for another week. A week soon passes. People turn away thinking of those who have disappeared in the water and are floundering about in distress, their limbs numb with cold, wrestling with death. The latest pool of icy water was colder than most of them have been recently. People had got used to Celle and Theresienstadt, to water that was not so cold, and they had adapted themselves accordingly.

The majority of those left in the camp were going about with a kind of *passe-partout* in their wallets, admitting them to Bad Celle or Bad Theresienstadt, and it was a great disappointment to many of them when they had to go to Auschwitz. It was as if they were on a pleasure ship bound for Madeira and went off course and hit an iceberg and found themselves in the water. They had never meant this to happen—they had never dreamt of it. Auschwitz was for the proletariat, for the poor who had no money for a pleasure cruise. It was not for the rich who could pour out money or for the powerful who could boast of their good contacts who had given them an introduction, enabling them to get a berth on the pleasure steamer.

Schlesinger was stopped by a guard. He had not taken off his hat when required to do so and was reprimanded. The guard who found fault with him has a grudge against the German Jews, like most of the guards, because the German Jews kick us on to the trains. So he was as pleased as Punch to be able to bring the head of the whole show down a peg. He was indeed brought down—he stood there stuttering and stammering and the guard fairly hugged himself with delight.

The Dutch Jews are gradually beginning to make up the majority in the camp. The Long-Term Residents are all away, except for about sixty. Dutch Jews, mostly persons who have been in hiding, are the only ones coming into the camp. The Dutch Jews are now being brought into the various jobs by degrees—the Barnevelders are given the preference, along with the members of the 1,000 List and the baptized. One more Theresienstadt and the old guard of the Long-Term Residents will have disappeared.

Wednesday February 9th: The carrying of the invalids from the hospital huts to the train yesterday beggars description. At two o'clock in the morning the nurses had already started to dress the people who were to be deported. OD men went in front with a horse and open cart and pushed the patients lying in their beds on to the open cart, alongside and on top of one another, just as one would push coffins into a hearse. While wet snow dripped from a dark sky and covered everything with a moist and clammy white bloom, in the gloom of a winter morning. They were driven like that to the cattle train, bumping and jolting, and there they had to stand out in the open air, waiting to be loaded, again just like coffins going into a hearse. Children with scarlet fever and diphtheria were carried weeping to the long snaking train. Children without parents from the orphanage. Perhaps the most abominable transport that has ever gone. You tend to lose sight of this owing to the large number and the general roughness and bestiality of it all, but this transport capped everything as far as lack of consideration for the sick was concerned. One patient died even before the transport departed. An empty wagon was travelling with the train, reserved for those who passed out on the way. [. . .]

There is now a new branch of the metal industry for dismantling pieces of wreckage from aircraft which have been shot down. They are brought here by barge along the Oranje Canal and include 'planes of all nationalities and types—Spitfires, Dorniers, Junkers, and so on. On the land behind the hospital the pieces of wreckage that have been brought in lie along the trench in front of the barbed wire. Metallurgical experts declare that the material from the German 'planes is first-rate, but that from the British and American 'planes is even better. With the Commandant's approval, they are collecting, especially from the latter, various pieces that can be used to renew parts of the camp vehicles which have been suffering from the general lack of first-class materials. Naturally a lot of residents have gone to have a look.

Secretly read copies of the "*Nieuwe Rotterdamsche Courant*" and the "*Asser Courant*" belonging to the last few days. Refreshing to be able to read after having been deprived of newspaper reports and articles for so long. The war news is excellent. The Germans admit the fall of Rovno and Lutsk. Speech by Hitler: great words, fear of Bolshevism.

Rumour going about that on February 9th another new revue will be put on at the camp. [. . .]

Thursday February 10th: Offer from Brauner to work in the transport department—carrying barrels and other items from eight o'clock in the morning till six o'clock at night. I declined politely. [. . .]

On Tuesday next it is the turn of Celle once more and it will affect, amongst others, any holders of Palestine certificates who are still here. Fräulein Slottke has once again given a choice to the Barnevelders who also have an option on Palestine, but picked Barneveld—Palestine or Barneveld? The intention seems to be to convert them and win them over for Palestine. They are in a quandary and are running from pillar to post, consulting everyone: 'What would you do?' A terribly difficult problem—nobody knows what Celle will mean for the certificate holders and nobody knows what the Barneveld privilege means. People with certificates stand under the protection of the British government, but nobody knows if things will ever reach the stage of an exchange, or if they will be able to remain in the camp at Celle. [. . .] They realize that one day they too may have to move to the east, or at all events to Germany. Weigh up your chances as far as these two unknown quantities are concerned, and take your pick! A gamble. Everyone must just try his luck.

Friday February 11th: A great surprise—the ban on parcels and post has been lifted with effect as from February 16th. We have been very well behaved—since the ban was introduced, not a single case of clandestine correspondence has come to the Commandant's notice. He has formally established this. Yes, we have such a kind Commandant—he rewards virtue out of the goodness of his heart. Even when dealing with the Jews, who, according to Hitler, are to be marked down for complete extermination. We feel like children who have paid attention in class. Shall we go on paying attention? That is not so easy in captivity where people feel a challenge to do all kinds of forbidden things. We are dying for a parcel with a piece of cheese, a piece of sausage, a cigarette. We feel as limp as can be—and how limp a man can feel! The camp is no longer a Transit or a Labour Camp, but officially a "Dispersal Camp".

Saturday February 12th: Yesterday morning and this morning went to the Outpatients' Department to see the doctor on the strength of a note from the work hut doctor. A put-up job. I made a clean breast of it—nine hours' work per day was too much for me, although I really didn't do a hand's turn. I wanted to rove about in the camp and chat with people and I needed a pretext for this. The doctor understood the situation and kindly played ball. [. . .]

But things are not perfect. In the unheated, icy cold passage of the Outpatients' Department I waited for an hour with many others. Opposite me was a little man with large glasses above a greying moustache. He fumblingly produced a cigar box from his pocket, a memento of Charles I of blessed memory. Everyone was looking—what could be inside? Here at Westerbork we are all curious about antiques. He opened the box very carefully and neatly with taut lips. Oh, you

250

should have seen it—a fat cigar lying between three cigarettes. [. . .] One of the waiting people said to the little man with the box: 'Plutocrat!' He looked up with a smile as if to say: '*Oggenebbish.*' Another asked: 'Can I buy a cigarette from you?' 'Buy? I like to buy them myself.' [. . .] We licked our lips at the sight of the fine cigar reposing like a Gulliver among the Lilliputian cigarettes. 'Have you any bread?' asked the little man. 'I will certainly sell you a cigarette for bread.' 'Bread did you say? I don't think so. Let me see. Well, perhaps I have.' [. . .] 'What will you give for a cigarette?' 'Let me see. A slice of bread with butter on it.' The little man considered for a minute. 'No, that's too little. Two, with butter.' The bread owner considered for a minute. 'All right,' he said. The deal was concluded. [. . .]

For a day or so I have been going about with a doctor's certificate in my pocket, saying that I am entitled to fresh vegetables. The vegetable-grower comes in from outside every week, on Thursdays or Fridays, and vegetables are collected for the sick. I am not sick, but, owing to the rapid decrease in the number of camp residents recently, hundreds of certificates have become available, almost for the asking. [. . .]

A crowd of people were bunched untidily in front of a narrow door, guarded by a few villainous-looking OD men. I meekly joined the tail-end of the crowd, armed with a cane basket. An OD man was attempting to introduce some order into the crowd. Yapping away, he pushed back the part sticking out to the right and tried to knead the human dough so that it could be turned into neat lines of three or four. All in vain—the people just stood tightly packed together in the soft mud which is what the ground is like here, all numb with cold. [. . .] Grumbles in the crowd: [. . .] 'That basket is digging into my back. Can't you hold it over your head?' 'I'm sorry, that's not easy.' 'Then you ought to have brought a bag.' 'And what if I haven't got a bag?' 'Something else then, but not a basket.' [. . .]

OD men tried in vain to control the traffic—they scolded and they cursed or dragged some individual out of the crowd and chased him away and here and there they hit someone. People from the crowd told the OD men about others who had pushed to the front, but they remained deaf to all complaints. [. . .]

You are powerless in face of the OD men—they are the

officially recognized keepers of the peace, but they understand nothing about the business of keeping order and only get going when there is something to be scrounged or when there is a girl to run off with. They are hated because of their brutishness and because people can get no legal redress from them. [. . .] The pushing went on and the complaining was endless. Old women were squashed and children disappeared in the mass of people and it was a wonder they were not smothered. OD men with their well-fed, sensual faces went along the crowd like wolves circling a group of horses—where can we find one to drag out? The people were standing there stiffly, their eyes filled with hatred and loathing. Sick folk who had come for their vegetables and in the struggle to get some were liable to get even sicker.

A shrill whistle blast. Pisk, the Basque pirate, the man sketched in charcoal, appeared on the scene with a couple of ruffians. He bellowed out a few commands full of rolled r's and shouted to the crowd. His OD men threw themselves on the masses, cut them sharply in two at a certain point and roughly chased the part that had been cut off up against the wall of the adjoining building. Curses in the crowd. Sighs. Imprecations. There you are—the traffic for the canteen is now under control. All those who had been standing at the rear were now in front, outside the door. The rest had been jumbled up together. Elderly people, for whom the vegetables were intended in the first place, children who had come on behalf of their ailing parents, were cast aside and trampled underfoot. Pisk surveyed the battlefield quite unmoved. The OD men made dirty jokes about girls. [. . .]

About eleven o'clock the OD announced that the canteen would be closed till one o'clock. Curses. The crowd broke up. I had waited exactly an hour and a half. I shall give away my certificate to anyone who wants it. [. . .] That is how people live here.

Sunday February 13th: Dr. Spanier told me something confidentially yesterday evening. I met him on the road and started up about the latest transport of invalids to Auschwitz. 'Horrible,' he said. 'And to think that things could have turned out quite differently. A week ago I gathered from certain statements by Aus der Fünten that they planned to empty the hospital out of sheer spite and send the patients to Auschwitz. I told the doctors at the time that I considered it was in the patients' best interests to send them back to the huts wherever possible. I told them that, not once, but several times. But they didn't do it.' I asked: 'Why not? Are your doctors so unintelligent that they can't understand a hint like that?' 'Yes, I'm afraid they are. It's disappointing.' Dr. Spanier was in a hurry and could not stand talking to me any longer. I said I would like an opportunity of meeting him again soon. He said: 'I'll bear it in mind.'

One wonders—did Dr. Spanier give out such a vague hint that his doctors did not understand him, and couldn't he have put it more clearly? Were the doctors taken by surprise when the German authorities announced their decision to send to Auschwitz invalids who were entitled to go to Celle because of their stamps? [. . .]

Yesterday evening a transport arrived from Amsterdam with 120 persons, mainly S-detainees.

Monday February 14th: The list is out again—1,000 are going to Celle. The original number planned was 600. From my hut alone 120 to 130 are leaving. A third of the population. [. . .]

The well-to-do folk are leaving—those who have made money and have travelled, those who have seen something of the world and know something of it. As they have travelled before, this journey does not weigh very heavily upon them, although everything is still shrouded in mystery for the moment and they would rather have stayed on their own native soil. No run on the Applications Office today. People have, in general, become reconciled to the idea that Celle is judged to be the best you can get under the present conditions. [. . .]

We who are left behind feel it will soon be our turn. We cannot escape any longer from the monster's claws, although, for the last of us who remain, those claws are covered with velvet. But the claws are still there under the velvet, the cruel claws that have mauled so many tens of thousands of us. Many a man who at one time fought against deportation and got a postponement now reasons with himself: 'For the few weeks that I can put off my deportation it's just not worth the trouble.' Nevertheless, many a man fights on to the last. 'As long as I can stay on Dutch soil,' he says, 'I'm going to stay on Dutch soil.' This attachment to his native soil has a heroic quality. It is the best and the bravest and the greatest lovers of

253

freedom who strive for this. 'Whatever fate hangs over my head, I'd rather it happened here than on the soil of my enemy.' Hope still plays a part in all this too. The war may be over any day and the invasion may come.

Tuesday February 15th: The actual departure was, in the end, much more harrowing than we had all thought it would be. No pen can express what really happens before and on a day of deportation such as this—however privileged the people may be—or what goes on inside us. At every handshake with a departing friend one soul seems to penetrate into the other, hands grasp and clasp each other as if they will never let go. The spoken word is either too much or too little. The queue lining up in front of the hut door is like a caravan solemnly going on a pilgrimage to a far country. In all the small squares of the window openings there are men and women crowded together, shouting a final greeting to those who are departing. At every window a last farewell, clusters of outstretched arms and hands, travellers rushing forward and grasping these hands and then quickly rejoining the queue. Every window-frame presents a compact living picture of people either moving or being moved. It is like a row of Jan Steen canvases placed side by side, but in a minor key.

Old women weep softly, mindful of the suffering inflicted on their children and grandchildren and dreading the fate still awaiting their sons and daughters in foreign parts at the hands of the tyrant. The young men and women who have grown hard as a result of the oppression under which they have been living for years, and have been strengthened by the misery into which their persecutors have plunged them, gnash their teeth in fury when they see their brothers and sisters and friends being led away and they curse their enemies. They spit out their hatred as if an adder had bitten their tongues. They clench their fists in impotent rage. The feeling of injustice that has slumbered all week is suddenly and violently stirred to life when they see their companions in misfortune being taken away and they give vent to their feelings without concealment, erupting like a crater shooting out its lava. There is a hurricane of contempt raging against the abductors.

Although those who are not "travelling" are officially forbidden by the *Obersturmführer* to leave the huts till after the train has departed, many try to get as close to the train as

254

possible as it is about to leave to wave a last farewell to their relatives and friends. OD men, who are the keepers of public order, chase them back again and again with harsh brutality, but they come back again and again, firmly resolved to see the train go. The OD men lose the game as their patience becomes exhausted and they give up in the end. From all the roads between the huts the people left behind finally come crowding into view like jacks-in-the-box and line up shoulder to shoulder along the Boulevard des Misères on the other side of the train.

A whistle blast announces its departure. At the windows of the compartments—partly piled up with luggage, rucksacks, cases, provisions—there are men, women and children, waving hands and handkerchiefs, not with sad faces, but with faces expressing a determination to be brave—triumphant faces. Along the Boulevard des Misères the waving men and women do not have sad faces either—nor do they betray any hint of determination in their features, just horror at the shameful crime that has been committed once more against their companions in misfortune. The train is a decent one, for human beings, but the journey is compulsory and the fate of the travellers is not known. The train slips away like a ghost; it glides past like a book with living pictures. We have seen old familiar faces for the last time—we have heard from them for the last time.

At the camp boundary, in front of the barrier, the train stops. There it is officially handed over to the German military occupation forces who have come on the train to accompany the "travellers". The Jews are counted one by one. Not a single Jew must be missing. Before the barrier the Commandant bears the responsibility for the consignment—after the barrier the occupation forces. But they are finally convinced that the consignment in kind is complete and no deduction has been made for the tare or discount. Business is business— *les affaires sont les affaires.*

Wednesday February 16th: Rauter was supposed to be coming from Amsterdam today, together with a few other high-ups, including Neumann, known and hated as an anti-Semite par excellence. The camp shivered and shuddered in anticipation. It was even worse than for a visit from Aus der Fünten, the Grand Inquisitor in miniature. The authorities gave instructions that everything that needed it had to be tidied up. The

Camp Commandant's Office was cleaned and scrubbed specially. The beds in the hospital huts were placed in orderly lines. On the wall of the waiting room at the hospital library in hut 6 a cloth was spread over pictures of the "*Le Rire*" type and caricatures: Dr. de Rooy walking with flat feet and with a gigantic thumb bulging from the pocket of his overcoat and the film artiste Kurt Gerron with the paper "*Erotik*" protruding from his coat pocket. There was an order that all girls and women between fifteen and thirty years of age should remain in the living huts. Rauter had to be led up the garden path—he must not find out that there are so many young working folk at Westerbork, but must get the impression that the work was being done by elderly people and men over middle age. In all probability he would demand that the young workers should be sent to Germany which commandeers every fit young person, Jew or Aryan, it does not matter which. Gemmeker prefers to keep them here for the sake of his own position. So the deceivers deceive each other. The Portuguese have been notified to appear in hut 9 today with the papers referring to their personal antecedents. There was a rumour that they were to have their craniums measured. Merriment throughout the camp. The place is full of different skull shapes, even among thoroughbred Jews with four grandparents of pure race.

This morning we sat waiting for the great men to arrive. But they just left us sitting there, as has happened so many times already. [. . .]

Received a newspaper for the first time since the lifting of the postal ban. The camp is alive again—the newspapers fly from hand to hand. People are once more discussing the war situation on the basis of reported facts and actual place names at the fronts. They are dissatisfied. The war is going too slowly. The Russians are making too little headway. On the Italian front the British are not making any progress and are suffering setbacks. There is no sign of the invasion coming. And the transports keep going on with the regularity of clockwork. There are only 4,700 Jews still in the camp. Unless the war soon comes to an end, it looks as if the camp will be completely emptied out and the final remnant of the Jews will be carried off to the east. [. . .]

Thursday February 17th: The best list of all has smashed—the gruel list. An order from the medical service: all gruel certificates are void with effect as from today. [. . .] Now only four hundred portions are being supplied daily—there is a great scarcity of barley and rolled oats. People who are not thirty per cent under the normal weight or can be assumed to have always been considerably underweight are having no more gruel given out to them, apart from those with stomach trouble, who are naturally all underweight.

Another list has smashed in the S-hut. Two practical jokers poking fun at all the different lists which have smashed one after the other established a *"Lau-Man-Tinnef"* List. (*"Lau-Man-Tinnef"* is slang. It means something like: "no good, man— rubbish.") New S-detainees who were brought in were told about this list and it was praised as being the best list and one which would give them a good chance of getting out of the S-hut. But—you don't get something for nothing. Complete information available for the price of one cigarette. The current price for every service of any importance or involving any effort. Many of the S-detainees who arrived walked into the trap and gave an offering. The operators of the list sometimes had good days—one day a profit of seven cigarettes was recorded. Until the fateful Tuesday came and they had to go on the transport. The list had smashed. [. . .]

One of the work leaders, a Dutch Jew, formerly a dealer in rags and a buyer-up of pawn tickets, continually urges us on to work on the orders of the German SS. He is on the 1,000 List and is endeavouring to stay on it and be sent to Theresienstadt instead of Auschwitz. [. . .] Today he broke out again: 'My patience is exhausted. It wouldn't worry me at all if I had to put you all down in my notebook. I'm not going to go on the transport just because of you folk.' [. . .]

The woman room leader is not a true blue type either. The wife of a teacher. On the 1,000 List too. Everyone comes here in blue overalls. She wears something different every day—a blue pullover with an ochre-yellow scarf on top, a brown suit, riding breeches with topboots. An impudent type. A highly coloured complexion—with a bit too much assistance given to nature. Outwardly sweet, with a honeyed tongue like a snake. She is thought to be pretty. [. . .] At the afternoon roll-call yesterday she checked the people as they came in, demanded their Camp Cards and gave out extra work. One of those punished who had come late because he had to help his sick mother burst out: 'Surely you don't mean that.' 'Indeed I do.' 'Then you should be ashamed of yourself. You're doing the work of the SS for them. We shall remember this.' She turned as pale as a sheet through all her make-up. 'Yes, but I have to because I'm ordered to do it.' 'Then, damn it all, you shouldn't take on a job like that.' She just stood there dumbfounded. She was thinking of her green stamp and the 1,000 List. Today she is just as lively as ever and is giving out orders as imperturbably as ever. [. . .]

Friday February 18th: Of over two hundred knives belonging to the potato peeling section that have been supplied over a period to hut 57 for picking off the foil there are only twenty-seven still left. Apart from a certain number which did not work and were useless, the knives have been spirited away little by little.

Just before the roll-call yesterday evening the *Obersturm-führer* paid an unexpected visit to hut 85 where the Barnevelders live. He was furious—it was a rubbish dump, it stank, they were a disorderly crowd. [. . .] The Commandant gave an order that the ladies and gentlemen present should prepare for an inspection on the following Sunday and spread out their goods and chattels in an orderly fashion on their beds. [. . .] The old clubroom type of life has passed its heyday. As a result, more space is becoming available in 85 and people have more freedom of movement. Until now hut 85 has been about the most pathetic thing in the whole of Westerbork—the fine flower of the Jewish middle classes flung on the scrapheap.

Westerbork is becoming a social centre. This afternoon yet another café was opened. [. . .] A small café with space for about fifty people. Since a week ago last Sunday chess contests have also been held in that room, on Sundays and on certain evenings during the week. Chess enthusiasts assemble there regularly.

Saturday February 19th: A transport for Theresienstadt is being made up. They are running short of people. The Commandant is tossing out travel tickets for Theresienstadt. Anyone who wants to go can go. [. . .] You can choose: Theresienstadt or Auschwitz. *Mesdames et messieurs, faites vos jeux!* Such an opportunity will never come again. But think it over well—anyone who turns down Theresienstadt because he wants to stay here longer will inevitably go to Auschwitz, to Poland. [. . .]

As I was walking along thinking things over this afternoon, a camp friend stopped me. 'It's a good thing I've met you. A telegram has arrived today at the Commandant's Office from Frederiks in The Hague, and he is asking for a certain number of Jews to be kept on in the camp so that they can be put on the Barneveld List. You are included.' I was speechless with amazement. That would perhaps change my status still further. If the Commandant agreed to that, I would get a nice safe little ice-floe to step on to, i.e. Barneveld, which after the baptized is the most highly privileged group of all, the Theresienstadt of Holland. Things have not got to that stage yet, but the prospect is interesting. What they will ultimately do with that group is not known, but for the time being they are remaining here. [. . .]

Sunday February 20th: Fetched vegetables this morning. Waited three-quarters of an hour in icy cold weather outside the canteen, after which I got a voucher inside and then I waited again in a biting east wind beside the wagon to collect the vegetables tossed out to us. [. . .]

Another amusing episode has occurred today—this time in hut 85, among the Barnevelders. Following his warning, the *Ostu* appeared, not at half past five, as he had said, but at half past eight. The Barnevelders had been cleaning and scrubbing all day long to make a proper show of things and had deposited their baggage tidily on their beds. The *Obersturmführer* appeared in full regalia, followed by Schlesinger, Todtmann, Mozes, the head of the Huts Administration, Stein, Grüneberg and other prominent personages. The *Ostu* pounced here and there. He made a well-known authority on Asiatic art open a suitcase and he rummaged about among the grimy laundry and brought out a pair of grimy shoes. 'What a thing to find on a cultured man! Well, well!' 'Excuse me, but these shoes belong to my wife.' 'Then you must have a dirty wife.' To another who had four suits he gave the ironical advice: 'Why don't you go and fetch yourself a fifth one from the Clothing Department.' He confiscated one of them, also an overcoat and a pair of shoes. The same sort of thing was repeated here and there. The Commandant was very sarcastic.

Outcome of the inspection—away with all the boxes! Each

individual was to have no more than a rucksack and a suitcase. Two sets of all undergarments and two suits for men were laid down as the number they ought to have. Confiscation of French and English books and for his own use a "History of the Jewish People". [. . .]

Jews did voluntary work at the Oranje Canal today again, unloading fragments of aircraft that were suitable for dismantling. The inducement offered was an extra meal, an extra stamp for a parcel from Amsterdam. People readily yield to this. The stomach governs the character of most people. Did not Esau sell his birthright to Jacob for a mess of pottage? People are like that. And some of them wanted to see what things looked like outside the camp. They wanted a diversion. To get this, they will readily abandon to some extent the following principle: Thou shalt not work voluntarily for the enemy! There was not a lot of work done. Some persistent lead-swinging, just as you find everywhere here. [. . .]

Tuesday February 22nd: Shoe inspection yesterday evening in hut 85. The Commandant had arranged to come at about nine o'clock and the whole hut shivered and shook with nerves for hours beforehand. Mozes and Grüneberg of the Huts Administration came an hour in advance to give instructions on what to do. It was like a class on First Aid. 'Watch carefully,' said the great man Mozes, 'this is how you have to hold up your polished shoes to show the Commandant.' And he wriggled his two giants of hands into a pair of doll-like shoes belonging to one of the ladies and then held out his hands wearing the shoes. 'Like this. First the top part. Then the part underneath.' And he turned over the two little shoes, with the soles facing upwards. In the meantime Grüneberg had been going about with a feather duster flicking round the various decorative features, such as borders and edges of things, lest the Commandant's wrath and anger should be stirred up by accumulations of dust. A Commandant like this one can make or mar you. Professor Dresden, the hut leader, was going about with beads of cold perspiration on his worthy forehead, making sure that everyone was hard at it—cleaning, cleaning, cleaning. Everyone was cleaning, the whole hut was like some sect of polishers. Male and female helpers were running to and fro, checking to see that everyone was there and in the right place. Girls were enthusiastically sweeping the narrow passages between the beds. Other girls were sweeping in exactly the opposite direction. They were all getting in one another's way, they were all shouting excitedly, anxious that everything should go well and turn out satisfactorily. Chance visitors were tossed to and fro like a bouncy rubber ball by scurrying men and women as they raced to and fro between the two wings of the hut. At half past eight there was an order from the hut Administration telling the men to stay in the men's room and the women in the women's. One of the administrative staff guarded the doors like a second Cerberus. 'Nobody else in. Off with you!' They were ready. The Commandant could come when he liked. They had done their best, everyone had done his bit of cleaning honestly and conscientiously. The room was all agleam with shining shoes.

Well after nine o'clock the Commandant appeared in uniform, followed once again by the aristocrats among the Jews: Schlesinger, Todtmann, Stein and so on. He came into the room like a bright comet appearing in the heavens. The comet disappeared into the narrow passage-way; its light was dimmed. In front of each space the Commandant stopped with his satellites who were proceeding along in circular formation behind him and faced his Jews, each of whom displayed one or two pairs of shoes, one pair on his feet and one pair on his hands. The men had to raise their feet like a horse being shod and turn their hands with military precision according to the Mozes method. It was all done in deadly earnest. Like a *Marche Funèbre*. [. . .]

On the stroke of twelve the inspection came to an end. The comet vanished from the firmament. The victims of the inspection were dead-beat after all the tension and fatigue they had undergone. Fifty-eight Barneveld men and fifteen Barneveld women had failed their examination. Too stupid to clean their shoes. Or too lazy. This evening they must sit the examination again. And if they do not pass this time all the occupants of hut 85 will have to turn out on the parade ground. Everything must be just so! People are inclined to think that the Commandant is not quite right in the head. But that is forbidden. However, there is definitely something wrong with him.

Wednesday February 23rd: The fate of the Portuguese has been decided. Yesterday afternoon the announcement came like a bombshell from a clear sky that they were to be going to

Theresienstadt on the following Friday with all their goods and chattels. So they were not going to Portugal. We had realized that this was just a little joke, a game. But why Theresienstadt? God alone knows! We must assume that in the end the German authorities did not know what to do in this particular case and therefore sent the Portuguese to Theresienstadt, like others they did not know what to do with. That was all they got for parading last Sunday before the German authorities who were kind enough to take note of their cranial structure and their facial angle, albeit superficially. What a performance! What grotesque lunacy! [. . .]

Some people on the 1,000 List have been put down for Theresienstadt too, those who are over sixty. A premature journey to what is represented as the Mecca of the Jews.

In the foil-picking section we have got a new room boss, a Friesian who used to be a dancing master. He started off by emitting a crowing noise. Like a triumphant cock he announced: 'Ladies and gentlemen, you must bear in mind that I like peace and quiet.' Thunderous hand-clapping and foot-thumping. Not the right approach to merchants, professors, teachers and housewives who sit absolutely mum here. He fancies himself, but we don't care a scrap for him. [. . .]

Yesterday the *Obersturmführer* kept hut 85 waiting in vain—the shoes were beautifully cleaned, but evidently something even more serious had cropped up to prevent him from inspecting his Jews. They were very disappointed.

Thursday February 24th: Yesterday evening the postponed inspection took place in 85. Oh dear, how hard they had polished their shoes! Every pair had already been held out to Professor Dresden who examined the shoes in the Administration corner with critical eyes, with critical professorial eyes—front, back, side and underneath part—to save his flock from further misfortune. The shoes were gleaming like black imps. The Commandant looked at them, one by one, with the patience of Job, as if he were attempting to classify newly discovered plants. He did not say much about his findings. There was not much he could say, for that matter. Everything was spick and span. No batman could have improved on the work of the dirty Jews. But the Commandant was not satisfied. 'Let me see,' he said. 'About sixty have not cleaned their shoes. Sixty people under fifty-five years of age are to go on outside work on Saturday afternoon and Sunday.' And so the shoe-cleaning drama came to an end. The Barnevelders under fifty-five years of age were snorting with rage. They knew perfectly well how his mind worked: 'I'll catch you privileged bourgeois folk; you are going to work, damn you! Frederiks or no Frederiks, I don't care a hang! You are Jews just like the others and not one whit better. And that's that!' The Jews thought to themselves: 'Oh for the Barneveld days!'

The proposed transport of Portuguese from the Barnevelders' hut and the hut for the baptized Jews was cancelled this morning. Great astonishment. [. . .]

Friday February 25th: Speech by the dancing master in the foil section. 'Ladies and gentlemen,' he said in his Friesian voice which was like the crowing of a cock, 'I have something further to say to you.' A meaningful chorus of coughs from the foil pickers. 'Too little is being produced and this cannot go on. It is in your own interest to produce more. Until now Jews have run this section and it must be kept like that.' (Whispering here and there—'he must see to it that he stays on the 1,000 List'— 'as if the transports won't be going on just as usual.') 'It is the duty of everyone to work. People who worked in the community in the past do the same here and those who were not in the habit of working then do not work here either.' ('Hm, hm,' among the audience.) 'So, ladies and gentlemen,' the cock went on, 'I shall no longer permit you to toast bread on the stoves after eight o'clock and eat your breakfast here. People may, if they wish, eat their breakfast here before eight o'clock in the morning. Everyone must watch his step from now on.' (Hissing from several of the benches. Whispers: 'That's how one slave speaks to another.' 'Ladies and gentlemen, take your partners for the next waltz!') [. . .]

The transport to Theresienstadt that had been postponed departed this morning—800 men, women and children. This time there was quite a rush for the train, a third-class one. There was a rumour that anyone who was not exempted and had a chance of getting to Theresienstadt and did not take advantage of it would irrevocably go to Auschwitz next time. Dr. Spanier gave this out late in the evening about bedtime to the hospital staff. There was a kind of panic. So even this morning, until shortly before the departure of the train, men and women were still putting their names down for the transport to Theresienstadt. A number of sick people, including a few who had only just had operations and could scarcely move, felt impelled to go on the transport too. [. . .]

There are still 4,230 Jews in the camp. Most of the huts are standing empty and lifeless. The occupied huts are usually overfull. On the day of the transport there is space to breathe in. On the following day everything is packed to the roof once more. Tomorrow the remnant from hut 62 is being spread out over the huts which are still being kept on—71 and 72 and 84. Some of the small living huts where members of the 1,000 List and a few other privileged persons, such as ex-members of the Jewish Council, reside are also lying empty. The camp is like a small boy with trousers that are far too wide for him and a cap hanging right down over his ears. The roads are empty. There is something threatening in the atmosphere now. We are beginning to feel that we have been left behind. Should we not have gone with the others, should we not have been in it with them? [. . .]

The Barnevelders are not being left in peace. The Commandant has given orders that all occupants of the hut up to the sixty-fifth year of age have to do outside work on Saturday afternoon and all day Sunday. He is obviously furious with the plutocrats, the bourgeoisie of 85. [. . .]

Saturday February 26th: Today there was another invasion of strangers from hut 62. [. . .] I feel out of my element, jammed in between walls of human beings whose language I do not speak, whose habits I do not share, whose meddlesomeness I detest. As chance would have it, a friend of my youth has arrived in my hut and has become my "room-mate", as was the custom in the barracks. But it is quite different now from what it was like then. In the old days there was a need for companionship which goes with the bloom of youth and the feelings of attachment that mark the formative years. Now there is a need to be alone with your mature thoughts, your own deliberations and deliberateness, a need for space created in the mind by the material prosperity of life. The proximity of a friend is a comfort because it recalls the familiarity of youth, but the only real support is still only to be found in yourself, in your beliefs or convictions or in your determination to get through these hard times.

Sunday February 27th: [. . .]

The inmates of hut 85 did outside work yesterday, dragging scrap metal along from crashed aircraft at a moderate tempo. At eight o'clock this morning they set out again to do the same sort of work in snowy weather, most of them in overalls.

For weeks on end we have been eating cabbage, of all varieties, accompanied by unpeeled potatoes of the cheap bogland type; on one single occasion we had barley soup for a change. Small helpings. Got a pound of sugar today plus a few spoonfuls of jam.

Monday February 28th: Everybody here steals and nobody is ashamed of doing it or upset if others do it. This morning a few respectable men and women who were standing waiting for potatoes to fall off when a wagon of them was being unloaded half-emptied a sack of potatoes without any action being taken by the man on the wagon who was also a Jew. The lines of demarcation between honesty and dishonesty are getting blurred. Life here shows how easily a respected citizen, male or female, a very pillar of social order and private property, can slide down the slippery slope into a world which lives on theft, when he begins to feel the pinch of hunger. You can think of it as a kind of game. It is like the naughty boy who steals a few apples or pears or chestnuts from a cart. This does not mean that he has criminal tendencies and it does not mar his future. So people here steal a potato or two from a wagon in the passing, or scramble for them in the roadway and roast them on the ashes, at work or in the hut, to supplement their meagre daily ration. I do this.

Like many others, I regularly go about with a few raw potatoes in the pockets of my overalls or munch a winter carrot. Anyone with the teeth for it can be seen gnawing at a winter carrot, starting with the children who have strong teeth to bite with. The whole camp is gnawing carrots. The whole camp is roasting potatoes. Can I do otherwise? Worthy fathers of families and first-rate mothers steal bagfuls of winter carrots or potatoes from which they make steaming hot meals to feed their offspring who are growing all the time and are not getting enough. Early in the morning, when the supervision is not so strict, they launch their attacks on the kitchen where the potatoes are waiting for the women to peel them. They break in and steal. They surreptitiously remove cabbages and hide them under their jackets or coats. They steal onions out of cases on the way from the cart to the kitchen or canteen.

Stealing is carried on on a small and a large scale and anyone who starts on a small scale will inevitably end up doing it on a large scale—or "wholesale". Mothers are ashamed of their sons who come home laden with spoils and do not know whether they ought to encourage or discourage them. Discouraging means going chronically short; encouraging means stimulating a bad trait of character which might get them into trouble when they return to a normal community life. The old standards of decency have faded or disappeared in a society where personal ownership no longer exists, where everyone who finds himself beside a source of supply takes what he can get, where everyone, or nearly everyone, who goes short or fears he will go short takes from the crowd without society itself opposing this in any way or the keepers of public order taking any stern action because they themselves are guilty of the same offence. These people, above all!

In this respect the society we live in is definitely rotten— man is good for nothing. Everyone here is a thief on a small or a large scale without, however, being a criminal. Anyone who manages to steal a batch of potatoes will also demand a place on the stove to cook them, often taking up the time of those who want to heat up their own lawful portions or helpings, with coal belonging to the community which gives in to this demand. Theft has become common to all and is authorized by the community. People boast of their spoils. [. . .]

266

PUBLISHER'S NOTE

THE handwritten manuscript of this diary is in the possession of mevrouw A. Jonkman in Amsterdam. It has been prepared for publication by mevrouw B. Imhülsen and J. H. Jansen. Obvious mistakes and slips of the pen have been amended without comment. Here and there a word has had to be filled in. A few passages have been omitted for reasons of discretion, and the English version has been slightly shortened with repetitions omitted and passages of a less interesting nature cut. Wherever these cuts occur, square brackets have been inserted. It cannot definitely be established whether the writer made any diary entries between November 7th 1942 and May 28th 1943 and between February 29th and March 15th 1944.